Alexander the Great and the Logistics of the Macedonian Army

Alexander the Great and the Logistics of the Macedonian Army

Donald W. Engels

University of California Press

BERKELEY · LOS ANGELES · LONDON

University of California Press
Berkeley and Los Angeles, California

University of California Press, Ltd.
London, England

Copyright © 1978 by
The Regents of the University of California

First Paperback Printing 1980
ISBN 0-520-04272-7
Library of Congress Catalog Card Number: 76-52025
Printed in the United States of America

4 5 6 7 8 9

For Carolyn

Contents

List of Tables and Maps   ix

Acknowledgments   xi

Frequently Abbreviated Works   xiii

Introduction   1

Chapter 1.   The Macedonian Army and Its Logistic System   11

Chapter 2.   Greece and Turkey   26

Chapter 3.   Syria, Lebanon, Israel, Egypt, and Iraq   54

Chapter 4.   Iran and Afghanistan   71

Chapter 5.   Uzbekistan, Tadzhikistan, Turkmenistan, Pakistan, and Southern Iran   99

Chapter 6.   Conclusion   119

Appendix 1.   Rations   123

Appendix 2.   The Site of the Pinarus   131

Appendix 3.   Approximate Chronology of the Gedrosian Campaign   135

Appendix 4.   Alexander's Route in the Gedrosian Desert   137

Appendix 5.   Statistical Tables   144

Note on the Maps   159

Maps   160

Bibliography   177

Index   190

Tables and Maps

TABLES

1. The Army's Grain Requirement for One Day   144

2. The Army's Grain and Forage Requirement for One Day   145

3. The Army's Grain, Forage, and Water Requirement for One Day   145

4. Approximate Troop Numbers in Alexander's Army: Hellespont to Gaugamela   146

5. Approximate Troop Numbers in Alexander's Army: Gaugamela to India   148

6. Approximate Troop Numbers in Alexander's Army: India   150

7. Alexander's March Rates   153

8. The Bematists' Measurements   157

MAPS

Northwestern Anatolia   160

Southwestern Anatolia   161

Central Anatolia   162

Cilicia   163

Battlefield of Issus   164

Syria and Palestine   165

Egypt   166

Mesopotamia   167

Western Iran   168

Media and Hyrcania   169

Eastern Iran   170

Afghanistan   171

Soviet Central Asia   172

India   173

The Gedrosian Desert   174

Southern Iran   175

Acknowledgments

Of the many individuals who have given me help and encouragement during the preparation of this study, I owe special thanks to the members of the Graduate Group in Ancient History at the University of Pennsylvania, and particularly to Dr. Michael Jameson, for their support and guidance. I would also like to express my gratitude to Professor Donald Lateiner, whose suggestions and advice have greatly improved the clarity and precision of the final draft. Thanks are also due to Professor J. D. Muhly for guidance in the geography of the Near East. I gratefully acknowledge the many suggestions of Dr. Robin Lane Fox and the kind encouragement of Dr. Eugene N. Borza. I would also like to express my gratitude to Dr. Ernst Badian for encouragement at a time when it was especially appreciated. But above all, I am indebted to Dr. Peter Green, who originally suggested this topic to me in his seminar on Alexander the Great in the fall of 1971 at the University of Texas. Since then, by frequent encouragement and infectious enthusiasm, he has become in large measure responsible for seeing it finally completed. I would also like to thank Miss Alexandria Juskiw for help with the proofs and Mr. Richard Bates for drawing the maps. Special thanks are due to Mr. August Frugé and the editorial staff of the University of California Press.

Although my research would have been difficult indeed without the aid and encouragement of these individuals, the conclusions of this work are entirely my own responsibility, as are any errors.

Frequently Abbreviated Works

AAAG	*Annals of the Association of American Geographers*
A.	Arrian, *Anabasis*
Arch. Mitt. Iran	*Archaeologische Mitteilungen aus Iran*
Army Veterinary Dept.	Army Veterinary Department, Great Britain, *Animal Management* (London 1908)
C.	Quintus Curtius, *History of Alexander the Great*
Clark and Haswell	Colin Clark and Margaret Haswell, *The Economics of Subsistence Agriculture* (London 1970)
D.	Diodorus Siculus, *Library of History*, Book 17
EW	*East and West*
Geo. Journ.	*Geographical Journal*
Geo. Rev.	*Geographical Review*
GGM	Karl Muller, *Geographi Graeci Minores* (Paris 1855)
Green	Peter Green, *Alexander of Macedon* (Harmondsworth 1974)
J.	Justin, *Epitome*
JRAS	*Journal of the Royal Asiatic Society*
JRGS	*Journal of the Royal Geographical Society*
Maurice	F. Maurice, "The Size of the Army of Xerxes in the Invasion of Greece 480 B.C.," *JHS* 50 (1930) 210–235

MDAFA	*Mémoires de la Délégation Archéologique Français en Afghanistan*
P.	Plutarch, *Life of Alexander*
Pett. Mitt.	*Pettermanns Geographische Mitteilungen*
PRGS	*Proceedings of the Royal Geographical Society*

Introduction

Although it has long been recognized that supply was the basis of Alexander's strategy and tactics,[1] a systematic study of the Macedonian army's logistics has never been undertaken. This neglect has been unfortunate since it has caused some erroneous assumptions about Alexander's generalship, especially in the Gedrosian campaign. Indeed, Tarn devoted only a fragment of a sentence to the problem: "as for commissariat, supplies were collected in each district as conquered and used for the next advance."[2] In fact, we hope to show that generally the opposite was the case. Because of the restricted capabilities of the methods of land transportation available to Alexander, only a limited amount of supplies could be carried from one district to the next. Hence, Alexander would have to arrange the collection of provisions in advance, and this was done with the local officials, who regularly surrendered to him before the army marched into their territory.[3] Tarn's simplistic view is not surprising, however, for the picture that emerges from the ancient authorities is that Alexander never needed any logistic planning at all, but secured his provisions as he went in some mysterious, automatic sequence. Burn denied that Darius attempted to cut Alexander's communications in Lydia because "Alexander's army was not, like a large modern force, to be paralyzed in a few

1. J. F. C. Fuller, *The Generalship of Alexander the Great* (London, 1958) 52–53.
2. W. W. Tarn, *Alexander the Great*, Vol. 1 (Cambridge, 1948) 13.
3. See below, p. 41.

weeks for lack of food and motor-fuel."[4] However, it will also become apparent that while Alexander did make full use of local resources, sometimes it was necessary to import food and water by sea—often from great distances—to support his men and animals. Berve[5] devoted a short section of his important work to logistics. Unfortunately, since he did not treat the topic systematically, his observations are of little value. He believed that the passages in Curtius and Diodorus[6] referring to the supplies Alexander ordered to be brought to him in Carmania from Parthia, Areia, and Zarangaea record an actual event and indicate an extensive logistic organization that was also employed in Sogdia and Bactria. However, it was physically impossible for pack animals to have carried supplies from those regions to Carmania, since they would have consumed all the supplies they were carrying long before reaching Alexander (see below, Chapter 1), and hence the passages are of no value in reconstructing Alexander's logistic system.

Fuller[7] understood that supply is the basis of strategy and tactics and that the Macedonian army could seldom have been supplied by foraging alone. Nor could Alexander have achieved his many rapid marches or traversed desert areas without a highly efficient logistic organization. Although Fuller deserves credit for recognizing the problem, he did not attempt to find any solutions.

Unlike some of his historians, Alexander himself was deeply aware of the importance of military intelligence and securing adequate provisions for his army. Even as a child Alexander seems to have displayed a precocious interest in the length of Persian roads and the nature of the journey into the interior of Asia.[8] An incident preserved by Vitruvius illustrates Alexander's understanding of the difficulties of provisioning cities (or armies which are moving cities) when remote from cultivable land. The relevant passage is worth quoting:

4. A. R. Burn, "Notes on Alexander's Campaigns 332–330 B.C.," *JHS* 72 (1952) 82.

5. H. Berve, *Das Alexanderreich auf prosopographischer Grundlage*, Vol. 1 (Munich, 1926) 191–192.

6. C. 9. 10. 17; D. 105. 7.

7. Fuller, op. cit., 52.

8. P. 5. 1; Plut. *de Fort. aut Virt. Alex.* 342C; Polyb. 12. 22. It was a commonplace among historians in antiquity that Alexander studied military strategy and the gathering of intelligence as a child, and given who his father was and the type of environment in which he grew up, this is not remarkable. Cf. J. R. Hamilton, "Alexander's Early Life," *GR* 12 (1965) 123; Green, 37f.

Alexander, delighted with this type of plan, inquired at once, if there were fields in the vicinity, which could supply that city with provisions of grain. When he found this could not be done except by sea-transport, he said: "Dinocrates, I see the unusual form of your plan and I am pleased with it, but I perceive that if anyone leads a colony to that place, his judgement will be criticized. For, just as when a child is born, if it lacks the nurse's milk, cannot be fed or led up the courses of growing life, so a city without fields and their produce abounding within its walls cannot grow, nor become populous without an abundance of food, nor maintain its people without provisions."[9]

The success of Alexander's expedition, the longest military campaign ever undertaken, was in no small part due to his meticulous attention to the provisioning of his army. This becomes all the more apparent when one remembers the ease with which the Macedonians traversed terrain such as the Anatolian Plateau and Palestine in summer, the Sinai in early autumn, the Dasht-i-Kavir, and the Zagros Mountains. Other armies following the same routes often lost a large portion of their men from starvation and dehydration alone. The Macedonians' successful passage of such regions contributes just as much to Alexander's achievement as his strategy at Issus, Gaugamela, or the Jhelum.

The purpose of this study is to attempt to solve two problems: How did Alexander secure provisions for his army throughout Asia? And how did the availability, acquisition, distribution, consumption rates, and transport of provisions affect Alexander's strategy, tactics, and the timing and direction of his army's marches? The following method will be used to answer these problems. The first step will be to reconstruct the Macedonians' logistic system to discover its capabilities and limitations. To begin, the army's consumption rates of food and water will be calculated, based on the known nutritional requirements of men, horses, mules, and camels. Of course, the army's gross consumption will vary with the numbers of troops, followers, cavalry, and baggage animals, and these aspects will receive special attention. But their precise numbers do not affect the army's *consumption rate* (the weight of food and water consumed per individual per day), which remains constant no mat-

9. 2. Preface 1–4.

ter how many personnel and animals are with the expedition. The minimum weight of the noncomestible supplies carried by the army (for example, tents, military gear) will also be calculated. Next, the efficiency of the various methods of transport used by Alexander will be measured in terms of the weight they can carry, their consumption rate of food, and the rate of speed they can achieve. Last, the relationship between the maximum weight of supplies capable of being transported by the army and the army's consumption rate of provisions under varying conditions of replacement will be expressed mathematically. This last procedure will produce a model of the Macedonians' logistic system, adjustable for different terrain, numbers of personnel, and animals.

The second task will be to apply this model to the human and physical geography and the climatic conditions of Alexander's route as they existed in his day. Far from being a mere line drawn on a map, each of the routes followed by the Macedonians is the result of a conscious decision by Alexander to best fulfill his army's strategic and logistic objectives. I hope to reconstruct Alexander's routes in eastern Iran, Afghanistan, and Turkestan with more accuracy than has been done previously and, more importantly, to discover the logistic and strategic reasons for Alexander's choice of these routes. To construct the routes I will use the geographical information provided by recent archeological, geographical, and paleoecological research as well as the ancient sources of Alexander's career and the bematists' measurements preserved in Pliny and Strabo. Occasionally, comparative information provided by other early armies that were supplied by the same methods as Alexander's and that traveled in the same areas can be used to help restore the Macedonian route.

Fortunately, all the countries through which the Macedonians traveled have received extensive, detailed geographical studies. First, each route followed by the Macedonians has received accurate, detailed descriptions by the nineteenth- or early twentieth-century travelers gathering military intelligence, which in those times consisted of the same type of intelligence needed by Alexander: climatic conditions, how long the mountain passes remain blocked in winter, harvest dates (which depend on climate), the easiest roads, which routes are the best provided with water and forage, the location of large areas of cultivable land, and the logistic problems of an army moving through the region. These travelers present a striking contrast with their modern counterparts speeding along all-weather highways in air-conditioned and heated vehicles, over routes which bear little or no relation to those taken by the Macedonians. The observational skills of these early travelers are unsurpassed, and they are still considered to be essential sources of information by modern geographers.[10] I have tried to obtain at least two independent travelers' reports for each section of Alexander's route, especially in critical areas such as Central Anatolia, Palestine, the Sinai, and the Gedrosia. I have never found the observations of any of these geographical sources to be inconsistent or contradictory to any other source, and they fully merit the confidence that modern geographers place in them.

In addition to travelers' reports there are the magnificent modern geographical handbooks for each Near Eastern country, notably the excellent British Naval Intelligence series, and the works of Humulum, Olufsen, and Spate. These works utilize the data scientifically compiled for decades, and sometimes for even a century, by teams of trained geographers, soil scientists, botanists, zoologists, geologists, ecologists, climatologists, economists, regional scientists, and epidemiologists.

Moreover, intensive surveys are now being conducted by archaeologists to reconstruct the ancient human geography of many regions along Alexander's route. These sources are especially important because of the direct relationship between human settlement, agricultural production, and the location of military routes capable of supporting large numbers of men and animals. Indeed, few travelers observing the desolate salt-encrusted moonscape of the central Tigris–Euphrates Valley today realize that this was an intensively urbanized and agriculturally productive region in Alexander's era. Such a reconstruction is only possible after years of intensive surveys, excavations, and detailed analyses conducted by soil scientists, paleobotanists, and trained archaeologists.

The combined use of these three groups of modern sources for

10. Naval Intelligence Division, Ģreat Britain, *Persia* (1945) 601–602. These early travelers have journeyed through, and described, virtually every route passable by man in each region traversed by the Macedonian army. In trying to determine which routes were followed by Alexander, I compared the merits of the different routes in each region as described by these travelers and analyzed the other sources discussed below.

each section of the Macedonians' route provides a firm geographical basis for interpreting the ancient sources of Alexander's expedition.

The major extant ancient sources for the life of Alexander are Arrian, Curtius, Diodorus Siculus, Plutarch, and Justin. Strabo occasionally supplies valuable geographical information. None wrote less than three hundred years after Alexander's death.[11] Arrian probably wrote during the reign of Hadrian or Antoninus Pius, and he attained the governorship of Cappadocia under the former emperor. Arrian's two major sources were Ptolemy, son of Lagus, and Aristobulus. The latter, a contemporary of Alexander, was well known as an apologist even in antiquity, and he presented a highly flattering account of the king, glossing over many incidents that portrayed him in an unfavorable light. Ptolemy also wrote a highly favorable account of the king in the early years of his reign to help secure his rule in Egypt as Alexander's only legitimate satrap and successor. Ptolemy probably used for his sources only his memory and personal notes, and perhaps the partially published work of Callisthenes (Alexander's court historian who was killed in Bactria or shortly after). On a superficial level, Ptolemy appears to have been a dry, military historian who never distorted his account. It is now recognized, however, that he does indeed distort the record, especially when he was personally involved. Arrian's account is generally devoid of geographical and chronological errors and inconsistencies, and his concise narrative is the basis for the geographical reconstruction of Alexander's expedition. He is, however, occasionally terse to the point of obscurity, and at such times Curtius is often of assistance in giving a fuller description from which a coherent reconstruction of events is possible.

Curtius, Diodorus, and Justin (who abridged Pompeius Trogus) contain many similarities, and it is generally acknowledged that they often follow the same source or tradition, which is commonly called the Vulgate. Unfortunately, the identity of this common source remains unknown; nor, given the limitations of our evidence, is it ever likely to be discovered. Occasionally, some primary

---

11. This account of the sources is based on Ernst Badian, "Alexander the Great, 1948–1967," *CW* 65 (1975) 37–56, 77–83; Eugene N. Borza, "Cleitarchus and Diodorus' Account of Alexander," *Proc. Afr. Class. Assoc.* 2 (1968) 25–45; L. Pearson, *The Lost Histories of Alexander the Great* (New York, 1960).

sources for the Vulgate tradition can be dimly discerned in Curtius and Diodorus. Those recognized include Cleitarchus, Aristobulus, Callisthenes, and both Nearchus and Onesicritus for geography. At one time, indeed, it was thought that this tradition was based on Cleitarchus, but it is now apparent that there is insufficient evidence to prove such an identification. Diodorus, the earliest extant source, wrote under Caesar and Augustus; and Curtius, in the first century A.D., perhaps wrote under Claudius or Vespasian. Pompeius Trogus wrote in the Augustan era, and Justin made an epitome of his *Historiae Philippicae* perhaps in the third century A.D.

Curtius often provides extremely valuable geographical material whose impressive accuracy has been confirmed by modern geographical research. Not only is his geography accurate and consistent (his few mistakes are also shared by Diodorus, indicating that their source was at fault), but his descriptions of the difficulties encountered in marching through specific regions of the expedition are identical to those described by modern travelers.[12] One cannot expect detailed geographical material from Diodorus' briefer account, yet he too sometimes provides valuable information lacking in the other authors. His account of the expedition to Ammon is the most detailed and coherent of all the sources.

Plutarch used a wide variety of sources for his account—he mentions the names of twenty-four authors altogether—including Onesicritus, Aristobulus, and perhaps Cleitarchus, Callisthenes, and Chares.[13] Like Arrian, his account is generally apologetic toward Alexander. As he informs us in the beginning of his life of Alexander, Plutarch had no intention of writing history, but rather planned to delineate character and depict models for behavior consistent with the moral values, beliefs, and attitudes of his own society. We are not surprised, therefore, when he mistakes Bactria for India,[14] nor are we annoyed at his almost complete lack of geographical consistency in the latter part of his biography. To give accurate geographical descriptions was not his intention.

At one time it was thought that Arrian was our best source and

12. See below, pp. 84, 101.
13. For the best account of Plutarch's sources, aims, and methods, see J. R. Hamilton, *Plutarch Alexander: A Commentary* (Oxford, 1968) li f. Plutarch wrote in the late first or early second century A.D.
14. See Chap. 4, n. 76.

that Curtius and Diodorus were less reliable. This was because Arrian presented generally favorable information about Alexander (since his account was based on apologetic and favorably biased sources such as Ptolemy, Aristobulus, and Nearchus), while Curtius and Diodorus included unfavorable incidents. It is now recognized, however, that these source evaluations were based on the subjective views of modern interpreters (such as Tarn) who wished to idealize Alexander and that they do not, therefore, reflect the intrinsic merits of our sources. In fact, there is worthless information in our "best" source (for example, Ptolemy's talking snakes during Alexander's return from the Oracle of Ammon) and valid information in so-called disreputable sources. Green observes:[15]

Yet the uncomfortable fact remains that the Alexander-romance provides us, on occasion, with apparently genuine material found nowhere else, while our better-authenticated sources, *per contra*, are all too often riddled with bias, propaganda, rhetorical special pleading, or patent falsification and suppression of the evidence. . . . The truth of the matter is that there has never been a "good" or "bad" source-tradition concerning Alexander, simply *testimonia* contaminated to a greater or lesser degree, which invariably need evaluating, wherever possible, by external criteria of probability. This applies to all the early fragmentary evidence quoted in extant accounts as well as, *a fortiori*, to the authors of those accounts themselves.

Before we discuss the Macedonian army's logistics, a word must be said concerning the difference between modern and ancient crop yields and fertility along the route. Few studies exist specifically concerning the agricultural productivity and paleoecology of the regions along Alexander's route in the late fourth century B.C. It is significant, however, that in two areas that have been intensively studied, the Negev Desert and the Tigris–Euphrates Valley, the respective yield rate was five times and twenty times higher than today, and the extent of cultivated area was about ten times greater. A similar situation existed in the Lower Helmand Valley, the Lake Seistan region, and the Indus Valley.[16] Frequently, where no studies

15. Green, 479.
16. For the Negev see Michael Evenari, *The Negev: Challenge of a Desert* (Cambridge, Mass., 1971). For the Tigris-Euphrates Valley see Thorkild Jacobsen and Robert McC. Adams, "Salt and Silt in Ancient Mesopotamian Agriculture," *Science* 128 (1958) 1251–1258; Robert McC. Adams and Hans J. Nissen, *The Uruk Country-*

on paleoecology exist, the relative agricultural productivity of a region along Alexander's route can be determined by the existence of cities and extensive irrigation complexes dating to his era, often in areas that are now desert or wasteland. The superior techniques of ancient farmers in arid regions should never be underestimated: their amazing abilities to produce abundant yields by using sophisticated complexes of cisterns, canals (often placed underground), catchment basins, and barrages are just recently becoming appreciated (and imitated) by modern farmers. Geographical and historical sources are unanimous in stating that the climate throughout all areas of the Near East has not changed from Alexander's day to our own.[17]

I hope to show the problems Alexander encountered in the marshaling, transportation, and distribution of provisions—often in deserts and barren terrain—did not have simple solutions, and prodigious long- and short-range planning and preparation were necessary before the army could advance stage by stage. These preparations included the forming of alliances, often combined with the installing of garrisons or the surrender of hostages, to insure the establishment of magazines of provisions in desolate regions, the provisioning of the army by the fleet that sailed beside it in barren terrain, the division of the army into several units when supplies would be difficult to obtain, forced-marching to conserve supplies, and the synchronizing of the march with the harvest dates throughout the conquered regions. Not only were considerations of supply

---

side (Chicago, 1972) 55f.; Franklin Russel, "The Road to Ur," *Horizon* 14 (1972) 90–103. The progressive salinization and alkalization of the once fertile areas of Mesopotamia, owing to the evaporation of irrigation water and the consequent precipitation of salts and alkalies, is perhaps the greatest disaster in Near Eastern history. For the Lake Seistan and Lower Helmand Valley, see below, p. 91f. For the Indus Valley, see below, p. 107.

17. L. I. Hlopina, "Southern Turkmenia in the Late Bronze Age," *EW* 22 (1972) 213; John Gray, *Archaeology and the Old Testament World* (New York, 1962) 4; Martin A. Beek, *Atlas of Mesopotamia* (London, 1962) 9; David Oates, *Studies in the Ancient History of Northern Iraq* (London, 1968); Louis Dillemann, *Haute Mésopotamie orientale et pays adjacents* (Paris, 1962) 67; K. W. Butzer, *Quaternary Stratigraphy and Climate of the Near East* (Bonn, 1958); W. B. Fisher, *The Near East, A Physical, Social, and Regional Geography* (London, 1961) 63f. One will note various spellings for Asian placenames in works cited in this study. I have used those spellings most common to English writers in this text. Since geographical sources are not consistent in their use of diacritical notations for place names, they will not be used here.

important to the Macedonians, but also the climate and geography of their route. Often, the army's movements were determined not so much by political or military events as by the severity of the winter, amount of snowfall (in Persis), or rainfall (in the Gedrosia), or other geographical factors. To a large extent these conditions dictated when the army would delay, when it would march rapidly, which route it would take, and, hence, the very nations Alexander would conquer.

Of course, not all of Alexander's tactical and strategic decisions were based solely on logistic considerations, but it is only the possible relationships between his movements and the army's provisioning problems that will be considered in subsequent chapters. Furthermore, this study is offered only as a beginning for the analysis of these relationships, not as a final answer.

1.

The Macedonian Army and Its Logistic System

In analyzing the logistic organization of the Macedonian army, the first problem is to estimate the numbers of troops, followers, and animals with the expedition. Although the numbers of infantry and cavalry can be reasonably estimated from the references in the sources (see tables 4, 5, and 6), difficulties arise in computing the followers and pack animals. Traveling with the Macedonians were bodyguards, older Macedonians exempt from combat duty, hostages, servants, seers, physicians, sophists, poets, a historian, a tutor, secretaries, surveyors, the transport guard, Egyptian and Babylonian soothsayers, Phoenician traders, courtesans, a harpist, a siege train, engineers, and as the expedition advanced further into Asia, women and children. In addition, by the time the expedition reached India, there were enough Egyptian, Cyprian, Carian, and Phoenician sailors to take charge of a 2,000-vessel fleet.[1] Neverthe-

1. Bodyguards: D. 65. 1; A. 1. 6. 5; C. 5. 1. 42; older Macedonians: D. 27. 1; hostages: D. 76. 8; C. 9. 1. 22; C. 6. 5. 21; A. 1. 27. 4; servants: D. 77. 4; P. 35. 3; P. 40. 1; P. 46. 1; P. 48. 1; P. 54. 1; the seers Aristander: P. 14. 5; A. 4. 4. 3; Demophon: C. 9. 4. 28; and Cleomantis: P. 50. 3; the physicians Philip: P. 19. 2; C. 3. 6. 1; A. 2. 4. 8; and Critobulus (or Critodemus): C. 9. 5. 25; A. 6. 11. 1. Doubtless there were many doctors with the expedition. The sophist Anaxarchus: P. 28. 2; A. 4. 9. 7; the poets Agis, Choerilus, and Cleo: A. 4. 9. 9; C. 8. 5. 7–8; Callisthenes the historian: P. 33. 1; A. 4. 10. 1; the tutor Lysimachus: P. 24. 6; engineers: Str. 15. 1. 30; A. 2. 26. 2; secretaries: C. 8. 11. 5; A. 3. 5. 3; surveyors: Pliny *NH* 6. 61; the transport guard: A. 3. 19. 3; Egyptian and Babylonian soothsayers: P. 57. 3; C. 4. 10. 4; Phoenician traders: A. 6. 22. 4; courtesans: C. 5. 7. 2; P. 38. 1–2; the harpist Aristonicus: A. 4. 16. 6; the siege train: D. 85. 7; D. 98. 4; women and children: J. 12. 4; D. 94. 4; A. 6. 25. 5; sailors: A. 6. 1. 6; A. 6. 2. 4.

less, despite the many different types of followers, Alexander attempted to limit their numbers wherever possible.

The army inherited by Alexander had been transformed by Philip into the most effective fighting force in Europe or Asia, and Alexander not only retained many of Philip's veterans but also the disciplinary measures and logistic organization he imposed on the army.[2] Philip had forbidden wagons to be used by the army and had limited servants to one for every ten foot soldiers and one for every cavalryman to carry hand mills (for grinding grain) and other gear.[3] With an infantry-cavalry ratio of about six to one (see tables 4, 5, and 6), this would indicate an overall ratio of one servant for every four combatants. Both Philip's and Alexander's troops carried their arms, armor, utensils, and some provisions while marching and did not use servants or carts to carry these items, as was the practice of contemporary Greek and Persian armies.[4] Furthermore, Philip apparently forbade wives and women to accompany the army, a practice continued by Alexander until the army turned inland away from the Mediterranean toward Mesopotamia.[5] At this time, it became apparent to the men that it would

2. Not only were many of Alexander's officers, such as Parmenio and Coenus, veterans of Philip's army, but many of the common soldiers as well: D. 16. 2; Front. Strat. 4. 2. 4; J. 12. 5; D. 9. 3; C. 8. 1. 23–27. These veterans retained Philip's discipline, Front. Strat. 4. 2. 4; J. 12. 5, as did Alexander himself.

3. Front. Strat. 4. 1. 6.

4. Alexander maintained Philip's practice of having the soldiers carry their arms, armor: P. 60. 4; C. 4. 9. 20; C. 8. 4. 15; C. 4. 9. 17; C. 8. 4. 5; C. 9. 10. 15; A. 3. 21. 3; A. 3. 21. 7; C. 7. 5. 16; D. 55. 4; Str. 15. 2. 6; Polyaen. Strat. 4. 2. 10; rations: A. 3. 2. 1; A. 3. 21. 3; C. 8. 4. 20; back packs with personal possessions: C. 4. 9. 19–21; and utensils: A. 3. 2. 1; A. 6. 6. 2. Because so many supplies were carried by soldiers and their attendants, generally only a light baggage train was required: C. 3. 3. 27.

In contrast, each Greek hoplite regularly had a personal attendant: Hdt. 7. 229; Thuc. 3. 17. 4; cf. Thuc. 7. 75. 5; 4. 16. 1; Theophrast. Char. 25. 4; and the Spartiate often had seven helot attendants; Hdt. 9. 10; 9. 29. One should also note Jardé's estimate of 15,360 combatants and followers in Xenophon's force of 8,140 troops, based on a three-day ration of grain given to them at Heraclea Pontica (Anab. 6. 2. 3. – 6. 4. 16), A. Jardé, Les céréales dans l'antiquité Grecque (Paris, 1925) 131, n. 4. The Persian army was burdened by an enormous baggage train (C. 3. 3. 8–25) of followers, equipment, and ox carts (Xen. Cyrop. 6. 2. 30–39; Anab. 1. 10. 18; 1. 7. 20; 2. 1. 6). In general, see William Kendrick Pritchett, Ancient Greek Military Practices, Part 1, University of California Publications: Classical Studies, Vol. 7 (Berkeley, 1971) 49–51; Berve, op. cit., 170–4.

5. Philip did not take women with him on campaign according to Athen. 557b, and Alexander continued this practice in the beginning of his campaign, since in Caria he sent the recently married troops back to Macedonia to rejoin their families

be a considerable time, if ever, before they saw their wives and families again, and hence the numbers of women traveling with the army would have gradually increased. Later in Hyrcania, Alexander allowed his men to marry whichever captive women they wanted so that they would be less desirous of returning home.[6] Even if only one soldier out of four took a wife, this would add many thousands of followers; and, of course, children would soon follow these unions, if they had not already. Philip's policy of allowing the men to return home frequently, adopted when the Macedonian army's campaigns were restricted to neighboring countries, could not be continued by Alexander.

Yet, even when the number of followers increased, Alexander attempted to limit them as much as possible. At Sousia, before marching through the Kara Kum Desert on his aborted Bactrian campaign of 330, he ordered all wagons and excess baggage to be burned, beginning with his own.[7] Xenophon followed a similar procedure before entering the mountains of Kurdistan in winter and noted that the consequent reduction of followers, drivers, and animals would save half the army's rations.[8] The fast march rates achieved by the Macedonian army (see table 7) as well as the speed and tactical genius Alexander displayed in all his campaigns is inconsistent with a large, unwieldy train of followers.

Any estimate of the numbers of followers in the Macedonian army can only be an approximation. We will use the ratio of one follower for every three combatants until Gaugamela, and one follower for every two combatants thereafter when the numbers of women and children increased. It will be seen that their precise numbers are not the major factor in determining the capabilities

---

(A. 1. 24. 1). However, important commanders such as Philotas may have been permitted to take a woman before the rest of the troops were allowed to do so in Hyrcania (P. 48. 4–5).

6. J. 12. 3; 12. 4.

7. C. 6. 6. 14–17; cf. Polyaen. *Strat.* 4. 3. 10; P. 57. 1–2; and below p. 86.

8. Xen. *Anab.* 4. 1. 12–13. Bonaparte followed the same procedure when retreating from Moscow. Cf. Gen. J. E. B. Stuart's leaving behind his wagon train for his lightning advance into Pennsylvania in June 1863. In the Gedrosian Desert, the army encamped by a dry river bed—this in the rainy season—and a torrent of water swept away most of the women, children, and pack animals, but no soldiers (A. 6. 25. 5). It is difficult to understand Alexander's decision to encamp here, but the possibility that it was done deliberately cannot be eliminated. There was a serious shortage of provisions in the desert, and Alexander may have been forced to decide who would survive, the women and children or his soldiers.

and limitations of the Macedonian logistic system. Of much greater significance is the ratio between the system's carrying capability and its consumption rate of provisions, which remains nearly constant no matter how many personnel are with the expedition (see discussion later in this chapter).[9]

The animals with the expedition included cavalry and baggage animals. The numbers of the former can be reasonably estimated (see tables 4, 5, and 6), but the numbers of baggage animals varied with the amount of supplies carried (more supplies would have to be carried in arid regions than in fertile terrain), the number of personnel and the amount of supplies they carried, the availability of suitable animals, and the proportion of different types of animals used. For example, a camel can carry more than a horse, and therefore a baggage train consisting largely of camels would be smaller than one of horses and mules carrying the equivalent weight.

The transport capabilities of the baggage train would depend on the types of animals used and the number of wagons employed by the army. Mules, horses, and, later, camels were the motive power for the Macedonian baggage train.[10] Donkeys, oxen, and ox carts were not used. A horse or mule can carry about 200 lb. and a camel 300 lb. for extended distances.[11] At first, only horses and mules were used; camels may have been first introduced in Egypt (where they

---

9. In any case, it is not the purpose of this study to argue the numbers of followers in Alexander's army. I have told the reader what figures I will use, if he disagrees, he may adjust the calculations based on these figures accordingly.

10. Most references to the Macedonian baggage train in the sources use the terms ὑποζύγια : D. 28. 1; A. 1. 5. 9; A. 1. 5. 10; A. 3. 17. 5; A. 3. 19. 3; A. 6. 22. 4; A. 6. 23. 4; A. 6. 24. 4; A. 6. 25. 1; A. 6. 25. 2; A. 6. 25. 4; A. 6. 25. 5; σκευοφόρα: A. 1. 13. 1; A. 3. 9. 1; A. 3. 14. 5; A. 3. 14. 6; A. 3. 15. 4; A. 3. 16. 2; A. 3. 18. 1; A. 3. 23. 2; A. 3. 23. 6; or *iumenta*: C. 3. 13. 16; C. 5. 6, 9; C. 7. 4. 25; C. 8. 4. 19; C. 9. 10. 12; C. 9. 10. 22. ὑποζύγια may not necessarily mean draught animal since it is a generic term for any beast of burden. In only one case, A. 6. 25. 2, does the term almost certainly refer to draught animals. It appears that camels were not included in the terms σκευοφόρα or *iumenta*: A. 3. 15. 4; C. 5. 6. 9; C. 8. 4. 19; mules: P. 37. 2; P. 39. 2; P. 42. 4; A. 6. 24. 5; A. 6. 25. 1; horses used as baggage animals: A. 6. 24. 5; A. 6. 25. 1; camels: C. 4. 7. 12; P. 37. 2; C. 5. 6. 9; C. 5. 2. 10; C. 8. 4. 19; A. 6. 27. 6. If donkeys or oxen were used, there is no reason why they would not also have been mentioned.

11. Clark and Haswell, 204; W. B. Tegetmeir, *Horses, Asses, Mules, and Mule Breeding* (Washington, 1897) 129; H. Riley, *The Mule* (New York, 1867) 49. The size of the average horse has not increased significantly since the early first millenium B.C., see below, Appendix 1. The average camel can carry 300 lb. for extended periods, Maurice, 223; Maj. Arthur Glyn Leonard, *The Camel* (London 1894) 187–206; William

are first mentioned as being used by the Macedonians) or perhaps after the battle of Issus where Darius' baggage train, which contained camels, was captured.[12] Camels never entirely replaced mules and horses as pack animals, since after Egypt all three are noted throughout the march. For the sake of convenience, we will estimate that the average pack animal in the Macedonian baggage train could carry 250 lb.

Philip forbade the use of carts by the Macedonian army and Alexander seems to have maintained this general policy until he reached Iran, where the first use of carts is mentioned.[13] However, Alexander soon returned to Philip's practice: in Areia it became apparent that the carts restricted the army's speed and mobility, and Alexander ordered all carts and their superfluous contents burned, beginning with his own. Nevertheless, a few carts carrying essential items such as siege machinery and the ambulance always remained with the army.[14] Ox carts were never used by Alexander since oxen can only achieve a speed of 2 mph and their hooves are unsuitable for traveling long distances. Their endurance is also less than that of a horse or mule: they can only work for five hours per day as opposed to eight for a horse or mule.[15] Hence, ox carts could not

Torry, "Life in the Camel's Shadow," *Natural History* (May 1974) 64. These figures are net weights and exclude the weight of the pack saddle itself, which weighed about 50 lb., K. R. Veenhof, *Aspects of Old Assyrian Trade and Its Terminology* (Leiden 1972) 45; cf. Army Veterinary Dept., 197, 293f. All three animals can carry heavier loads for short distances.

12. C. 4. 7. 12; C. 3. 3. 24. The camels may have been captured in Darius' baggage at Issus, C. 3. 11. 20, or at Damascus, C. 3. 13. 4.

13. For Philip's practice: Front. *Strat.* 4. 1. 6. In Alexander's campaigns, almost all references to carts (*vehiculae, ἅμαξαι*) occur when the army is in Iran: P. 57. 1–2; A. 3. 23. 2; A. 3. 23. 6; C. 6. 2. 16; C. 6. 6. 15. One reference occurs in Afghanistan (C. 6. 11. 3) in a speech referring to carts belonging to Philotas and used as an example of his excessive luxury, and another in the Gedrosian Desert, where they were used as ambulances (A. 6. 25. 2). It is surely no coincidence that shortly after wagons began to proliferate, they were ordered to be burned (C. 6. 6. 15), and scarcely appear thereafter. Wagons were not included in the term σκευοφόρα A. 3. 23. 2; A. 3. 23. 6.

14. Siege machinery was transported by the army (D. 85. 7; 98. 4), probably on wagons as in the Roman army, I. A. Richmond, "Trajan's Army on Trajan's Column," *BSR* 13 (1935) 11–12. Wagons were also used as ambulances (A. 6. 25. 2).

15. Lynn White, *Medieval Technology and Social Change* (Oxford, 1963) 38; Clark and Haswell, 205; Leonard, op. cit., 283 f. Although the average two-oxen cart can pull 1,000 to 1,200 lb., it will only move less than half as far per day (at 2 mph. working 5 hr.) as a horse (at 4 mph. working 8 hr.), and the team will require 100 lb. of food per day, Army Veterinary Dept., 299. Besides being slow and lacking

achieve the speed necessary to keep up with the army's daily march rates, which average some fifteen miles per day (see table 7).

Another reason for the restricted use of carts by Philip and Alexander was the inefficient throat and girth harness used for horses and mules in antiquity; the throat harness was placed directly over the animal's windpipe, and the harder he pulled, the more it choked him, so that much less weight could be pulled than with a modern rigid shoulder harness.[16] Carts were also liable to break down, and their movement would be impeded in rough and hilly country since the animals would have to pull harder—and hence choke more. They were also slower and often required special routes since they were not always capable of traveling the same paths as the pack animals.[17] For these reasons there was a general belief among ancient commanders that the use of carts would impede an army's speed and mobility and encourage the possession of excessive baggage by the common soldiers.[18] Because so many supplies were carried by the troops and their attendants, the Macedonian baggage train would contain a limited number of pack animals and very few carts.

Some pack and draught animals would be needed to carry the army's noncomestible supplies, such as tents, hammocks, medical supplies, the ambulance, siege machinery, firewood, booty, and

endurance, oxen are often unpredictable and frequently dangerous; they may refuse to work for no apparent reason, and if goaded, they may attack their drivers. While donkeys are patient and enduring, they do not make good army transport animals since they are slow and can only carry light loads, Leonard, op. cit., 289f.; Army Veterinary Dept., 274–275. Hence, the carts in Alexander's army were probably drawn by horses or mules.

16. Lefebvre des Noettes, *L'attelage: le cheval de selle à travers les âges* (Paris, 1931) 12–16, 68–71, 162–164; R. J. Forbes, *Studies in Ancient Technology*, Vol. 2 (Leiden, 1965) 84–87. Because of the inefficiency of carts and wagons, human porters and pack animals were regularly employed for long distance transport instead of wagons in preindustrial societies, Clark and Haswell, 204; Fernand Braudel, *The Mediterranean and the Mediterranean World in the Age of Philip II*, Vol. 1 (New York, 1972) 282f.; James Morier, *A Second Journey through Persia in the Years 1810 and 1816* (London, 1818) 197. See below, Appendix 1.

17. A. 3. 23. 2; A. 6. 25. 2; Clark and Haswell, 204.

18. When Scipio Africanus the Younger was given the command at Numantia, he expelled all superfluous followers, forbade excess baggage to be carried by the soldiers, and ordered all wagons and their useless contents to be sold (Appian *Iber.* 14. 85). Metellus Numidicus (Sallust. *Jug.* 44.) and Marius (Front. *Strat.* 4. 1. 7; Plut. *Mar.* 13. 1) made similar reforms. Cf. James A. Huston, *The Sinews of War: Army Logistics 1775–1953* (Washington, 1966) 216–217.

perhaps some of the women and children.[19] In the Roman imperial army, one pack animal carried the tent, hand mills, kettles, and tool kits for each eight-man *contubernium*.[20] Additional animals transported the catapult carried by each legion and the effects of the military tribunes, legate, and centurions.[21] About 800 pack animals were required by each legion to carry its noncomestible supplies, or about one animal per seven combatants. In the Macedonian army, many items were carried by servants rather than pack animals, and hence the ratio of pack animals carrying noncomestible supplies to combatants was lower than in the Roman army. It should be remembered that because of the inefficient throat and girth harness, manpower was as effective as horsepower in antiquity. For although the former could carry only one-third the weight of the latter (about 80 lb. for extended distances),[22] a man only needs one-third the amount of grain provisions of a horse. Nevertheless, bulky items such as tents, hammocks, and the ambulance were probably carried by animals in the Macedonian army. A Roman eight-man tent weighed about 40 lb.,[23] and therefore a single pack

19. The Macedonians carried tents: A. 1. 3. 6; A. 3. 29. 4; C. 6. 2. 16; hammocks: D. 90. 7; the ambulance: A. 6. 25. 2; siege machinery: D. 85. 7; D. 98. 4; the royal treasury: D. 71. 2; cf. C. 3. 3. 24; and fuel: A. 1. 19. 9; C. 5. 4. 14; all or most of which were probably carried by pack animals or carts. Booty: P. 20. 6; P. 24. 1-2; D. 70. 2-3; C. 3. 11. 20; medical supplies: D. 95. 4; road building tools (picks, shovels, and axes): C. 5. 6. 14; cf. A. 1. 26. 1; C. 6. 5. 20; C. 6. 6. 28; C. 8. 2. 24; C. 9. 5. 19; other tools: the engineering corps would have tools for the construction of siege machines and towers: A. 2. 26. 2; A. 2. 19. 6; A. 2. 18. 6; and for the repair and manufacture of arms and armor, and tent pegs: A. 4. 19. 1 could have been carried by the troops or their attendants. The Macedonian army, like their Roman successors, apparently also carried stakes for palisades to fortify their camps. The Macedonian camp was regularly fortified with a ditch and palisade: A. 1. 6. 9; A. 3. 9. 1; A. 4. 29. 2; cf. D. 95. 1-2; C. 4. 12. 2; C. 4. 12. 17; C. 4. 12. 24; C. 4. 13. 26; C. 5. 5. 1; C. 5. 5. 8-9; C. 9. 3. 19. Before Gaugamela, Alexander fortified his camp with a ditch and palisade (A. 3. 9. 1.), in a treeless region (C. 4. 9. 10) where it would be impossible to cut stakes, indicating that they were carried by the army. Palisade stakes would not be carried unless they were frequently used. The Roman practice of fortifying camp with a ditch and palisade was apparently borrowed from the Macedonian practice (Front. *Strat.* 4. 1. 14).

20. J. Harmand, *L'armée et le soldat à Rome* (Paris, 1967) 156; Richmond, op. cit., 11-12; Hyginus, *De Munitionibus Castrorum* 1.

21. Richmond, op. cit., 11.

22. Clark and Haswell, 202-205. Like the pack animals, men can carry heavier weights for shorter periods.

23. Harmand, op. cit., 156; cf. James McIntyre and I. A. Richmond, "Tents of the Roman Army and Leather from Birdoswald," *Transactions of the Cumberland and Westmoreland Antiquarian and Archaeological Society* 34 (1934) 62-90.

animal could carry about six of them or enough to cover 50 men. We will use the ratio of one pack animal carrying noncomestible supplies for every 50 personnel in the Macedonian army, although this is a minimum estimate.

Now, a minimum ration for each adult male on the expedition would be 3 lb. of grain per day or its nutritional equivalent and at least 2 qt. of water per day.[24] This would be the minimum amount of water necessary for men marching through hot terrain with grain products as a major staple of their diets. To be fed adequately, the horses and mules would need in addition to their usual forage (10 lb. of straw or chaff), a ration of 10 lb. of grain per day, and each working animal would require 8 gal. of water per day.[25] The requirements are higher for camels, which need about 10 gal. of water per day—although if the animal has gone three or four days without water, he might require 20 gal. at one time.[26] For the sake of convenience, we will estimate that the average pack animal's ration will be that of a horse. Of course, rations for both men and animals could be reduced for short periods depending upon the terrain and climate, but to reduce them for an extended period would invite the effects of malnutrition and starvation. This is not the way to maintain an army's fighting trim, and like all competent generals, Alexander took great pains to assure adequate provisions for his army at all times. From the foregoing information, we can determine how the Macedonians' logistic system functioned under actual marching conditions.

After crossing the Hellespont, there were about 48,100 soldiers in Alexander's army and about 6,100 cavalry horses (see table 4). If there was one follower for every three combatants, they would number over 16,000, for a total of about 65,000 personnel. If one animal were needed to carry the noncomestible supplies (that is, tents, hammocks, blankets, fuel, personal possessions) for every 50 individuals, 1,300 baggage animals would be required. Thus, if the army at the Hellespont traveled through terrain in which there was abundant water and forage (chaff or straw) for the horses so that only grain needed to be carried, the number of pack animals needed to carry one day's supply of grain would be calculated as

24. See Appendix 1.   25. See Appendix 1.   26. See Appendix 1.

follows: 269,000 lb. (the total weight of the grain requirement of the personnel, cavalry horses, and baggage animals for one day) divided by 240 lb. (the 250-lb. carrying capacity of the animal minus his grain ration for one day). Hence, the number of pack animals necessary to carry one day's supply of grain would be 1,121. If a two-day supply of grain needed to be carried, we would divide 538,000 lb. (the weight of the two-day grain requirement for the personnel, cavalry horses, and pack animals carrying noncomestible supplies) by 230 lb. (250 lb. minus 20 lb.). This gives a total of 2,340 pack animals, and so on (see table 1).

It would be theoretically possible for the army to carry all its own grain provisions for 25 days since by that time the pack animals will have eaten all the supplies they carried at a consumption rate of 10 lb. per day. In actual practice, however, the army could only carry about a 10-day grain ration since the numbers of pack animals required to carry a larger amount would be phenomenal: 40,350 to carry a 15-day ration and 107,600 for 20 days. It is doubtful whether this many suitable animals existed in the whole of Greece. A horse, mule, or even a donkey was expensive for the ancient farmer to maintain since he normally existed on a subsistence basis and had little agricultural surplus to spare.[27] Hence, the availability of pack animals for the Macedonians was always limited. Another difficulty would be the acquisition and distribution of provisions for so many animals by the primitive methods of transport available to the army. A day's supply of grain for 40,350 horses would weigh over 200 tons, and unless this could be transported by water, there would be little possibility of it reaching the animals overland since it would have to be carried by other pack animals who would be consuming the supplies they were carrying. Few regions on earth in the fourth century B.C.—or even today—could generate a sufficient surplus to feed so many animals for any length of time. But the greatest problem would be the sheer size of the baggage train itself if many animals were used: if there were 107,600 animals and they traveled in single file, their line would extend for 306 miles.[28] Even if the animals traveled 10 abreast, the line would extend 31 miles, an interesting logistic

27. Clark and Haswell, 24, 212. If the personnel could carry 30 lb. of supplies apiece, the army could carry a 14-day grain supply; see below, Chapter 1, nn. 31, 35.
28. Five yards per animal is the common interval in marching order, Maurice, 223.

problem in itself since the fastest march rate recorded for the entire Macedonian army was 19.5 miles per day (see table 7). For these reasons it is highly improbable that the Macedonians ever employed more than 20,000 pack animals anywhere along their route.[29]

Now, suppose the army at the Hellespont were to march through terrain where there was abundant water but neither forage for the animals nor any grain. To find the number of animals necessary here, we divide 343,000 lb. (the weight of the grain requirement for the men and animals plus the latter's requirement of fodder for one day) by 230 lb. (250 lb. minus 20 lb.) Thus 1,492 animals would be needed to carry the army's requirement of grain and fodder for one day (see table 2). Once again, it would be theoretically possible for the army to carry a 12½ days' supply of grain and fodder since by this time the pack animals would have consumed all the supplies they were carrying. But in actual practice, no more than a seven-day supply could be carried because the number of animals would have been prohibitive.[30]

If the army were marching through desert (such as the Sinai), where neither grain, fodder, nor water would be found and all had to be carried, the number of pack animals needed to carry a day's supply is calculated by dividing 1,260,000 lb. (the weight of the army's grain, forage, and water requirement for one day: 1 gal. of water weighs 10 lb.) by 150 (the 250-lb. carrying capacity of the animal minus 80 lb. for its water and 20 lb. for its grain and fodder requirement for one day), which equals 8,400 animals (see table 3).

These last figures are significant, for there were indeed areas through which the army passed that were devoid of water, grain, and forage (and these will be discussed at the appropriate times), but we see that if rations were not reduced, it would be impossible for the army to carry more than a 2½-day supply of provisions with them. The number of pack animals would be 2,520,000 divided by zero or infinity: in other words, the pack animals would

29. Although other commanders are reported to have carried 30 days' provisions (e.g., Agesilaus for his invasion of Asia Minor, Xen. *Hel.* 3. 4. 3), a closer analysis will show that these provisions were either carried by ship or do not refer to grain rations but to money for food. Cf. Pritchett, op. cit., 35f.

30. If the personnel could carry 30 lb. of supplies apiece, the army could carry a nine-day ration of grain and forage.

have eaten up all the supplies they carried on the third day. If rations were reduced by half, an extremely dangerous procedure in a desert, 8,400 animals could carry a two-day supply. On the third day, however, 18,900 animals would be necessary (1,890,000 divided by 100), and on the fourth day 50,400 animals were needed (2,520,000 divided by 50). It would be impossible to carry a five-day ration since by that time the pack animals will have consumed all the provisions they were carrying, leaving none for the rest of the army.

Even if each man, woman, and child on the expedition carried, in addition to everything else,[31] 30 lb. of supplies apiece, it would still be impossible to carry five days' provisions even at half rations, no matter how many pack animals were with the army. It works out thus: for a three-day expedition, the personnel could actually carry all the requirements of the army.[32] For a four-day expedition, however, 11,400 pack animals would be necessary,[33] and it would be impossible to carry provisions for 5 days.[34] Again, the pack animals and personnel will have consumed all their provisions by the fifth day, even at half rations. This ratio between the army's consumption rate and its carrying capability remains constant no matter how many personnel or pack animals are used to carry supplies. Nor would it help if the cavalry horses carried

31. Each soldier on Alexander's campaigns carried his helmet, shield, leather breastplate, greaves, spear or sarissa, and utensils (Polyaen. *Strat.* 4. 2. 10; above n. 4), and the heavily armored troops carried in addition a cuirass and wore a kilt of leather strips covered with bronze. They also carried personal possessions in back packs (C. 4. 9. 19–21), swords, and perhaps some road-building tools, blankets, medical supplies, and tent pegs. The soldiers' attendants were weighted down with hand mills and ropes (Front. *Strat.* 4. 1. 6), and probably some of the gear recorded in n. 19. An estimate of 50 lb. carried by each soldier and attendant does not seem unrealistic when one remembers that the weight of a metal breastplate alone is 50 lb., A. M. Snodgrass, *The Arms and Armor of the Greeks* (Ithaca, 1967) 122–123; 30 lb. of provisions would bring the total weight carried to 80 lb.—the maximum an individual can carry for extended periods without injuring his health, Clark and Haswell, 202–203.

32. The army's total requirements for three days at half rations would weigh 1,890,000 lb., while the personnel could carry 1,950,000 lb. (65,000 × 30).

33. The army's total requirement will weigh 2,520,000 lb., while the personnel will only be able to carry 1,950,000 lb.; 11,400 pack animals (570,000 divided by 50) will be necessary to carry the remaining 570,000 lb. of supplies.

34. The army's total requirement will weigh 3,150,000 lb., while the personnel will be able to carry 1,950,000 lb. Infinity animals (1,200,000 divided by 0) will be necessary to carry the remaining 1,200,000 lb. of supplies.

supplies: after the fourth day, they would only be so much meat on the hoof.[35]

From these computations we can formulate a general principle that is valid for large and small expeditions alike: an army whose supplies are carried by animals and men cannot advance through desert where neither grain, fodder, or water is available for more than four days. If the army were fed full rations, it could not advance for more than two full days without incurring heavy casualties.

However, Alexander did indeed traverse deserts where little or no provisions were obtainable for over four days without casualties. Thus for each location he must have found a unique solution for the provisioning problem depending on the human and physical geography of the region. One of the purposes of this study is to discover what these solutions were.

In analyzing the Macedonians' logistic system it becomes apparent that Philip and Alexander created a new type of army, fundamentally different from those in contemporary Greece and Persia. In Greek armies, the number of followers often approached the number of combatants, and, as we have seen, arms and armor were carried by servants or baggage animals and not by the soldiers themselves. Philip trained his soldiers to carry their full panoply as well as some provisions on the march and forbade carts and women to accompany the army. Much equipment was carried by servants and not by pack animals or carts. This army organization

35. These relationships can be expressed by the following formula:

$$N = \frac{d(a + b + c) - (yz + 200\ x)}{250 - d(e + f + g)}$$

where N = the number of pack animals; a = the army's total ration of grain in lb.; b = the army's total ration of fodder in lb.; c = the army's total requirement of water in lb.; d = the number of days the provisions needed to be carried; e = a pack animal's ration of grain; f = a pack animal's ration of fodder; and g = a pack animal's ration of water. If the personnel could carry supplies, then y = the number of personnel; z = the average weight a person could carry. If the cavalry horses could carry supplies, then x = the number of horses. When the personnel and cavalry horses can carry supplies, if the resulting number above the division bar is negative, the carrying capacity of the personnel and cavalry horses will be greater than the amount of supplies needed to be carried, and therefore no pack animals will be required. It is doubtful, however, that cavalry horses were regularly used as pack animals since nothing will break their spirit faster than to be used in this way.

was developed by Philip in response to his campaigns in the mountainous regions of Thrace, Paeonia, and Illyria, where the use of carts would be impractical if not impossible over mountain paths, and where large numbers of followers would not only slow the army down (see table 7) but also make the army especially vulnerable while crossing mountain passes (see Appendix 2). Macedonia was a poor country; the phalanx was composed of peasants who could not afford expensive hoplite armor.[36] Few Macedonian peasants possessed expensive oxen, horses, or mules, and those that did could not afford to see their work animals requisitioned for an army expedition. The consequence of Philip's reforms was to make the Macedonian army the fastest, lightest, and most mobile force in existence, capable of making lightning strikes against opponents "before anyone had time to fear the event."

This organization was retained by Alexander, as far as possible throughout his campaigns, and was largely responsible for his army's astonishing speed and mobility which so terrified his adversaries.[37] Even when the size of his army increased, Alexander took great pains to retain its lightness and mobility by destroying wagons and excess baggage and by eliminating followers. Only horses, mules, and camels were used in Alexander's baggage train because they have greater speed and endurance than oxen or donkeys. Philip's and Alexander's troops were much like "Marius' Mules," heavily encumbered with arms, armor, rations, and per-

36. Snodgrass, op. cit., 114–115.
37. D. 4. 5: So much the rapid moves and energetic action of the young man shook the confidence of those who opposed him [entering Boeotia]; P. 26. 7: And the high spirit which he carried into his undertakings rendered his ambition finally invincible, so that it subdued not only enemies, but even times and places; A. 1. 4. 3: The Getae did not sustain even the first charge of the cavalry; for Alexander's bold stroke came as a great shock to them, in that he so easily crossed the Ister, the greatest of rivers, in one night without so much as bridging the stream; A. 1. 7. 5: The Thebans did not learn of his passage of the Gates until his arrival with all his force at Onchestus; A. 3. 17. 4: They (the Uxians), however, astounded at Alexander's swiftness, and overmastered at the very position in which they had chiefly put their trust, fled without so much as coming to close quarters; A. 3. 25. 7: Satibarzanes, for his part, learning of Alexander's proximity and astounded at the swiftness of his approach, fled with a few Areian horsemen; A. 7. 28. 3: And all that had to be done in uncertainty he did with the utmost daring; he was the most skilled in swift anticipation and gripping of his enemy before anyone had time to fear the event; C. 5. 7. 1: That intrepidity in encountering dangers, his promptness in forming and carrying out plans; C. 7. 4. 1: But Bessus [was] greatly terrified by Alexander's speed. . . .

sonal possessions but marching with a light baggage train.[38] Other contemporary armies spared their soldiers from carrying heavy burdens but paid for this amenity with a large, unwieldy baggage train of carts, pack animals, and followers which sharply reduced their speed and mobility. Because many supplies were carried by the troops and a restricted number of servants, the Macedonian army would need far fewer pack animals than another contemporary force carrying an equivalent weight of baggage, and hence the problems of acquiring sufficient numbers of animals and feeding them were also reduced.[39] The restricted use of carts would not only increase the army's mobility in rough terrain but also reduce the number of drivers and the need to carry or acquire replacement parts and lumber for repairs—an important consideration in the treeless areas of eastern Iran, Afghanistan, and Turkestan.[40] In short, the logistic organization of Alexander's army was brilliantly adapted for campaigning in Asia, where the acquisition of pack animals and provisions would often be difficult in barren terrain and where speed and mobility were frequently important tactical advantages.

Only the geographical and logistic problems Alexander encountered will be considered in subsequent chapters: areas where no problems occurred (in the Nile Valley, Tigris-Euphrates Valley, and the Indus Valley) will receive little attention. Conversely, regions where climate, geography, or lack of provisions may have

38. Marius reduced the numbers of pack animals by having the soldiers carry their own cooking utensils and provisions, and hence they were called Marius' Mules (Front. *Strat.* 4. 1. 7; Plut. *Mar.* 13. 1). Both Marius and Philip made these reforms for similar reasons: to increase their armies' speed and mobility and to reduce the numbers of pack animals in regions where animals were difficult to acquire.

39. For example, if the Macedonians carried their arms and armor on pack animals, and if the average weight of the soldier's panoply was 30 lb. and there were 50,000 troops in the army, their combined panoply would weigh 1,500,000 lb. This would require 6,000 animals to carry it and 240 additional animals to carry their grain ration for one day. All these additional animals or their equivalent in carts were not required by Alexander.

40. According to Xenophon (*Cyrop.* 6. 2. 32–39), carts would not only require drivers but a quantity of lumber for replacement parts, skilled carpenters and tools for repairing them, and a shovel and mattock per cart, probably for road building. Only a limited quantity of these men and materials would be needed by Alexander's force.

been significant factors in influencing Alexander's strategic decisions will be studied in depth.

Much in this reconstruction of the Macedonian logistic system is hypothetical for there are many unknown variables that cannot be calculated. Nevertheless, if the solutions to the Macedonian army's logistic problems are ever to have a scientific basis, it is first necessary that hypotheses be advanced which explain the recorded events, however inaccurate they may later prove to be.

2.

Greece and Turkey

Our sources do not indicate from what location Alexander and the Macedonian army left for their expedition. When Arrian begins his account of the army's march into Asia, the Macedonians are marching east past Lake Cercinitis to Amphipolis and the mouth of the Strymon.[1] The army may have started from Therma, the next large town west of Lake Cercinitis and Amphipolis. There are several reasons why Therma would make an excellent point of departure. It was on or near major routes of communication from Thessaly, Epirus, Thrace, and Northern Macedonia via the Axios Valley. It is near abundant supplies of water from the Axios and the springs and streams from Mount Khortiatis, which were sufficient to supply Xerxes' army.[2] Most significant, it was a port, and foodstuffs could easily be shipped to the army while it marshaled in the town. Sea and river transport were always much more efficient than land transport in antiquity since a large merchant ship could carry about 400 tons, while a pack horse or mule could only carry 200 lb. and would consume 20 lb. of foodstuffs daily while traveling.[3] This is why large armies could not remain stationary for extended periods

1. A. 1. 11. 3.
2. Hdt. 7. 127. Naval Intelligence Division, Great Britain, *Greece*, Vol. 3 (1945) 123–124.
3. The largest merchant ships of the fifth century B.C. could transport 10,000 talents (about 400 tons), Thuc. 7. 25. 6. See Chapter 1 for the capabilities of the methods of overland transport available to Alexander.

when remote from sea or river transport: they would rapidly deplete the surpluses of the immediately surrounding territory, and it would become increasingly difficult to transport supplies overland as the distance from the army increased.[4] Xerxes was no doubt attracted to the site of Therma for these reasons, since he halted his army here for a considerable period.[5]

The Macedonians left in early spring of 334 and carried a 30-day supply of provisions with them.[6] These provisions probably only consisted of grain and not water or forage, since in early spring the rivers of this region are in flood and its rich, fertile land would possess abundant fodder and pasture lands.[7] Taking a 30-day supply of grain at the beginning of the march makes excellent logistic sense for two reasons. First, it was always standard practice in antiquity for an army to live off the territory of the enemy and not off one's friends and allies.[8] Second, since it was early spring (either the last week of March or April) and the harvest would not begin until June, the towns along the Thracian coast would be on short rations themselves and could ill afford to provision the Macedonian army. The months before harvest were particularly agonizing for the ancient farmer when "things grow but a man cannot eat his fill."[9] The phenomenon of preharvest hunger is widespread among populations engaged in subsistence agriculture. Before harvest time, the individual's caloric intake drops below the quantity needed for physical maintenance, and the average body weight also declines sharply.[10] Populations living under these conditions seldom have enough surplus available at such times to feed themselves, let alone to supply an army, even if compelled to do so. The synchronization between the march and the harvest date is evident here. If the army left in late March or April, 30 days' provisions would last them to May, when the crop, although only "milk-ripe,"

4. This is why Alexander never spent the winter, or even more than a few weeks, with his entire army in a region remote from a seaport or navigable river; see below p. 61.

5. Hdt. 7. 127–130.

6. P. 15. 1, following Duris of Samos.

7. Naval Intelligence Division, *Greece*, Vol. 3, 116–154.

8. Onasander 6. 13; cf. Xen. *Hel.* 2. 1. 1–2; Amm. Marc. 24. 4. 9; J. K. Anderson, *Military Theory and Practice in the Age of Xenophon* (Berkeley, 1970) 51.

9. Alcman *Frag.* 56.

10. Clark and Haswell, 22f.

could be harvested and eaten.[11] The relationship between the timing and direction of Alexander's marches and the harvest dates and agricultural calendars of the various regions he conquered is of fundamental importance.

We have already seen that it would have been impossible for the Macedonian army to have carried more than a 14-day supply of grain overland, no matter how many pack animals were with the army.[12] Hence, the provisions will have been carried by ship, and this is why the army's itinerary included the coastal towns of Amphipolis, Abdera, Maroneia, probably Aenos, and Sestos.[13] Thanks to the information provided by Arrian, the approximate chronology of the army's itinerary through Thrace can be reasonably restored.

At Therma, the army could take a three days' ration to Amphipolis, some 57 miles away.[14] The envisioned march rate here—19 miles per day—would not be difficult over flat terrain in the spring.[15] Next, the expedition could march directly to Abdera (about 71 miles from Amphipolis) in four days, or it could make the march in two stages: first halting at Neapolis (38 miles from Amphipolis)

11. "Wheat," *Encyclopaedia Britannica* 23 (1943) 558f. The grain is milk-ripe 4 to 5 weeks after fertilization occurs and is fully ripe 8 to 9 weeks after. Xerxes also synchronized his march into Greece with the harvest date (Hdt. 7. 50), as did Lee for the advance of the Confederate Army into Pennsylvania in late June 1863.

12. See Chapter 1, n. 27.

13. A. 1. 11. 3–5.

14. Wherever possible, I have used the distances scientifically measured by those actually traversing the route. However, such measurements are rare, for few people now travel between Abdera and Maroneia, or from Prophthasia to the City of the Arachosians. But when these measurements are available and have been used, they will be noted. Where precise measurements are not available, the following method of measurement has been used. First, the most accurate map of the area is obtained. Next, an engineering measuring caliper is placed on the map's scale at a ten-mile interval. The caliper is then walked along the route shown on the map, which enables virtually all the curves and angles of the route to be measured. 5% is then added to the measured distance to compensate for vertical motion (e.g., movement up and down in mountainous areas) and curves not depicted on the map or not measured by the caliper. This technique is accurate within about 2% when checked against the actual traveling distance and is more accurate than using a hank of string or other primitive methods. Care must be taken to have the initial measurement accurate. It may be checked by walking the caliper along the scale. Where there is a problem as to the route Alexander took, it will be discussed in the appropriate place. When measurements derived from this method are used, they will not be noted.

15. Naval Intelligence Division, *Greece*, Vol. 3, 127–133. The entire Macedonian army achieved a march rate of 19.5 miles per day from Gaza to Pelusium; see table 7.

and then in Abdera (another 33 miles). From Abdera to Maroneia is only 36 miles—a two day march—and after revictualing from the latter town, the Macedonians could carry a three days' supply of provisions to the Hebrus (probably near Aenos), a journey of 55 miles. From Aenos to the Melas River is also about 55 miles, and perhaps the fleet provisioned the army at Leuce Acte at the mouth of the Melas, the same location at which Xerxes' army was revictualed by the Persian fleet some 150 years before.[16] It probably took the army three days to travel over the rocky, broken terrain from the Melas to Sestos, a distance of 47 miles.[17] In addition to the time spent marching, the army would have to halt for at least one day in seven. These halts are necessary because cavalry horses and pack animals cannot withstand the pressure of loads on their backs for more than seven consecutive days without rest.[18] They are also necessary to give the animals time to graze on grasses or greenery, an opportunity they seldom have while the army is marching, since horses, mules, and camels will only eat during the day. Hence, in addition to the 18 days spent marching from Therma, at least two additional days were needed for halts: bringing the total march time to 20 days.[19]

When the army crossed the Hellespont, it would still possess a ten-day supply of grain, no doubt stowed aboard the many cargo vessels remaining with the expedition.[20] This was excellent logistic and strategic planning, since the additional ten-day supply would not only allow the grain in the fields further time to ripen but would also give the Macedonians time to secure a bridgehead and defeat any Persian advance force sent to stop them before they had to begin requisitioning grain from the cities under Persian control. Once the Persian advance force was defeated, the Anatolian towns would not offer much resistance to the conqueror and would give him any supplies he needed.

The Macedonians might have been provisioned from the fleet at Arisbe, Percote, and again near Lampsakos, where the army began

16. Hdt. 7. 25; Maurice, 219.
17. Maurice, 213.
18. Clark and Haswell, 204; Leonard, op. cit., 165, 193, 294; Army Veterinary Dept., 137. See also table 7.
19. The march time is given in A. 1. 11. 5.
20. A. 1. 11. 6.

to turn inland.[21] After passing the latter city, the 30 days' provisions would be about used up, and hereafter the army would have to rely on foraging and requisitions to continue. Hence, Memnon's strategy of laying waste all the territory through which the Macedonians would have to pass would have been extremely effective if carried out.[22] Since he would have ravaged the territory before the crops were harvested, he would not only have deprived Alexander's foraging parties but would have also prevented the towns from replenishing their own limited reserves, from which the Macedonians would also acquire provisions. Persian control of the sea would have effectively blocked supplies from Greece reaching the army by ship.

After the victory at the Granicus, the first topological problem concerning Alexander's route occurs. Most maps illustrating Alexander's route take him due south in almost a straight line from Dascylion to Sardis, oblivious of rugged mountains, steep canyons, and barren scrub land.[23] This path seems to be a distortion of the route of the Roman road that proceeded from Dascylion down the Macestus Valley to Pergamon and hence to Sardis via Thyatira. However, there are good reasons for Alexander to have taken a different route.

First, there is no evidence that Alexander was ever in Dascylion. Arrian[24] wrote that Alexander sent Parmenio to take the town, and it is unlikely that he would bother sending Parmenio when he himself would follow immediately. But even if Alexander was in Dascylion, he would not have chosen the route from there via Pergamon and Thyatira to Sardis. The Macedonian army could not follow any arbitrarily chosen trail: it was strictly limited to terrain where supplies would be sufficient and its baggage train could travel. The upland region between Dascylion and Sardis consists of uninhabited

21. For the Macedonian route here see Walter Leaf, *Strabo on the Troad* (Cambridge, 1923) 101. Robin Lane Fox, *Alexander the Great* (New York, 1974) 515, would amend *par' akten* (along the coast) for the River Praktios in A. 1. 12. 6. However, the passage would then read: "On the next day, he passed Lampsakos and encamped along the coast, which flows from Mount Ida and runs into the sea that is between the Hellespont and the Euxine Sea." This scarcely seems possible. See Green, 169.

22. A. 1. 12. 9.

23. E.g., those based on *CAH*,[1] Vol. 6, 357. Others, e.g., Fritz Schachermeyr, *Alexander der Grosse* (Vienna, 1972), 167, go direct from Zeleia to Sardis.

24. A. 1. 17. 2.

waste land with rugged, barren, crystalline mountains forming acidic soils only capable of supporting scrub vegetation.[25] Communications between northern and southern regions are extremely difficult except along the Aegean coast, since the entire area is broken up by precipitous gorges and mountains.[26]

Alexander, then, was unlikely to have traveled from Dascylion to Sardis directly, and in all probability, he chose the same coastal route followed by all armies traveling north to south in the Troad. Xerxes, Xenophon, Scipio Africanus the Elder, the Arab commander Maslama, the Second Crusade led by Louis VII, and early modern Turkish armies have all traveled along the coastal route past Ilium to Antandrus and Adramyttium.[27] Alexander probably chose the coastal route for the same reasons as these other experienced commanders: large areas of productive land under cultivation in the Scamander Valley and the coastal plains from Antandrus to Adramyttium; abundant water supplies from the Scamander, Euenos, and other smaller streams; the presence of the large towns of Sigeum, Thymbra, Neandria, Assus, Antandrus, Astyra, Killa, Thebe, and Adramyttium on or near his route; and a relatively smooth track, passable for his primitive carts and pack animals. Ancient towns were centers of consumption and foci of food collection and transport networks,[28] and hence the army's problems of acquiring food would be reduced when their route passed through towns wherever possible rather than uninhabited country. Also, towns possess transport facilities such as harbors, ships, pack animals, and roads that would be readily available to import more food if it were needed. Furthermore, because of the limitations of overland transport in antiquity, almost all agricultural production oc-

25. Leaf, op. cit., xvii–xxiv; J. C. Dewdney, *Turkey, an Introductory Geography* (New York, 1971) 164; Naval Staff, Intelligence Department, *A Handbook of Asia Minor*, Vol. 2 (London, 1919) 162, 180, 197, 206: "Plenty of water and wood but no land under cultivation." 274: "Supplies are scarce." 322: "Country [from Bigadich to Kyrkaghach] is generally bare, covered largely with rocks and scrub and supplies are scanty."

26. Naval Staff, *Asia Minor*, Vol. 2, 162; Leaf, op. cit., xxii; Dewdney, op. cit., 163–165.

27. Xerxes: Hdt. 7. 42; Xenophon: Xen. *Anab.* 7. 8. 7–8; Scipio Africanus: Liv. 37. 37. 3–4; Maslama (717 A.D.): Maj. George Oakey, *Military Routes of Communication in Asia Minor* (M.A. Thesis, University of Pennsylvania, 1958) 50; Louis VII in 1148: Steven Runciman, *A History of the Crusades*, Vol. 2 (Cambridge, 1952) 270; early modern Turkish armies: Maurice, 212.

28. M. I. Finley, *The Ancient Economy* (Berkeley, 1973) 125.

curred within a small radius of human settlements.[29] There was no cultivation where there were no settlements, and since 90 percent of ancient populations were engaged in agriculture, settlements necessarily imply agricultural production.[30]

South of Adramyttium, the Macedonians could have turned inland at Pergamon or further south at Myrina, past Magnesia to Sardis—an ancient, well-traveled road.[31] Both routes are abundantly supplied with water, and the alluvial land of the coastal region is the most valuable farmland in Turkey and was always densely settled.[32] Alexander's following the coastal route would also be consistent with his policy of capturing the ports to prevent the Persians from establishing naval bases. Although this practice first receives attention from the sources at Miletus,[33] there is little doubt that Alexander knew from the beginning that the Persian fleet would soon enter the Aegean and had formulated this policy early, as his alliances with Tenedos (surely made when Alexander was in the vicinity of Troy), Dascylion, and Mytilene indicate.[34] The Persian fleet, like Alexander, probably synchronized the beginning of its operations with the harvest date. With 200 men per vessel and 400 vessels, the Persian fleet would consume 120 tons of grain alone per day. Hence, one of the reasons for Alexander's early start (which he was able to achieve because he collected 30 days' provisions to

29. Michael Chisholm, *Rural Settlement and Land Use, an Essay in Location* (London, 1968). This is true today for modern agricultural villages and towns, and it was a fortiori true in antiquity, when the more primitive methods of transport were a greater constraint.

30. In the first modern censuses taken, that of Sweden in 1750 and the United States in 1790, 85–90% of the population lived on farms and were engaged in agriculture. Thus, in the fourth century B.C., with a much less developed commercial or industrial structure than in Europe or the United States in the late eighteenth century, an even larger percentage of the population would be engaged in agriculture. The percentage of the population engaged in cultivation in regions such as Mesopotamia, the Nile Valley, the Lower Helmand Valley, and the Indus Valley may have been somewhat less, since the greater surpluses there could potentially support larger nonagricultural populations. However, agricultural economies based on hydraulic engineering require much higher labor inputs per acre than dry farming. Important commercial centers such as Tyre may have also had a smaller percentage.

31. W. M. Ramsay, *Historical Geography of Asia Minor* (London, 1890) map facing 105.

32. Dewdney, op. cit., 163f.

33. A. 1. 20. 1.

34. Tenedos: A. 2. 2. 2; Mytilene: A. 2. 1. 4. Dascylion was not on the coast but its port, Myrlea, was. The town was captured by Parmenio after the battle of Granicus, A. 1. 17. 2.

last to the harvest) was to anticipate the Persian fleet, which could not be provisioned adequately before June.

There is yet another indication that Alexander followed the coastal route. Tarn was probably correct in stating that Alexander intended to found the town of Alexandria Troas after the battle of the Granicus.[35] Alexander personally examined each site where he founded a city,[36] and there is no reason to doubt that he did so here. There are two occasions when he could have examined the site of Alexandria Troas. The first may have been after he visited Ilium, about 15 miles north of the site. However, this would entail a two-day excursion and waste valuable time when the army was in the precarious position of establishing a base on the Asian coast of the Hellespont. Indeed, Arrian wrote that Alexander proceeded directly from Ilium to Arisbe to rejoin his army.[37] It is more likely that Alexander visited the site after his victory, when his position in north western Anatolia was secure.

After receiving the city of Sardis in surrender and confiscating its badly needed treasury, Alexander advanced to Ephesos, covering the 60-mile distance in four days.[38] The army probably took the Persian Royal Road connecting the two cities which crosses the spur of Mount Tmolus at Kara Bel and proceeds hence down the Cayster Valley.[39] No water or supply problems would be encountered in this rich, productive region, especially now during the harvest.

After settling the affairs of Ephesos and receiving the towns of Magnesia on Maeander and Tralles in surrender, Alexander

35. W. W. Tarn, *Alexander the Great*, Vol. 2 (London, 1948), 240.
36. The Alexandrias that Alexander personally surveyed and that are recorded by the sources on his life are: Alexandropolis in Thrace (P. 9. 1); Alexandria in Egypt (A. 3. 1. 5); Alexandria of the Caucasus (A. 3. 28. 4); Alexandria Margiana (C. 7. 10. 15); Alexandria on the Jaxartes (A. 4. 1. 3); Alexandria Bucephala (C. 9. 1. 6; C. 9. 3. 23; A. 5. 19. 4); Alexandria Nicaea (C. 9. 1. 6; C. 9. 3. 23; A. 5. 19. 4); Alexandria of the Oreitans (A. 6. 22. 5). Other Alexandrias that Alexander is recorded to have founded but that the sources on his life do not mention his having visited are: Alexandria Troas; Alexandria Areion; Alexandria by Issus; Alexandria-Bactra; Alexandria-Prophthasia; Alexandria of the Arachosians; Alexandria on the Oxus (Termez); Alexandria on the Tigris; Alexandria by Babylon; Tarn, op. cit., Vol. 2, 232f. All of these towns were directly astride his route, as given by the sources on his life or the bematists, and it would have been difficult for him not to have seen them.
37. A. 1. 12. 6.   38. A. 1. 17. 10.
39. Ramsay, op. cit., 30, 42, 167; Hdt. 5. 100.

marched south to besiege Miletus, perched on the end of steep, craggy Mount Latmus. Here, the Persian fleet sent to relieve the city encountered its own supply problems when it anchored by Mycale. The Persians had to obtain water from the mouth of the Maeander, but when a small force was sent to prevent their disembarkation, they found themselves virtually besieged in their ships and had to reprovision at Samos.[40] The Macedonians were likely to have had supply problems here too, for the promontory of Mount Latmus possesses neither fields nor rivers and the city of Miletus always obtained its provisions from the Maeander Valley. This may have been one of the reasons Alexander only took a small division to besiege the city.[41] Grain and water would have to be collected from considerable distances in the interior, and once when the sailors from the Macedonian fleet were detailed for gathering fuel and provisions and for convoying stores, they were surprised by a Persian sneak attack.[42] The fleet probably played a major role in transporting supplies here as it did later at Halicarnassos.[43] After the city was captured, the fleet sailing with the army was dismissed except for 20 war ships and several cargo vessels used to transport siege machinery and to supply the army with grain.[44] The fleet was too expensive to maintain in its entirety, and Alexander decided that he could conquer the Persian fleet by capturing their naval bases.[45]

By autumn, the Macedonians reached Halicarnassos via Iassus and undertook a siege lasting about two weeks.[46] This location would give the king his first real test in logistic planning and organization, for the Bodrum Peninsula is a desolate area. Most of it consists of barren hills covered with scrub and small clumps of stunted pines. Fresh water is virtually unobtainable except within the confines of the city itself, and the tiny rivulets would provide

40. A. 1. 19. 7–8.   41. A. 1. 18. 1–3.
42. A. 1. 19. 9.   43. D. 24. 1.
44. D. 22. 5; 24. 1. Of course, Alexander still kept his Hellespont squadrons intact, for they saw action six months later under Amphoterus and Hegelochus (C. 3. 1. 19).
45. A. 1. 18. 9; A. 1. 20. 1.
46. Green, 194, nn. 23, 24. For Alexander's route here see Freya Stark, "Alexander's March from Miletus to Phrygia," *JHS* 78 (1958) 102–120; "Alexander's Minor Campaigns in Turkey," *Geo. Journ.* 122 (1956) 294–305; *Alexander's Path from Caria to Cilicia* (London, 1958). She is incorrect, however, in stating that his route from Miletus to Halicarnassos was via Alabanda and Lagina, as the evidence from Iassus shows.

only a trickle in autumn.[47] Alexander established camp 5 stades (about 1,000 yards) from the city, opposite the Mylasia Gate.[48] This would place it at Yokusbasi near Torba Bay, the terminus for all routes leading to the city from the east.[49] A camp here would not only cut off land communications with the city and serve as a terminus for Alexander's own communications but also the nearby bay would be a convenient harbor for the reception of supply vessels. Although Diodorus only mentions the transport of grain,[50] it is obvious that water and forage would also have to be transported by the fleet: the cargo vessels remaining with the army were being put to good use.

After he captured Halicarnassos, Alexander left a force of 3,000 Greek mercenary infantry and 200 cavalry to garrison Caria and divided the rest of the army. Parmenio received a squadron of the companion cavalry, the magnificent Thessalian cavalry, the allied troops, and the baggage train to conduct a winter campaign against the tribes of Phrygia, while Alexander himself marched into Lycia and Pamphylia to capture the coastal towns.[51]

Parmenio, in addition to his other duties, may have been Alexander's transport officer, who was given general supervision of the baggage train.[52] He would be responsible for its protection, proper marching order, care of the animals, and the correct packing and balance of the saddle bags. He is in charge of the baggage train here and later in Persis and is responsible for the supervision of the captured Persian baggage trains after Issus and Gaugamela. Later, he was given the extraordinary responsibility of transporting the 7,290 tons of treasure stored at Persepolis, Susa, and Pasargadae to Ecbatana on 20,000 mules and 5,000 camels—a task which implies considerable skill, experience, and knowledge of logistic organization.[53]

47. C. T. Newton, *Discoveries at Halicarnassos, Cnidus, and Branchidae* (London, 1863) 573–601; Naval Intelligence Division, Great Britain, *Turkey*, Vol. 2 (1943) 136, 141.

48. A. 1. 20. 2; A. 1. 20. 4.

49. G. E. Bean and J. M. Cook, "The Halicarnassos Peninsula," *BSA* 50 (1955) 131.

50. D. 24. 1.

51. A. 1. 24. 3.

52. For the importance of this officer see Army Veterinary Dept., 135f. Cf. Xen. *Cyrop.* 6. 2. 35.

53. Parmenio has the supervision of the baggage train in Lycia, A. 1. 24. 3; in Persis, A. 3. 18. 1; C. 5. 6. 11; and he was given the task of transporting the treasure,

When Parmenio was no longer with the army, his position may have been taken by Craterus or perhaps Erigyius.[54]

The king also dismissed the recently married soldiers for a leave of absence to visit their families, which implies that there were no wives or children with the army as yet. Since it was now winter, one of the reasons Alexander may have divided his army was to conserve provisions in the mountainous regions of Lycia. It was standard procedure for Alexander to divide his army in smaller units in areas where the acquisition of supplies was difficult.[55] Another reason for dividing his army here was to increase its maneuverability in the narrow valleys and mountain passes of Lycia.

Alexander's divisions now entered the rich but narrow valleys of Lycia and Pamphylia, whose towns would have ample stores for the army's reduced numbers.[56] The Macedonians would never be more than ten miles from an important source of drinkable water since both regions are abundantly supplied with rivers and fresh-water lakes. After subduing Aspendus and conducting operations against the Termessians and Sagalassians, the king marched north through the valleys of Pisidia, all of it productive farmland containing copious supplies of water.[57] At Celaenae, Alexander left one of his most able commanders, Antigonus Monophthalmus, with 1,500 troops to garrison the citadel,[58] a major site of great strategic importance, guarding the routes south to Pamphylia, west to

A. 3. 19. 7; D. 71. 1-2; P. 37. 2; Str. 15. 3. 9. He was in charge of the enemy's captured trains after the battle of Issus, A. 2. 11. 10; C. 3. 12. 27; and Gaugamela, A. 3. 15. 4.

54. Craterus: A. 4. 28. 7; A. 5. 21. 4; C. 5. 6. 11; Erigyius: A. 3. 23. 2; C. 6. 4. 3.

55. Other examples of Alexander dividing his army where supplies would be insufficient for the whole force were: Miletus: A. 1. 18. 1-3; during the expedition to the Oracle of Ammon: C. 4. 7. 6; before entering Persis, "a sparse land and rugged": C. 5. 3. 3; Hdt. 9. 122; during the minor campaign into the interior of Persis: C. 5. 6. 12; before entering the Dasht-i-Kavir Desert in pursuit of Darius: A. 3. 20. 1; before attacking the mountain strongholds of Sogdia: A. 4. 17. 3; before reentering Persis: A. 6. 29. 1.

56. For the nature of the land see Stark, "Minor Campaigns," 296–302; Dewdney, op. cit., 175–180; Xavier de Planhol, *De la Plaine Pamphylienne aux Lacs Pisidiens* (Paris, 1958). Parmenio took one squadron of Companion cavalry, the Thessalian cavalry, and the allies, or about one-fourth of the army. The number of recently married soldiers is, of course, unknown. Thus Alexander seems to have had somewhat less than three-quarters of his army for his Lycian expedition, or less than 34,000 troops.

57. Stark, "Minor Campaigns," 119.

58. A. 1. 29. 3.

the Hermus and Maeander valleys, and north to Gordion.[59] This fortress was an important link in Alexander's communications, and, later, Antigonus used it as a base to fight three hard battles against the Persians.[60] From Celaenae, the Macedonians probably followed the old military route through Amorium, Pessinus, and Germa to Gordion.[61] Since only part of the army wintered with Alexander at Gordion, they would not make an intensive demand upon the agricultural resources of the surrounding territory.

When did Alexander begin his march from Gordion across the Anatolian Plateau, a place "abounding in villages rather than cities?" (C. 3. 1. 11). Most of Phrygia and Cappadocia is steppe, suitable only for grazing, except for thin strips of intensive cultivation near the valleys of the Sangarius, Halys, and Cappadox (Delice Irmak).[62] Since the harvest begins here in late July or August,[63] it is unlikely that the king left Gordion much before late July for the reasons noted above.[64] Another reason for delaying the march until the harvest was to simplify the army's problem of acquisition, since after that date the crops would have already been collected in the villages or towns, saving the army the arduous task of harvesting it themselves. The passage of the Macedonian army placed a severe burden on the slender agricultural resources of the Plateau, and Curtius noted that it would have been impossible for the army to retreat over the same route by which they advanced since they had eaten all the crops along the way.[65] The army was in a real sense a moving city, larger than almost any in the ancient world, except for the extraordinary urban conglomerations of Mesopotamia, and its requirements of food and water were correspondingly high. If the Macedonians took a month to subdue Phrygia and Cappadocia and to march the 417 miles from Gordion to Tarsus, they would require 4,000 tons of grain alone,[66] at a consumption rate of 130

59. Green, 209f.

60. C. 4. 1. 35.

61. Ramsay, op. cit., 29–30, 49; Frederick S. Starr, "Mapping Ancient Roads in Anatolia," *Archaeology* 16 (1963) 163.

62. Naval Intelligence Division, *Turkey*, Vol. 2, 136; Dewdney, op. cit., 195.

63. Naval Intelligence Division, *Turkey*, Vol. 2, 135; William J. Hamilton, *Researches in Asia Minor, Pontus, and Armenia*, Vol. 2 (London, 1842) 222.

64. See p. 27.

65. C. 3. 5. 6.

66. 63,000 personnel × 3 lb. × 31 da. = 5,859,000 lb. of grain. 6,280 cavalry horses × 10 lb. × 31 da. = 1,946,800 lb. of grain. 1,300 baggage animals × 10

tons per day. This figure becomes more meaningful when it is compared with the average gross yield rates of antiquity. With a two-field system, the average annual yield per acre of wheat would be .25 tons at most, or 160 tons per square mile.[67] Hence, the Macedonians on their march would consume the total crop production of 25 square miles, and they had a very restricted area upon which they could draw because of the limited area of cultivated land and because none of the rivers of the region were navigable.

There is no indication in our sources of which route Alexander took from Ancyra in Phrygia to the Cilician Gates, which he would have to cross to capture Cilicia and its important harbors, but there were essentially two routes he could have followed. The first is the southern route following the south bank of the Halys, later to become famous as the Pilgrims' Route; the second was the Persian military route of the Royal Road followed by Xerxes, which proceeded east from Ancyra, crossed the Halys slightly north of El-madag, thence to Tavium and down the Delice Irmak Valley, and crossed the Halys once again north of Caesarea-Mazaca.[68] It is more probable that Alexander chose the latter since it was the major military route in Anatolia during the Persian Empire and since the southern route does not appear in history until the Roman period.[69]

---

lb. $\times$ 31 da. $=$ 403,000 lb. of grain. 5,859,000 $+$ 1,946,800 $+$ 403,000 $=$ 8,208,000 $=$ 4,104 tons of grain. This excludes the rations for any pack animals carrying food-stuffs. If the army marched at 15 miles per day and halted for one day in seven (see table 7), they would cover the 417-mile distance in 31 or 32 days.

67. Clark and Haswell, 152; Jardé, op. cit., 31f. This corresponds to a gross yield rate of 20 bushels per acre. In modern Persia, however, farmers using modern agricultural techniques consider a yield of 8 to 11 bushels per acre high. And arable land is often left in fallow for three and even four years before producing a crop, Naval Intelligence Division, Great Britain, *Persia* (1944) 439. Yield rates in Mesopotamia, the Nile Valley, and the Indus Valley were higher.

68. Starr, op. cit., 163; John Garstang, "Hittite Military Roads in Asia Minor," *AJA* 47 (1943) 40f.; John Garstang and O. R. Gurney, *The Geography of the Hittite Empire* (London, 1959) 2–31; J. G. C. Anderson, "Explorations in Asia Minor During 1898," *BSA* 4 (1897–98) 72–78; J. G. C. Anderson, "The Road System of Eastern Asia Minor with the Evidence of Byzantine Campaigns," *JHS* 17 (1897) 22–30; Ramsay, op. cit., 254f.; D. H. French, "A Study of Roman Roads in Anatolia," *Anatolian Studies* 24 (1974) 143–149; Rodney S. Young, "Gordion of the Royal Road," *Proc. Amer. Philosoph. Soc.* 107 (1963),348–364; Victor W. Von Hagen, "The Horror of the Tomissa Crossing," *Geographical Magazine* 48 (1976) 278–281; Hdt. 5. 52. This route was the most important communications route from the Hittite period to the Persian Empire.

69. Ramsay, op. cit., 256.

It must be stressed again that a military route is not a mere line drawn on a map but a narrow corridor with sufficient agricultural and water resources in the immediate vicinity with which large numbers of men and animals can be supported. The Delice Irmak Valley is wide and fertile, while the Halys often flows through narrow gorges with precipitous banks. Spring flooding in the latter makes cultivation hazardous, and because of the steep banks, irrigation of the surrounding plain was impossible until the construction of modern dams.[70]

Whichever route Alexander chose, he would somehow have to reach the Cilician Gates from the lower bend of the Halys River sometime in August, the driest time of year in the most arid and desolate region of Anatolia.[71] In terms of water and agricultural resources, the most feasible route for Alexander to have chosen went from Caesarea-Mazaca via Moustilia to Tyana, a journey of 82 miles.[72] A route further west would take the Macedonians near the Salt Lake (Tuz Golu) where fresh water is unobtainable in summer since the region is virtually true desert.[73] Except for small pockets of cultivation at Incesu and Yeşilhisar, the whole route from Mazaca to Tyana in August was, as Hamilton attests, "barren and uncultivated and the burnt up pasture scarcely afforded food to a few flocks of sheep."[74] Although we are not told how long the army took to march the distance (and often when the army was short of supplies, Alexander forced it to march rapidly), judging from the difficulty of the terrain and the hot climate, it would probably take a minimum of five to six days.

70. Dewdney, op. cit., 35, 50–53, 219–235; V. Flottwell, "Aus dem Stromgebiet des Qyzyl-Yrmaq (Halys)," *Pett. Mitt. Ergänzungsheft* 24 (1894–95) 114; John Macdonald Kinneir, *Journey Through Asia Minor, Armenia, and Kordistan* (London, 1818) 78–105; Maj. Robert Whitney Imbrie, "Crossing Asia Minor, the Country of the New Turkish Republic," *Natl. Geo. Magazine* 46 (1924) 464. Naval Intelligence Division, *Turkey*, Vol. 1, 165f.

71. Dewdney, op. cit., 35, 50–53, 195f.; Hamilton, op. cit., 213–304; Naval Staff, *Asia Minor*, Vol. 4, pt. 2, 263–272; Sirri Erinc, "Climatic Types and the Variation of Moisture Regions in Turkey," *Geo. Rev.* 40 (1950) 225; Naval Intelligence Division, *Turkey*, Vol. 1, 164f.; J. H. M. Cornwall, "A Journey in Anatolia," *Geo. Journ.* 64 (1924) 218. Hamilton's account is especially valuable since he traveled the route at about the same time as Alexander, in August.

72. For the distance: Naval Staff, *Asia Minor*, Vol. 4, pt. 2, 270.

73. Hamilton, op. cit., 213–304; Dewdney, op. cit., 195f.; Naval Intelligence Division, *Turkey*, Vol. 1, 164f.

74. Hamilton, op. cit., 294.

The worst problem would have been water: the small stream running through Yeşilhisar would have been entirely inadequate in August to supply the almost 100,000 gallons of water the Macedonians consumed each day.[75] It is worth noting that only one-third of the available supply of water from a river could be utilized since it is flowing away while being drawn upon.[76] If Alexander fed his troops full rations after leaving Mazaca, their rations would run out in two and a half days in the vicinity of Yeşilhisar. Few supplies could be obtained for the remaining three or four days' journey to the vicinity of Tyana, which would have caused a heavy loss of life among the pack animals and personnel from exhaustion and dehydration. If the army were fed half rations from Mazaca, a dangerous procedure under such conditions, the food and water would run out in four days when the army reached Misli; still a two-day journey to Tyana.

To resolve this shortage of supplies, Alexander certainly had magazines of provisions established along his intended line of march. Advance depots are necessary for even small expeditions traveling through regions where neither grain nor water would be available along the route.[77] In this location, food and water could be carried by camel from Mazaca to Incesu and north from Tyana to Misli. Water depots could be created by damming up small streams or by filling their empty beds with water brought from elsewhere.[78] For magazines to be established, however, Alexander must first secure the alliance of the peoples along the intended route since they would be responsible for supplying the depots and for maintaining security along the route. If advance depots were not established in terrain such as this, or if they were destroyed by marauders, first the pack animals and then the followers and men would die, desert, or refuse to march further, thus placing the entire expedition in peril.

75. Ibid., 284, 294, for the state of the river in late July; 63,000 personnel would require 31,500 gal. of water per day; 7,580 cavalry horses and baggage animals would require 60,640 gal. of water per day at 8 gal. per day. 31,500 + 60,640 = 92,140 gal.

76. Maurice, 221.

77. Lt. Arthur Conolly, *Journey to the North of India Overland from England*, Vol. 1 (London, 1838) 188, 349; James Morier, *A Journey Through Persia, Armenia, and Asia Minor to Constantinople in the Years 1808 and 1809* (London, 1812) 147; C. 8. 10. 13.

78. As in the Gaza-Beersheba campaign of 1917. Water could be brought south from the Halys and Kara Su and north from the springs near Tyana.

However, it was not sufficient for Alexander to merely secure an alliance with the peoples along the route where magazines would be established. The taking of hostages or the establishment of garrisons was also required to insure that the new allies' responsibilities were fulfilled properly in regions such as this where supplies would be difficult to obtain.[79] Thus, the Cappadocians surrendered lands on the far side of the Halys and probably gave hostages as well before Alexander entered their country.[80] We have already noted the limited ability of the Macedonian baggage train to transport supplies overland for long distances. Therefore, since only a restricted amount of supplies could be carried from one district to the next, Alexander would have to arrange the collection of provisions for the army in advance all through his campaigns; and doubtless this was done with the local officials, who regularly surrendered to Alexander before he entered their territory.[81] Supplies would be acquired by gifts, requisition, or by purchase by the troops at markets.[82] Not to have surrendered to Alexander before he entered a district was considered a hostile action,[83] and special operations were required to assure the army's food supply in such cases.[84]

79. The Macedonian army would experience supply difficulties and would probably need advance depots of provisions in the following locations: (1) between the lower bend of the Halys to Tyana; (2) from the Nahr el Kebir to the Nahr el Arash in Syria; (3) from Tyre to Gaza; (4) in the Sinai; (5) from the mouths of the Nile to Paraetonium; (6) from Hamah to Aleppo; (7) from Persepolis to Isfahan; (8) in the Kara Kum Desert for Alexander's attempted campaign into Bactria in 330; (9) for the Gedrosian Desert; (10) for Hephaistion's expedition along the Iranian coast of the Persian Gulf.

Of these, locations 3, 4, 5, and 10 were probably established by the fleet. For 1, 2, 3, 7, and 8, alliances were made with the peoples occupying the territory through which the Macedonians would march, and for location 1, hostages were taken by the Macedonians (C. 3. 1. 23); for 2, a temporary garrison was established (A. 2. 13. 7); for 7, a garrison was established (A. 3. 25. 2); while for 8, Alexander won over the towns by his fair dealing before the main force marched through (D. 73. 1). Since 6 was already in Macedonian hands by the time the army marched through, no alliance would need to be made. Location 9 represents a special case which is given its own separate study in Chapter 5.

80. A. 2. 4. 2; C. 3. 1. 23.

81. Surrenders before the Macedonians' advance into a territory: C. 4. 7. 1–4; C. 9. 7. 12–13; C. 9. 8. 7; C. 8. 10. 1–2; C. 8. 13. 1; A. 1. 23. 8; A. 1. 24. 5; A. 1. 26. 2; A. 1. 28. 1; A. 1. 17. 3; A. 1. 24. 4; A. 3. 1. 2; A. 5. 21. 6; A. 5. 3. 5; A. 3. 25. 1; A. 6. 17. 2–3; A. 3. 23. 4; A. 4. 22. 6. One could add many other examples.

82. Purchases: A. 6. 23. 1; A. 6. 23. 6; cf. Xen. *Anab.* 1. 5. 10; 2. 3. 24; 2. 4. 5. Requisitions: C. 9. 10. 5. Gifts: C. 4. 2. 2; C. 8. 12. 6; A. 5. 3. 5.

83. D. 76. 3; C. 6. 5. 11; A. 3. 17. 1–3; A. 6. 15. 5–6; A. 6. 21. 3.

84. See p. 72.

The march through Cappadocia passed without incident and after encamping at the Camp of Cyrus (Pozanti),[85] they passed through the Cilician Gates after they had been abandoned by the feckless Arsames. Considering the immense difficulties armies experience in crossing mountain passes (see Appendix 2), Alexander considered the Persian abandonment of the Cilician Gates one of the greatest strokes of luck of his career.[86] Arsames, belatedly following the example of Memnon of Rhodes, began devastating the land around Tarsus,[87] an action which did not affect the Macedonians' logistic situation since it was quickly halted by Alexander's rapid approach. Alexander entered Tarsus, the most malarial location in Anatolia,[88] on about the first week of September 333,[89] a little over a month after leaving Gordion.

Immediately after entering the city, the king was apparently infected by pernicious malaria,[90] which incapacitated him for almost two months. Darius, meanwhile, had been marshaling his forces at Babylon, and when he heard of the death of Memnon by the first week of September, he left Babylon on the 577-mile journey up the Euphrates to Sochoi (Darab Sak on the Amuq Plain), a march which probably took about 48 days, including the necessary halts and the five days it took to cross the river.[91] When Alexander had

85. W. M. Ramsay, "Cilicia, Tarsus, and the Great Tarsus Pass," *Geo. Journ.* 22 (1903) 383f. See also Schachermeyr, op. cit., 663–671, on the Cilician Gates.

86. C. 3. 4. 11.

87. C. 3. 4. 3.

88. Naval Staff, *Asia Minor*, Vol. 4, pt. 2, 34. It is also the hottest; average summer temperatures are 113° F. in the shade and 122° F. in the sun while moderating to 104° F. at night.

89. A. R. Bellinger, *Essays on the Coinage of Alexander the Great*, Numismatic Studies, 11 (New York, 1963) 10–11; Marcel Dieulafoy, "La bataille d'Issus, analyse critique d'un travail manuscrit du Commandant Bourgeois," *Mem. Inst. Nat. France Acad. Inscr. et Belles-Lettres* 39 (1914) 56–57; Green, 220; Judeich, in Kromayer and Veith, *Antike Schlachtfelder* 4 (Berlin, 1929) 355.

90. I have written an analysis of Alexander's illness which will appear in *Classical Philology*. It should be noted that the First Crusade deliberately avoided entering Cilicia in early September because of the deadly malarial conditions there at that time of year, Runciman, op. cit., Vol. 1, 190.

91. Darius began his march from Babylon shortly after he received word of Memnon's death (C. 3. 2. 1; D. 30–31. 1). Alexander received word of Memnon's death shortly before his own illness, about the first week of September (D. 31. 4); hence, sometime in the fourth week of August or early in the first week of September. Curtius (3. 3–4. 1) describes the death of Memnon and Darius' march just before Alexander entered Cilicia. Now, if Alexander received intelligence of Mem-

almost recovered from his illness, he received intelligence that the Persians were within a five days' march of Cilicia.[92] Five days later, perhaps in the fourth week of October, the king had fully recovered,[93] and he sent Parmenio with the allied infantry, the Greek mercenaries, the Thracians, and the Thessalian cavalry—at most one-fourth of the army[94]—to picket the passes leading into Cilicia from the surrounding mountains.[95] Parmenio also occupied the Kara Kapu Pass, which connects the Adana Plain with the Plain of

---

non's death at this time, Darius, by the splendid Persian postal service (Xen. *Cyrop.* 8. 6. 17–18), would also receive the message at about the same time or a little later. He is already on the march by the time he receives word of Alexander's illness (C. 3. 7. 1). The *terminus post quem* for Memnon's death is given by Curtius (C. 3. 1. 21) and Plutarch (18. 3). Curtius wrote that Alexander was still unaware of Memnon's death while he was at Gordion, which, we have seen, he probably left no earlier than late July, and Plutarch wrote that he heard of Memnon's death after leaving Gordion in late July. Hence, Memnon's death probably occurred in mid-August with the message reaching Alexander and Darius in the last week of August or the first week of September.

It is 577 miles from Babylon to Sochoi by the Euphrates route which Darius apparently took (C. 3. 7. 1; C. 3. 3. 7). It would take Darius 48 days to achieve this distance at 15 miles per day including 5 halts and the 5 days it took to cross the Euphrates (C. 3. 7. 1). Sochoi is to be located at Darab Sak on the upper Kara Su; René Dussaud, *Topographie historique de la Syrie antique et médiévale* (Paris, 1927) 445.

Tarn, op. cit., Vol. 1, 26, misled once again by Curtius' rhetoric, believed that Darius' force was smaller than Alexander's or about the same size. However, the passages he cites do not say that Darius' force was small, but only that because of the restricted nature of the battle field, the full numbers of the Persian army could not be used with effect. Arrian (2. 8. 5–7) lists 130,000 infantry and 30,000 cavalry in Darius' force, and Curtius (3. 9. 1–6) lists 119,000 infantry plus cavalry. Curtius, 4. 9. 3 and 4. 12. 13 also give a total of about 160,000 for the Persian army at the battle of Issus. Arrian (2. 8. 8) wrote that some said that Darius' force numbered 600,000, but this is apparently not what he believed.

92. C. 3. 5. 10; cf. C. 3. 5. 6; D. 32. 2; D. 31. 6.

93. C. 3. 6. 8; C. 3. 6. 16.

94. At the Hellespont, Alexander has 24,800 Macedonians, 12,600 Greeks, 900 Thracians and Paeonians, 8,000 other Balkan troops, and 1,800 Thessalians (D. 17. 3–5, table 4). He loses 129 at the Granicus (J. 11. 6. 12), all the Argives at Sardis (A. 1. 17. 8), picks up 300 Greeks at Miletus (A. 1. 19. 6), leaves 3,200 Greeks behind at Halicarnassos as a garrison for Caria (A. 1. 23. 6), and loses 56 unidentified troops at the city during the siege (A. 1. 20. 10–1. 22. 7), loses another 21 troops at Sagalassus (A. 1. 28. 8), leaves a garrison of 1,500 unidentified troops at Celaenae (A. 1. 29. 3), receives 3,300 Macedonians, 150 Greeks, and 200 Thessalians at Gordion (A. 1. 29. 4), and some Agrianians before Issus; see table 4. Even if no Greek, Thessalian, or Thracian died at the Granicus, Halicarnassos, Sagalassus, or was left in the garrison at Celaenae—which is extremely improbable—all these contingents together would still only amount to 27% of the whole army.

95. A. 2. 5. 1; D. 32. 2.

Issus, and captured the latter town (Kara Huyuk).[96] By this time, the Persians had encamped at Sochoi, and Parmenio had to drive out the Persian pickets already occupying the Syrian Gates.[97] Darius had chosen his location with care, since the Amuq Plain offered unrestricted maneuverability for his large force and, at first, abundant supplies. It was also strategically located between the Beilan Pass and the Amanic Gates, an excellent vantage point from which to check the Macedonians as their column slowly and with difficulty trickled down from either pass.

Alexander himself, although he knew of their presence, did not march against the Persians but instead went into western Cilicia where he first subdued Soli and in a week-long campaign overcame the mountain tribes of the region.[98] After completing this operation, which was probably intended in part to secure his rear in the impending battle against Darius, the king returned to Soli, where he conducted sacrifices to Asclepius, held a review of his army, a relay race with torches, and athletic and literary competitions to show "with what great confidence he scorned the Persians."[99] Then, marching east again, he reached Tarsus and Magarsus (Dort Direkli near Karataş),[100] where he sacrificed to Athena, and hence

96. C. 3. 7. 6–7. After exhaustive and diligent surveys of the Cilician Plain, Kara Huyuk emerges as the only conceivable candidate for the town of Issus, M. V. Seton-Williams, "Cilician Survey," *Anatolian Studies* 4 (1954) 159. It is also very near to where the literary sources place the town: C. L. Murison, "Darius III and the Battle of Issus," *Historia* 21 (1972) 406–407, nn. 22, 23, conveniently sums up the literary evidence.

97. D. 32. 2; C. 3. 7. 7. It was impossible for Alexander, with his excellent intelligence and communications systems (Eugene N. Borza, "Alexander's Communications," *Proceedings of the Second International Symposium on Ancient Macedonia* (1973); Green, 404f.; see below p. 71) not to have known the location of the Persian army at Sochoi when it encamped toward the end of October. It was impossible to keep the location of the Persian king and his army of perhaps 160,000 men a secret. It was impossible for the barbarians occupying the Pillars of Jonah and Beilan Passes, whom Parmenio drove out, to have no knowledge of the Persian army encamped just over the passes on the Amuq Plain. It was impossible for Parmenio, who later occupied these passes, or for any sentient human being, not to see the Persian army on the Amuq Plain. To have Alexander ignorant of Darius' location until he reached Mallus flatly contradicts C. 3. 5. 10; C. 3. 5. 6; D. 32. 2., and common sense, and it would be a situation unparalleled in the annals of military history.

98. A. 2. 5. 6.

99. C. 3. 7. 3.

100. L. Robert, "Contributions à la topographie des villes de l'Asie Mineure méridionale," *CRAI* (1951) 257; Seton-Williams, op. cit., 154; Helmut Th. Bossert, *Journ. of the Turk. Hist. Soc.* 14 (1950) 662.

to Mallus (near Kiziltahta),[101] where he conducted more sacrifices.

Alexander, after recovering and learning of Darius' whereabouts, so far from immediately advancing to meet the Persians, pursued a policy of deliberate delay, flaunting his unconcern for the huge Persian army encamped just a short distance away by holding dress reviews, games, and literary competitions. This policy was undertaken deliberately to provoke Darius into entering the narrow regions of Cilicia, restricted by mountains and swamps, where he would lose his important tactical advantage of open space. Little wonder that the Persian command's fighting blood ran hot after learning of the displays at Soli.[102] Yet, there is another reason why Alexander knew that Darius would advance into Cilicia, one that can be determined by a comparison with another army in a similar situation, although far removed in time.

Consider the position of the Confederate Army at Gettysburg on July 1–3, 1863. The army of 75,000 troops, almost all of which were infantry under the command of Robert E. Lee, advanced into southern Pennsylvania in late June, the harvest date for the winter wheat that was grown extensively in the region, and secured an area of over 300 square miles surrounding Gettysburg. Southern Pennsylvania is among the most productive agricultural regions in the United States. Far from being engaged in subsistence agriculture, developments in the science and technology of crop production as well as the spread of efficient means of transport such as the railroad and efficiently harnessed horse-drawn wagons had enabled the region to become a breadbasket for Washington, Baltimore, and Harrisburg. The Confederate Army had a well-organized commissariat of wagons drawn by efficiently harnessed mules and horses.

Nevertheless, despite all these advantages, in two days after the army had concentrated at Gettysburg, the food began to run low. This is because when any army remains stationary and is remote from river or sea transport, it will quickly exhaust the supplies of the surrounding territory, no matter how productive that territory is and no matter how great the capability of the animal-drawn trans-

---

101. *FA* 5 (1950) 120; *FA* 6 (1951) 3360; Robert, op. cit., 267; Seton-Williams, op. cit., 161; Bossert, op cit., 661–666.

102. C. 3. 8. 10–11; A. 2. 6. 3–5; P. 19. 1. The south coast of Cilicia is marshy for 10 to 15 kilometers inland from Tarsus to Karrataş, today as it was in antiquity, Seton-Williams, op. cit., 121, 128.

port system. Lee understood that because of the shortage of supplies, he could not conduct a lengthy defensive operation against the Federal troops in their strong positions and hence was forced to launch the disastrous attacks of July 2 and 3.[103]

Darius was also remote from the Euphrates and the sea, and the logistic capabilities of his commissariat were far less than were the Confederate Army's of 1863, no matter what type of wagons or draught animals he used.[104] Alexander, however, was able to delay in Cilicia without supply problems since he had access to the sea transport facilities at the ports of Tarsus, Soli, and Magarsus. It is likely, then, that the Persians were rapidly exhausting the resources of the Amuq Plain since they had remained there for at least two weeks,[105] and, as Alexander well knew, Darius was compelled either to attack or to order a demoralizing and humiliating retreat.[106] Supply was the basis of Lee's strategy as it probably was for Darius.

At Mallus, Alexander received intelligence that Darius still remained at Sochoi, and the Macedonian king began to advance eastward. The site of Mallus was discovered over 25 years ago and should no longer need discussion.[107] A problem arises here con-

103. For the battle of Gettysburg see Douglas Southall Freeman, *Lee's Lieutenants: A Study in Command*, Vol. 3 (New York, 1944) 20–189. Lee himself wrote, "We were unable to await an attack, as the country was unfavorable for collecting supplies in the presence of the enemy who could restrain our foraging parties by holding the mountain passes [10 miles west of Gettysburg]." Compare Gen. J. Early's attack at Cedar Creek on October 17, 1864; he wrote, "I was now compelled to move back for want of provisions and forage, or attack the enemy in his position with the hope of driving him from it, and I determined to attack." (Freeman, 597). Darius faced the same decision (C. 3. 8. 7–9) and met the challenge the same way as these other brave and experienced commanders.

104. For the limitations of ancient transport see above, Chapter 1.

105. This is the minimum length of time it would have taken to march from Tarsus to Soli, conduct a week-long campaign against the mountaineers, and march back to Mallus. It may indeed have taken longer; Judeich, op. cit., 358, n. 2, estimated three to four weeks.

106. Darius would not be able to utilize sea transport from the Syrian coast: the Orontes River is not navigable (Naval Intelligence Division, Naval Staff, Great Britain, *Handbook of Syria* [London, n.d.] 402), and Sochoi—60 miles from the coast—is too far to be effectively supplied from vessels at the coast. At this time the Phoenician fleet was in the Aegean (D. 29. 2) and so could not convoy stores. Unprotected merchant ships would be attacked by elements of Alexander's own small fleet (A. 2. 7. 2; D. 22. 5; D. 24. 1) if they tried to provision Darius. For the 60-mile radius for effective transport of provisions overland, see below p. 56. Alexander could afford to wait; Darius could not.

107. See n. 101.

cerning the Macedonians' march rate from Mallus to Myriandrus (Ada Tepe?),[108] a distance of 87 miles.[109] Some, following Arrian (2. 6. 2), assert that the distance was covered by the army in two days,[110] while others maintain that this rate of speed was impossible and that the march took from three to six days.[111] The fastest average march rate ever recorded for the entire Macedonian army with all its baggage, cumbersome wagons, and followers was 19.5 miles per day. It was physically impossible for Alexander, with the forces he had at Mallus and those divisions that later joined him at Issus, to have marched from Mallus to Myriandrus in two days, and those who compare this rate with Alexander's march rate from the Caspian Gates to Hecatompylos, or with the return from the Kalat-i-Nadiri to Artacoana, or with his march to Maracanda,[112] make a serious error. One does not compare the march rate achieved by 500 mounted infantry in hot pursuit over open country with the rate of an entire army with all its baggage, wagons, and followers traversing rough terrain and two mountain passes. Yet, it appears that many are unaware that such distinctions even exist. It is far worse to compare the march rates of a Macedonian army of the fourth century B.C. with fast, lightly equipped units of the eighteenth or nineteenth centuries A.D. under completely different geographical conditions, methods of transport and harnessing techniques, and with only a small fraction of the number of combatants. Yet such comparisons have been made, much to the detriment of historical accuracy.[113] Since the Macedonian army could not have

108. Seton-Williams, op. cit., 127. See Murison, op. cit., 407, n. 23, for the literary evidence. Although no pre-Hellenistic remains have yet been found at Ada Tepe in the surveys conducted there, surveys, of course, can only establish the *presence* of time periods, not their *absence*. Ada Tepe seems to be the only conceivable candidate for Myriandrus, and its location there is supported by the literary evidence.

109. Naval Staff, *Asia Minor*, Vol. 4, pt. 2, routes 10, 50, pp. 209–210, 312–314. Ada Tepe is 10 km. south of Alexandretta, Seton-Williams, op. cit., 127.

110. Murison, op. cit., 409; Franz Miltner, "Alexanders Strategie bei Issos," *Oest. Jh.* 28 (1933) 73–74; Dieulafoy, op. cit., 58–59.

111. A. Bauer, "Die Schlacht bei Issos," *Öst. Jh.* 2 (1899) 123: five to six days; W. Dittberner, *Issos, ein Beitrag zur Geschichte Alexanders des Grossen* (Berlin, 1908) 79: three days.

112. E.g., Miltner, op. cit., 73–74. See table 7.

113. E.g., C. Neumann, "A Note on Alexander's March Rates," *Historia* 20 (1971) 196–198. The accumulation of examples is of no value unless one understands the general principles governing a large army's movement. For the problem of Alexander's march rates, see table 7.

traversed 87 miles in two days, as Bauer saw long ago,[114] what did happen?

First, it is not at all certain that Arrian wrote that the Macedonian army traveled from Mallus to Myriandrus in two days. His sequence of events (2. 6. 1–2) is as follows: First, Alexander at Mallus hears a report that Darius is still encamped by the Assyrian Gates. Then Alexander assembles a council of war (we are not told where), and his commanders urge him to march against the enemy. The next day, he marches against the Persians, and in two days (we are not told from where) he passes the Gates (we are not told which) and encamps near Myriandrus.[115]

Quintus Curtius supplies the flesh and blood to the skeleton Arrian has provided (see map, p. 163). He wrote (3. 7. 5–10) that first Alexander advanced from Mallus to Castabalum in two days to contact Parmenio, who had earlier captured Issus. The distance between Mallus and Castabalum (Bodrum)[116] is about 53 miles, and Alexander probably took only a cavalry escort and/or a company of light armed troops. Alexander and Parmenio with the forces given to him returned to the main army via the pass of Kalekoy and marched into Issus. At Issus, a council of war was held to plan the strategy against the Persians. From the town, the army passed the Pillars of Jonah (note the correct spelling) Pass and advanced to Myriandrus, about 38 miles away.[117] Thus, if we accept Curtius' statement (3. 7. 8) that the strategic council occurred at Issus, Arrian's two-day march for the whole army would have been from Issus to Myriandrus (38 miles) instead of from Mallus to Myriandrus (87 miles). From these sources as well as the geography

114. Bauer, op. cit., 123. He assumed it was so obvious that a large army could not cross two passes and march 87 miles in 48 hours that he did not give any explanation. Unfortunately, his assumption was incorrect.

115. The phrase Ἔνθα δὴ συναγαγὼν τοὺς ἑταίρους . . . is of no chronological value since ἔνθα δὴ means 'then,' 'thereupon,' or 'hereupon': cf., e.g., Hdt. 1. 159; Xen. *Hel.* 2. 4. 39; Aesch. *Pers.* 490; Plato *Prot.* 324A.

116. E. L. Hicks and J. Theodore Bent, "Recent Discoveries in Eastern Cilicia," *JHS* 11 (1890) 234; Seton-Williams, op. cit., 150; A. Dupont-Summer, "Une inscription araméenne inédite de Bahadirli (Cilicie)," *Jahrbuch fuer Kleinasiatiache Forshung,* 2, *In Memoriam Helmuth Theodor Bossert* (Istanbul, 1965) 200–209. Although the site was securely located over 85 years ago from epigraphical evidence giving the name of the town and its patron deity, it is still misplaced on some maps of the battle.

117. Naval Staff, *Asia Minor*, Vol. 4, pt. 2, 316–322.

and topography of the region, we can restore the following movements of Alexander before the battle of Issus:

Day 1 (the second week of November). Alexander left Mallus in the morning with some light armed troops for Castabalum, located strategically at the entrances of the Bahçe and Hasanbeyli passes, to confer with Parmenio, who would possess the latest intelligence concerning Darius' force. The main army at Mallus, consisting of at least three-quarters of the entire army, also left in the morning for Issus. The main army took the major route of communication between the Plain of Adana and the Plain of Issus. First, they went northeast from Mallus along the Pyramus River to the ford at Mopsuestia (Misis),[118] the same site at which Xenophon had crossed the Pyramus with Cyrus some 70 years earlier.[119] From there they traveled east-southeast through the strategic Kara Kapu Pass. It is certain that the army went through this pass since it is the only pass between the Adana Plain and the Plain of Issus, and Curtius specifically stated (3. 7. 6–7) that Parmenio had occupied the pass through which the army would travel to reach Issus.[120] The army did not take the coastal route past the flank of Misis Dag (which is 83 miles from Mallus to Myriandrus)[121] because this route does not go through the Kara Kapu Pass.[122] The coastal route is also wretched,

118 Ramsay, *Asia Minor*, 385; Ramsay, "Cilicia," 365; Seton-Williams, op. cit., 164.

119. Xen. *Anab.* 1. 4. 1–4. This site is indicated by Xenophon's statement that it was 15 parasangs from Tarsus to the Pyramus where he crossed it. At approximately 3 miles per parasang, this would give 45 miles. The actual distance between Tarsus and the Pyramus east of Misis is 47 miles (Naval Staff, *Asia Minor*, Vol. 4, pt. 2, routes 7, 44; Kinneir, op. cit., 129–133). The location is proven by Xenophon's statement that the Pyramus was one stade, about 600 feet wide, where the army crossed it. At only one point is the Jihan (Pyramus) 600 feet wide; directly east of Misis (Naval Staff, *Asia Minor*, Vol. 4, pt. 2, 718). At all other locations, upstream and downstream, the river varies from 80 to 100 yards wide or less. Although the river is widest at Misis, it is also the only ford of the river south of Yarsuat, many miles upstream, because while wider it is also shallower and has a slower current. It will be noted that the Macedonians deliberately avoided the Adana Plain.

120. Kinneir, op. cit., 135; John Williams, *Two Essays on the Geography of Ancient Asia* (London, 1829) 112; Ramsay, "Cilicia," 365; Naval Staff, *Asia Minor*, Vol. 4, pt. 2, 312–314; 209–210; Murison, op. cit., 420; A. Janke, "Die Schlacht bei Issos," *Klio* 10 (1910) 139. Likewise, the army must have passed through the vicinity of Mopsuestia to reach the pass since it lies at the entrance of the valley leading to the Kara Kapu defile.

121. Naval Staff, *Asia Minor*, Vol. 4, pt. 2, routes 50, 21, 11, 15A, 13.

122. Ibid., p. 235.

narrow, and completely lacking water or cultivable land,[123] while the Pyramus route is well supplied with both.[124] By the evening of the first day, the main army would have reached Mopsuestia, about 17 miles from Mallus.

Day 2. By the evening of this day, the main army would have reached the vicinity of the Kara Kapu Pass, some 20 miles from Mopsuestia, and Alexander would have reached Castabalum to confer with Parmenio and his reconnaissance squads.

Day 3. In the morning Alexander would leave Castabalum with Parmenio and the forces given to him and rejoin the army that was marching through the Kara Kapu Pass. Alexander and Parmenio need not have gone through this pass to rejoin the main army on the road to Issus since they could go directly to the town via the Kalekoy Pass. It would have taken the main army at least 12 hours to have crossed the Kara Kapu Pass[125] before they marched the remaining 12 miles to Issus. That evening, Alexander conferred with Parmenio and his other commanders. Parmenio suggested that the Macedonians continue to delay in Cilicia to draw the Persians into the narrow passes where they would be at a disadvantage. No doubt he also pointed out the difficulty the Macedonians would have in deploying against the Persians if they were forced through the narrow passes of Beilan, Bahçe, or Hasanbeyli. However, the consensus was that the Macedonians had delayed long enough and it was now time to march against Darius.[126] It will be noted that Cyrus the Younger's force also took two days to march from Mopsuestia to Issus.[127] Also on the morning of this day, just after Parmenio's last reconnaissance, the Persian army began marching north for the 40-

---

123. Ibid.
124. Ibid., p. 19; Seton-Williams, op. cit., 139.
125. It took the Macedonians nine hours to cross the Pillars of Jonah Pass (Appendix 2) before the battle of Issus. But here they crossed without their baggage and followers. Although the army at Mallus only had three-quarters of all the troops, they also had baggage animals and followers to make the crossing, and if they marched at the standard marching rate for infantry, 2.5 mph (see n. 135) it would have taken them at least 12 hours to cross. From the description in Kinneir (op. cit., 135), it is clear that the Kara Kapu is just as narrow as the Pillars of Jonah, if not more so. The same "funnel effect" would be encountered if the army went through the narrow coastal route past the flank of Misis Dag.
126. A. 2. 6. 1; C. 3. 7. 8–9.
127. Xen. *Anab.* 1. 4. 1.

mile journey to the Hasanbeyli or Bahçe Pass (the army may have used both).[128]

Day 4. By morning, Alexander and his whole force left Issus for Myriandrus, 38 miles away, and by evening, they reached the Pillars of Jonah: the same time it had taken Cyrus' force to reach the Pillars from Issus 70 years before.[129] On this day also, the Persians began crossing the Amanic Gates.

Day 5. At dawn, the army began crossing the Pillars of Jonah, which would have taken them another 12 hours, and at night, the army encamped by Myriandrus: again, the same length of time it had taken Cyrus' force to travel from the Pillars to Myriandrus.[130] On this day also, the Persian column had entered Issus and slew and mutilated the Macedonian invalids who were left there to recover.[131]

Day 6. Alexander received intelligence that Darius was at Issus and was now marching toward the Pinarus (Payas) River.[132] Alexander picketed the Pillars of Jonah and marched the army north to the base of the pass.

Day 7 (third week of November).[133] At dawn, the Macedonians

128. Alexander's intelligence here resembles that of Gen. Longstreet on the morning of July 2 at Gettysburg. Shortly before dawn, this Confederate officer sent scouts to Little Round Top to see if it were occupied by a Union force. The scouts reported that it was not. However, shortly after the scouts left—perhaps only minutes later—the position was occupied by a powerful Union brigade. Longstreet's intelligence cannot be "blamed" here, nor can Alexander's.

129. Xen. *Anab.* 1. 4. 4.

130. Ibid., 1. 4. 6.

131. This incident implies that Alexander had removed all his pickets from the Amanic Gates, since Alexander did not receive intelligence of Darius' advance. He left his invalids at Issus, thinking it was a place of safety in his rear, which also implies that he was advancing toward Darius via the Beilan Pass. Leaving invalids in a place of safety is common military procedure, since it spares them a cruel journey in a horse drawn wagon over rough terrain. Cf. the carrying of the mortally wounded J. E. B. Stuart to Richmond (Freeman, op. cit., 427).

Three days would be a fast march rate for the entire Persian army to achieve the 65 mile distance from Sochoi to Issus, although this speed could easily have been achieved by light, advance units of the Persian army (see table 7). An alternative reconstruction of the chronology before Issus would have the Macedonians make a day-long halt at Issus on day four in which to conduct their strategic council, and then begin marching to Myriandrus on day five. This would give the Persians four days to reach Issus from the Amuq Plain instead of three.

132. For the location of the Pinarus, see Appendix 2.

133. The battle occurred in November, A. 2. 11. 10.

began crossing the Pillars once again and by a mighty effort reached the Pinarus by 4:30 P.M. At that time, a general engagement occurred in the narrow plains of the Pinarus, and the Macedonians were victorious; pursuit, however, was cut short by nightfall. Just as he had planned and prayed, Alexander's tactics of delay had been successful.[134]

Thus, it took the Macedonians at least five days to march the 87 miles from Mallus to Myriandrus. It had taken Cyrus' force four marching days to travel from Mopsuestia to Myriandrus, and it took the Macedonians the same amount of time. We have noted that it would have taken the Macedonians at least 24 hours to have crossed both the Kara Kapu and the Pillars of Jonah Pass. Now, if the Macedonians took 48 hours to march from Mallus to Myriandrus, the time spent on crossing the narrowest parts of the two passes would leave only 24 hours remaining in which to accomplish a march of 86 miles. However, the average marching rate for infantry is 2.5 mph,[135] and the Macedonians could scarcely have done better over the rough terrain they had to march through (the Pillars of Jonah alone are almost a mile high);[136] further, there would be no time to halt for food, water, or even a brief rest (see table 7)—and all this before a major battle. But, at 2.5 mph, the army could only achieve 60 miles in 24 hours. Therefore it was impossible for the Macedonians to have marched from Mallus to Myriandrus in 48 hours, no matter which route they took.[137]

134. C. 3. 8. 19; cf. A. 2. 7. 3; P. 20. 3.
135. Dieulafoy, op. cit., 64; Neumann, op. cit., 197–198.
136. Roman Oberhummer and Heinrich Zimmerer, *Durch Syrien und Kleinasien* (Berlin, 1899) 104.
137. Arrian's treatment of the events before the battle of Issus (and, presumably, that of his sources, Ptolemy in particular) is deliberately vague since the sequence of events shows Alexander not as bold and dashing, but calculating, cautious, and perhaps even fearful. Nor should this picture detract from his generalship, since these thoughts and emotions are common to many brave and experienced commanders before a major battle. Alexander's strategy may also indicate the high position of Parmenio in the king's councils, since he supported these tactics (C. 3. 7. 8–9), and perhaps even planned them himself. Significantly, the Macedonian strategy at the Granicus was, albeit belatedly, based on Parmenio's planning, Green, 494f. The tactics in Cilicia are characteristic of a mature and not a young commander (Freeman, op. cit., 522f.).
Although Alexander delayed in Cilicia for excellent strategic reasons, many of the contemporaries for whom Ptolemy and Aristobulus wrote thought otherwise (cf., e.g.,

Aeschines *Against Ctesiphon* 164). They believed that Alexander was "penned in" by Darius, afraid of meeting him on even ground where he would be trampled by the Persian cavalry. It was to counter these beliefs that Ptolemy was deliberately vague about the length of Alexander's delay in Cilicia and about his knowledge of the Persian camp at Sochoi. Then, too, according to Ptolemy, none of Alexander's strategic decisions were determined by his logistic considerations (let alone those of the Persian king), a view we are attempting to refute.

Murison, op. cit., 420–422, in his useful article on Darius' strategy before Issus, believed that the Persian king attempted to split Alexander's army in half by entering Cilicia via the Amanic Gates. However, consider the position of the Persian army under such circumstances. As the Persian column slowly trickled through (see Appendix 2 for this metaphor) the Bahçe and Hasanbeyli passes, right under the eyes of the Macedonian pickets and Parmenio and his powerful force at Castabalum, they would find Parmenio and his force on their right, Alexander the Great with his force on the left, the sea in front, and the mountains in back. Even if Parmenio allowed the Persian column through the passes—which is extremely improbable— this is scarcely an enviable position: it is a trap.

3.

Syria, Lebanon, Israel, Egypt, and Iraq

After the battle of Issus in November, Alexander continued his policy of securing the coasts from the Persian fleet by marching through the Beilan Pass and then south through the Amuq Plain to subdue the Phoenicians. Parmenio and Memnon were sent to Coele Syria to protect Alexander's left flank as he proceeded down the coast.[1] At Damascus, Parmenio captured 7,000 Persian pack animals, some of which were camels.[2] Like the Macedonians, the Persians also used men as well as animals to carry supplies.[3] We have already noted that manpower was just as effective as horsepower in antiquity because although the former can only carry one-third the weight of the latter (about 80 lb. for extended distances), a man only consumes one-third as much grain as a horse.

The Syrian coast receives abundant rainfall from October to April and possesses much valuable farmland. However, for a distance of 70 miles between the Nahr el-Kebir, near Latakia, and the Nahr el-Abrash, north of Tripoli, there are no perennial streams, and although rainfall is abundant, springs are scarce.[4] It is probable that the Macedonians would need depots of water along this section of their route, and no doubt Straton, the prince of the

1. For Alexander's route in northern Syria see M. Abel, "Alexandre le Grand en Syrie et en Palestine," *Revue Biblique* 43 (1934) 528–545.
2. C. 3. 13. 16; C. 3. 3. 24.
3. C. 3. 13. 16.
4. Naval Intelligence Division, Great Britain, *Syria* (1943) 44–59; Naval Intelligence Division, Naval Staff, Great Britain, *A Handbook of Syria* (London, n.d.) 421.

Aradians who governed the territory between Latakia and Amrit,[5] was made responsible for supplying them when he surrendered to Alexander before the Macedonians marched into his territory.[6] Alexander also garrisoned Syria temporarily with the allied cavalry before entering the country.[7] From the Nahr el-Abrash to Tyre, there are many small rivers and wells which would have been sufficient to supply the army with water. However, along the 50-mile section of the coast between Tripoli and Beirut, there are but a few narrow pockets of cultivable land since the coastal range plunges precipitously into the sea. Because the army would find little grain or fodder for the horses, either a three days' supply was carried by the army or they obtained supplies from the large cities in the region (Tripolis, Berytus, Byblus), which would possess ample stores themselves and contain sea-transport facilities to import grain from other areas.

At Tyre, which the Macedonians besieged from January to July of 332 B.C., provisions would have to be brought from great distances. The river Litani, five miles north of the city, was adequate for the water requirements of the army,[8] but grain would have to be imported from the Anti-Lebanon, Syria, Palestine, and beyond. The Macedonian combatants, followers, and cavalry horses would need 28,172 tons of grain for the seven-month siege.[9] The requirements for the crews of the allied navy of 200 vessels that joined the Macedonians during the siege would raise the total even higher. The coastal plain of Tyre, however, is only 13 square miles and hence its gross annual grain production would only be about 2,080 tons.[10] The city of Tyre itself imported much of its food from Palestine.[11] The logistic situation of the army would be exacerbated

5. Abel, op cit., 539–540; Dussaud, op. cit., 97, 149.
6. A. 2. 13. 7–8.
7. A. 2. 13. 7.
8. The minimum volume of the Litani is 50,000,000 gal. per day, Naval Staff, *Syria*, 404.
9. A seven-month supply of grain for the army would weigh: 69,000 personnel × 3 lb. × c. 210 da. = 43,470,000 lb.; 6,130 cavalry horses × 10 lb. × c. 210 da. = 12,873,000 lb.; 43,470,000 lb. + 12,873,000 lb. = 56,343,000 lb. = 28,172 tons of grain.
10. Naval Staff, *Syria*, 533; see above, p. 38 for the yield rates.
11. John Gray, *Archaeology of the Old Testament World* (New York, 1962) 7–8; G. A. Cook, *A Textbook of North Semitic Inscriptions* (New York, 1903) nos. 5, 11, 19; *Acts of the Apostles* 12. 20.

because the harvests in this region do not begin until June, and hence the army would have to requisition grain from the granaries in nearby towns, which would be depleted in the months just before harvest.[12] In this context, the letter Alexander wrote to the high priest at Jerusalem, demanding provisions and an alliance while he was besieging Tyre, is certainly authentic.[13] Arrian also stated that Palestine made an alliance with the Macedonians during the siege of Tyre.[14] The raid into the Anti-Lebanon region, led by Alexander himself to secure supplies of timber,[15] may also have had for its objective the opening up of supply lines to that fertile region.

Because of the law of diminishing returns, however, it would be impractical to import grain overland for more than a four-day journey (or about 60 miles) using the methods of transport available to Alexander.[16] While the productive Plain of Jezreel in Palestine (with a total cultivable area of fifteen square miles)[17] and part of the Anti-Lebanon region are within a 60-mile radius of Tyre, they do not possess a sufficient cultivable area to produce 28,172 tons of grain. Hence, the allied navy probably had a hand in supplying the army at Tyre as it did at Halicarnassos. Naval con-

12. See above, p. 27. For the harvest date: Naval Staff, Syria, 257, May or June.

13. Josephus, Jewish Antiquities 11. 317–319.

14. A. 2. 25. 4. Palestine had προσκεχωρηκότα ἤδη before Alexander marched through.

15. A. 2. 20. 4; C. 4. 3. 1.

16. If a pack animal were to be driven on a five-day journey with a load of grain weighing 200 lb., the animal would consume 100 lb. of grain during the trip and on the return journey. Hence, the driver would receive payment for the delivery of 100 lb. of grain, which would be just enough to cover the expense of feeding the animal on the trip. This assumes that sufficient fodder and water for the animal could be found on the journey and excludes the cost of the driver's own maintenance. Cf. Finley, op. cit., 33–34. Compulsion may be used, but it would be ineffective. To supply the army for 10 days with grain by overland transport from a radius of 75 miles or a five-day journey (typical caravan speed; cf. table 7) would require over 28,000 pack animals, who would devour as much food as the entire army combined. Their numbers would be: 69,000 personnel × 3 lb. × 10 da. = 2,070,000 lb.; 6,130 cavalry horses × 10 lb. × 10 da. = 613,000 lb.; 1,380 baggage animals × 10 lb. × 10 da. = 138,000 lb.; 2,070,000 + 138,000 + 613,000 = 2,821,000 lb.; which would require 2,821,000 divided by 100 lb. = 28,210 pack animals. See Chapter 1 for the method. Cf. Huston, op. cit., 28, for the 70-mile radius for the effective procurement of supplies by Washington's army at Valley Forge.

17. Joint Palestine Survey Commission, Agricultural Colonization of Palestine (Boston 1928) 22.

tingents from Sidon, Byblos, Rhodes, Soli, Lycia, and Cyprus arrived at intervals,[18] and they surely carried or convoyed supplies.

Alexander's march through Palestine is not even mentioned by the sources, but it must have provided him with a formidable problem in logistics. Not that the grain supply would present difficulties: the siege of Tyre ended in July,[19] and the army undoubtedly made the 160-mile march from Tyre to Gaza in that month or perhaps in early August—just after harvest time. Athough the coasts of Palestine are generally sandy and marshy, the productive farmlands of the Philistine Plain, Galilee, and the valleys of Esdraelon and Jezreel are within easy access of the coast and would have been more than sufficient to supply the 1,600 tons of grain needed by the army for an 11-day march.[20]

But it was the water supply that would have presented an insurmountable obstacle. The few perennial streams along the route would be little more than stagnant pools from July to August,[21] and the intermittent wadis would be dry. The wells and springs supplying the coastal towns of Accho, Dor, Joppa, and Ascalon depend on the rains and thus would contain little water during the summer months.[22] The supplies contained in rainwater cisterns in the towns would also be depleted during the months just before the return of the rains in October. The major problem the Macedonians faced, however, was the distribution of well water to the army during its march.

For example, if some soldiers lowered a four-gallon capacity bucket into a well, filled it with water, raised the bucket, and placed the water in a receptacle once every 15 seconds, in 24 hours they would only remove 23,040 gal. of water (assuming that the well did not give out), while the army's water requirement at this stage would be almost 100,000 gal. per day.[23] This is why rivers are so important to the army; they reduce these distribution problems

18. A. 2. 20. 1–3.   19. A. 2. 24. 6.
20. Survey Commission, op. cit., 22. The coastal plain from Haifa to Beersheba contains 794 square miles of cultivable land. See table 7 for Alexander's march rates.
21. Naval Intelligence Division, Great Britain, *Palestine and Trans-Jordan* (1943) 24–25.
22. Naval Intelligence Division, *Syria*, 59; Naval Staff, *Syria*, 485.
23. 71,000 personnel × ½ gal. = 35,500 gal.; 6,130 cavalry horses × 8 gal. = 49,040 gal.; 1,420 baggage animals × 8 gal. = 11,360 gal.; 35,500 + 49,040 + 11,360 = 95,900 gal.

by allowing a great many individuals to draw water simultaneously. In the 100-mile coastal section of Palestine between Haifa and Gaza, there are only 35 water sources total, many of which have very low yield rates of from one to two cubic meters per hour.[24] Of course, yields would be lower in summer. Since the army only marched about 15 miles per day, it is unlikely that more than a few major wells would be accessible to them along their daily march. Hence, it does not seem possible that the army could procure and distribute the 1,100,000 gal. of water required for an 11-day march through Palestine, since the region did not possess the facilities necessary to water large numbers of men and animals.[25] For these reasons, in addition to water depots being established where possible by local inhabitants, it is probable that the fleet provided much of the army's water along the Palestine shore, for it coasted alongside the army during its march.[26] The fleet was commanded by Hephaistion, who was often in charge of the Macedonians' commissariat.[27] Abundant quantities of water could have been collected at the Litani or the other perennial rivers of Syria and transported easily down the coast.

The two-month siege of Gaza[28] presented the most difficult logistic problem Alexander had faced so far. While there were wells in the city, these would not be accessible to the besiegers, nor would the few wells in the vicinity of the town be adequate to supply the 6,000,000 gal. of water necessary to sustain the army for two months.[29] Other wells were located at Beersheba, 31 miles from

24. Joint Palestine Survey Commission, op. cit., 412–413; Naval Intelligence Division, *Palestine*, 248.

25. The water of the Jordan River is unsuitable for drinking: it is both salty and muddy, Naval Intelligence Division, *Palestine*, 29. The water of the Sea of Galilee is drinkable once filtered, but here one encounters the logistic problems of bringing water to the coast, 38 miles away on animals which needed to drink the water they carried. Since it would take about four days round trip from the Sea of Galilee to the coast, not more than one depot of Galilee water could have been established on the coast—and this assumes that the camels bringing the water were all trained to go without water for four days.

26. A. 3. 1. 1; C. 4. 5. 10. A merchant ship of the largest type could carry 53,360 gal. of water including the weight of the amphorae. Cf. Arr. *Ind.* 40. 11, where Alexander's fleet collected and transported a five-day water supply in the Persian Gulf, which would be in the vicinity of 50,000 gal.

27. A. 6. 28. 7; C. 8. 2. 13.

28. D. 48. 7.

29. The daily requirement would be about the same as in n. 23. 100,000 × c. 60 da. = 6,000,000 gal.

Gaza, but without modern compression pumps, they could scarcely provide water at an adequate rate to supply the army. The Ghazza Wadi provides only a trickle of water from September to October.[30] It is likely that the army would need to import its entire requirement of grain also, for although it was just after harvest time, the grain in the vicinity of the city would have been taken from the fields and stored behind its massive fortifications. Again, the fleet seems to have been instrumental in supplying the Macedonians. Siege engines were brought from Tyre by the fleet,[31] and undoubtedly provisions were brought also.

"Alexander now set out for Egypt—his original goal—and marching from Gaza, he arrived at Pelusium on the seventh day."[32] Thus Arrian, in so many words, describes the most arduous march undertaken by the Macedonian army until the Gedrosian Desert. Earlier and later armies alike have experienced great difficulties in crossing the Sinai Peninsula and have required massive preparations before their advance. For the invasion of Egypt by Cambyses in 525, the establishment of advance depots of water and, apparently, the use of a primitive pipeline were required. Artaxerxes Ochus lost part of his army in the quicksand crossing the Sabkhet el-Bardawil because of a failure to obtain advance intelligence during his invasion of Egypt in 350. Later, in 306, Antigonus carried part of his army's supplies by a fleet which was partially wrecked in a storm while crossing the coast of the peninsula at about the same time of year as did Alexander. The difficulties Bonaparte experienced in his crossing are well known. Immense and difficult must have been the preparations before the Macedonian army crossed in late September or October, yet, as usual, not a single word of these preparations appears in our sources.[33]

In analyzing how the army crossed the desert, it is first necessary to establish approximately when the march was made. Tyre was

30. Naval Intelligence Division, *Palestine*, 25, 27.
31. A. 2. 27. 3.
32. A. 3. 1. 1.
33. Cambyses: Hdt. 3. 5–8; Artaxerxes: Diod. 16. 46. 5; Antigonus: Diod. 20. 73–74. Bonaparte crossed the Sinai with 13,000 troops in February and again in May only after depots of water and provisions were established, J. Christopher Herold, *Bonaparte in Egypt* (New York, 1962) 267f. Ancient Greek historians seldom display any interest in the supply problems of armies, A. W. Gomme, *A Historical Commentary on Thucydides*, Vol. 1 (Oxford, 1945) 16, and this is especially true of Alexander's campaigns.

taken in July,[34] and it would be generous to allow a month for Alexander to settle the administrative affairs of the city and to make the 160-mile journey from there to Gaza. The siege of Gaza lasted two months, probably from sometime in August to sometime in October. There is no reason for the Macedonians to have lingered in the city after it was captured, and no source indicates that they did. Thus, the army will have journeyed from Gaza to Pelusium sometime in October, if not earlier. Of all the months of the year, September and October are absolutely the worst to travel in the Sinai. Rains do not begin here until November, and the few wells along the coast, which are often too brackish to drink in any case, would be dry or virtually dry just before the onset of the rains.[35] The coast of Sinai from Gaza to Pelusium is entirely covered with sand dunes, and the army would have to march along the shore wet by the ocean lest the horses and wagons sink in the sand.[36] There is no vegetation along the coast from Raphia to the Bitter Lakes. Even if supplies were collected at Gaza, the rations would not last more than four days.[37] The fleet sailed alongside the army by the coast,[38] and they undoubtedly set up magazines of provisions before sailing on to Pelusium. Notably, the march passed without incident, and Alexander covered the 137 miles in only seven days—undoubtedly to conserve provisions.[39]

---

34. A. 2. 24. 6.

35. D. G. Hogarth, "The Geography of the War Theatre in the Near East," *Geo. Journ.* 45 (1915) 464; P. G. Elgood, *Egypt and the Army* (London, 1924) 267; G. W. Murray, "The Land of Sinai," *Geo. Journ.* 119 (1953) 142–143. The fresh water in wells and pools along the coast is often only a foot deep and floats on salt water.

36. Murray, op. cit., 142–143; Naval Staff, *Syria*, 462–463; Maj. C. S. Jarvis, *Yesterday and Today in Sinai* (Boston, 1932) facing p. 26; Topographical Section, General Staff, Great Britain, *Sinai Peninsula*, 1: 250,000, Sheets 17 E-I, 17 D-K.

37. See above p. 21.

38. A. 3. 1. 1. Ὁ δὲ ναυτικὸς στρατὸς παρέπλει αὐτῷ ἐκ Φοινίκης ὡς ἐπ᾽ Αἴγυπτον.

39. Marching rapidly to conserve provisions is standard practice. Cf. Xen. *Anab.* 1. 5. 7; Lieut. Col. J. A. Grant, "Route, March, with Camels, from Berber to Korosko in 1863," *PRGS* 6 (1884) 326–334. Alexander knew of this procedure and used it during his expedition into Bactria from Sousia: C. 6. 6. 19, "the scarcity of supplies caused him (Alexander) to hasten." This probably describes the terrain between the Kalat-i-Nadiri to Sousia. Other locations where Alexander force-marched his troops where supplies would be scarce were: in the Dasht-i-Kavir: A. 3. 20. 1–4; the return from the Kalat-i-Nadiri to intercept Satibarzanes: A. 3. 25. 6; in the Gedrosian Desert: A. 6. 25. 3; C. 9. 10. 14. Alexander may have had many reasons for force-marching his troops at any given moment, but only possible relationships between his movements and his provisioning problems are considered in this study.

Once the Nile Valley was reached, the army would not encounter any supply problems, so no time will be spent on their movements here. It is significant, however, that wherever Alexander winters with his army, he will choose a location with abundant cultivable land in the vicinity and with a close proximity to a navigable river or ocean harbor.[40] Where these criteria could not be fulfilled (for example, in Gordion, Persis, and Sogdiana), he will divide his army into smaller units which would winter in separate locations.[41] Even Tarsus and Babylon, where Alexander did not spend the entire winter but halted for a considerable period for other reasons, were equipped with river- and sea-transport facilities.[42] Once again, the reason for this was the limited capabilities of overland transport and the low crop yields of antiquity: the army would soon starve if it remained stationary when concentrated in a region remote from a navigable river or port.

The Siwah expedition represents a significant logistic problem since it is a test case for the principles developed in Chapter 1. For his journey to the oracle of Ammon, Alexander needed an armed escort to protect him from marauding Bedouins in the 340-mile journey into the wilds of the unsubdued Libyan Desert.[43] However, the expedition's precise numbers are not important since the conclusions derived from the expedition remain true for any number. It took the force eight days to travel from Paraetonium (Mersa Matruh) to Siwah, where the oracle was located,[44] a distance of some 160 miles. Judging by the speed it made, the expedition probably consisted of light armed infantry; and a baggage train of

40. Winter of 333/332: Tyre; 332/331: Egypt; 331/330: the majority of the army wintered in Susa near the navigable Karun; 330/329: Zarangaea; 329/328: Bactra near the navigable Oxus.
41. Gordion: A. 1. 24. 3; Persis: C. 5. 3. 3, and below, p. 72f. In the winter of 328/327 Alexander divided his forces between Maracanda, Bactra, and Nautaca: A. 4. 17. 3; A. 4. 18. 2; C. 8. 2. 13.
42. Tarsus: Naval Staff, *Asia Minor*, 727; Babylon: Hdt. 1. 194.
43. C. B. Welles, "The Discovery of Sarapis and the Foundation of Alexandria," *Historia* 11 (1962) 279, estimates that Alexander may have had as many as 5,000 troops accompany him on the expedition on the basis of A. 3. 1. 4. However, this large number would tax the limited water resources and would cause the distribution problems noted above p. 57, at the five wells along the 160-mile journey. Curtius 4. 7. 6 says *paucis* went, and this is reasonable.
44. D. 49. 3-5.

camels was used.[45] This is the first mention of the use of camels by any of the sources.

The regiment set out from the mouths of the Nile and marched along the coast about 178 miles to Paraetonium. Very little of this area can now be cultivated, and the large cisterns one now sees along the route are Roman.[46] It is possible that a detachment of the fleet supplied the expedition with water and grain as it traveled along the coast. At Paraetonium, Alexander and his caravan were supplied with grain and water for the march into the interior,[47] probably once again from the fleet. It would not be necessary to carry forage since the small oases along the route contain sufficient fodder for small expeditions even in July.[48] On the way to the oracle, however, the Macedonians encountered a violent *Khamsin*, a severe windstorm which often afflicts Egypt during the last week of March and April. During these storms, which are caused by the differential heating of the Libyan Desert in contrast to the rest of the Near East in spring, south wind velocities often reach gale force, temperatures rise 30° to 40° F. in a matter of minutes, and the humidity quickly falls to 10 percent or less—wilting or killing all vegetation. The storms are accompanied by severe electrical disturbances and, in the desert, violent sand storms.[49] The storm obliterated all traces of the route, and the guides, instead of leading the party to the next spring, completely lost their way. On the fourth day, the water ran out, the day the camels' abundant requirements had to be met. Fortunately, and by divine intervention, so our sources believed, a sudden rain storm enabled them to replenish their water with another four-day supply at this critical moment. Aristobulus wrote that two crows flying ahead of the army acted as guides for the rest of the journey to the oracle, and it is not without significance for the continuity of traditions in the region that today a flight of two crows—not one crow nor more than two—is regarded as a lucky omen by natives about to embark for Siwah.[50] For the return trip, the caravan undoubtedly followed

45. C. 4. 7. 12.
46. C. D. Belgrave, *Siwa: The Oasis of Jupiter Ammon* (London, 1923) 6, 44.
47. D. 49. 3; cf. A. 3. 3. 3.   48. Belgrave, op. cit., 44, 47, 49.
49. W. B. Fisher, *The Middle East, A Physical, Social, and Regional Geography* (London, 1961) 44–46 for a description of the storm. Str. 17. 1. 43; A. 3. 3. 4.
50. Crows: Belgrave, op. cit., 43; Aristobulus: A. 3. 3. 6. Water ran out: D. 49. 3; C. 4. 7. 12. Rain: D. 49. 3–5.

the correct route back to the Mediterranean, where there are springs within a three-day march of each other along the track. A journey from Siwah 330 miles overland directly to Memphis is difficult without trucks or automobiles since there is a 120-mile waterless interval. Travelers' reports of this route make it clear that the water and agricultural resources are inadequate to support even a small military patrol.[51]

In the Siwah expedition, we see the principles developed in the first chapter taking effect under actual conditions where neither water nor grain were available for a four-day march. If the expedition loaded up with an eight-day grain supply and water for the men only, expecting to replace the water from the springs along the route, our logistic model predicts that water will not last more than four days,[52] which is precisely what happened. Indeed, I have not been able to find a single account of a caravan that proceeded more than four days without replenishing its water in terrain where no water or grain was obtainable.[53] This expedition also shows that a baggage train consisting entirely of camels is in no better logistic condition than one of horses and mules for a journey of four days or longer; for while camels can carry more, in four days they will also need to consume more food and water to stay alive.

Alexander left Memphis perhaps by mid-April of 331 for his journey to Tyre.[54] Between Memphis and the 136 miles to Pelu-

51. Wilfred Jennings-Bramly, "A Journey to Siwah in September and October, 1896," *Geo. Journ.* 10 (1897) 597–608, barely made it with three men and three camels. Cf. Welles, op. cit., 278–279; Eugene N. Borza, "Alexander and the Return from Siwah," *Historia* 16 (1967) 369.

52. Even if the expedition took the maximum amount of water they were capable of carrying, the water would still run out in four days, no matter how many personnel or pack animals were on the journey. The men would carry 3 lb. of grain for 8 da. = 24 lb. + 6 lb. = .6 gal. of water. The camels would carry 10 lb. of grain for 8 da. = 80 lb. + 220 lb. of water = 22 gal. In four days, however, the men would require 20 lb. of water and the camels, 200 lb. See Appendix 1. Hence, when the water rations were distributed on the fourth day to the men, to the camels carrying food and water, and to the camels carrying baggage, no water would be left. This excludes rations needed for any horses on the expedition.

53. Cf. Grant, op. cit., 326–334; Belgrave, op. cit., 47–58, note the suffering of the camels on their third day without water. G. A. Hoskins, *Visit to the Great Oasis of the Libyan Desert* (London, 1837) 47.

54. A. 3. 6. 1. Ἀλέξανδρος δὲ ἅμα τῷ ἦρι ὑποφαίνοντι ἐκ Μέμφιος ᾔει ἐπὶ Φοινίκης. . . . Alexandria was founded on April 8, or very near that date, C. B. Welles, op. cit., 284; P. M. Fraser, *Ptolemaic Alexandria*, Vol. 1 (Oxford, 1972) 4, n. 9, and it would

sium, the army had to cross bridges over the Nile and all the canals along the way.[55] Since it takes a great deal of time for large masses of soldiers to move through restricted spaces like bridges and mountain passes,[56] the Macedonians probably would not reach Pelusium until mid-May; which is also the date of the harvests in Egypt and southern Palestine.[57] Once again, preparations must have been made for crossing the Sinai, and it is probable that the fleet, which also traveled from Egypt to Tyre,[58] supplied the army in this area. Water would not have been a problem in Palestine during spring when the streams would be in spate and the wells and rainwater cisterns full. It was important for Alexander to have left during the present year's harvest, not only for the reasons already noted[59] but also since the army undoubtedly had placed a severe burden on the last year's harvest during the sieges of Tyre and Gaza.

Alexander probably reached Tyre by mid-June, and he stayed there for a considerable time, occupied with important military and administrative concerns.[60] Perhaps he left the city for Thapsacus (Carchemish)[61] on the Euphrates by the first week of July and

take some time for Alexander to sail up river to Memphis and organize the journey. Welles is probably correct in stating that the city was founded after Alexander's return from Siwah on about April 8, because if it were before, there would not be enough time for Alexander to march the 680 miles there and back, visit the oracle, and return to Memphis before early spring. Cf. Borza, op. cit.

55. A. 3. 6. 1.

56. It took Darius' army five days to cross the Euphrates, C. 3. 7. 1, and also the Lycus, C. 4. 9. 9. It took the army of Xerxes seven days and seven nights to cross the two Hellespont bridges, Hdt. 7. 56. Later, it took Alexander's light armed force five days to cross the Oxus, C. 7. 5. 1; C. 7. 5. 18, and about 16 days for his whole army to cross the Hindu Kush, D. 83. 1; C. 7. 3. 21. See Appendix 2.

57. Fisher, op. cit., 489; Naval Intelligence Division, *Palestine*, 248; Naval Staff, *Syria*, 257.

58. A. 3. 6. 1.

59. See above, p. 27.

60. C. 4. 8. 11–16; A. 3. 6. 1–3. Alexander also made an expedition into Samaria (C. 4. 8. 10) before arriving at Tyre. It is about 300 miles from Pelusium to Tyre.

61. Carchemish is indicated as the site of Thapsacus by Xenophon's account (*Anab.* 1. 4. 11–1. 7. 1), the measurement of Eratosthenes of the distance between Thapsacus and Babylon down the Euphrates (Str. 2. 1. 36), and Alexander's own crossing (A. 3. 7. 3). According to Xenophon, it was 50 parasangs, or about 150 miles, from Thapsacus to the Araxes River and 35 parasangs, or about 105 miles, from the Araxes to the Mascas River where it joins the Euphrates. The Euphrates was 4 stades, or 800 yards, wide at Thapsacus. Now the Balikh River, where it joins the Euphrates, is 150 miles from Carchemish via Harran, the route followed by Julian

arrived there by the first week of August.[62] There were essentially two routes the Macedonians could have followed to the Euphrates: through Coele Syria via Damascus, Homs, Hamah, and Aleppo, a region which was much more agriculturally productive in antiquity than at present;[63] or up the Phoenician coast to Seleucia, the port of Antioch, and inland by the route essentially followed by Cyrus the Younger, Crassus, Trajan, and Julian through the Amuq Plain to the Euphrates.[64] The latter route would, of course, simplify the army's logistic organization by utilizing sea transport. After reaching Thapsacus, Alexander may have stayed there for a

(Amm. Marc. 23. 3. 1–23. 6. 6) and apparently by Xenophon himself (W. J. Farrell, "A Revised Itinerary of the Route Followed by Cyrus the Younger through Syria," *JHS* 81 [1961] 153), for easier acquisition of supplies. It is about 137 miles down the Euphrates Valley to the Balikh from Carchemish. It is about 100 miles between the Balikh and the Khabur where it meets the Euphrates down the Euphrates Valley. The Euphrates bed is about 800 yards wide at Carchemish (D. G. Hogarth and C. L. Wooley, *Carchemish*, Vol. 1 [London 1914] 37), but only 300 yards wide at Meskene, another suggested site for Thapsacus (Farrell, 153). Xenophon mentions two rivers flowing into the Euphrates between Thapsacus and Cunaxa, the Araxes and the Mascas. There are two and only two rivers between Jerablus and Babylon: the Balikh and the Khabur. Either the Araxes is the Balikh and the Mascas is the Khabur or Xenophon is wrong. The Syrian name for the Khabur was Maskas (W. Wright, *Catalogue of Syriac Manuscripts in the British Museum*, Vol. 3 [London, 1872] 1130). If the Mascas were where R. D. Barnett put it (*JHS* 83 [1963] 5), south of Abu Kemal, then Cunaxa, which was 102 parasangs or about 306 miles south of the Mascas, would be about 40 miles *south* of Babylon. There is nothing remotely resembling a 100-foot-wide river at the site of Abu Kemal. Eratosthenes, an exacting geographer, measured 4,800 stades, or 552 miles, between Thapsacus and Babylon down the Euphrates route. The actual distance is about 558 miles between Carchemish and Babylon. Alexander kept the Euphrates and the Armenian mountains on his left after crossing the river, which suits a crossing at Thapsacus. Carchemish is above the 10-inch isohyet, so there would be fodder for the horses in the neighborhood. Eratosthenes again gives 2,400 stades between Thapsacus and the shortest route to the Tigris (Str. 2. 1. 38), or 276 miles, which is about the correct distance between Carchemish and the Tigris by the shortest possible route, see below, p. 69.

62. A. 3. 7. 1. Alexander arrived at Thapsacus in Hecatombaeon, when Aristophanes was archon at Athens, that is, between July 10 and August 8, W. B. Dinsmoor, *Archons of Athens* (Cambridge, 1931) 359, 429. A time near the latter date is indicated by the preceding chronology and subsequent events.

63. Howard Crosby Butler, "Desert Syria, the Land of a Lost Civilization," *Geo. Rev.* 9 (1920) 77–108; cf. R. Mouterde and A. Poidebard, *Le Limes de Chalcis* (Paris, 1945). Water depots may have been needed between Hamah and Aleppo if this route was followed. The First Crusade avoided the inland route from Antioch to Jerusalem via Damascus because of the lack of water along the way, the difficult terrain, and the easier access to sea transport along the coastal road, Runciman, op. cit., 268, 275.

64. Cyrus: Xen. *Anab.* 1. 4. 9–19; Crassus: Plut. *Crassus* 19. 3 (Antioch to Zeugma); Trajan: Dio Cass. 68. 26. 1 (Antioch to the Tigris); Julian: Amm. Marc. 23. 2. 6.

time planning strategy against Darius. The army may have taken five days in crossing the river by the two bridges constructed over the Euphrates.[65] Hence, it would have been the second or third week of August before the entire army had crossed over.

During the Macedonians' journey inland, Alexander removed Arimmas, the viceroy of Syria, because, according to Arrian, he had failed to collect sufficient supplies for the projected conquest of the interior.[66] This is the only reference in any of the sources to advance logistic planning by Alexander, and it shows that he had planned the conquest of Mesopotamia a considerable time earlier. It also raises an interesting question about Alexander's logistic planning and his original strategy for the conquest of Mesopotamia. What sort of supplies could a viceroy of Syria provide? What kind of supplies would the army need for a conquest of Mesopotamia? Food and perhaps pack animals seem to be the only answer. Military equipment could just as easily be obtained in Phoenicia or from Greece and Macedonia by ship—as it was later.[67] If Arimmas was to have provided a substantial quantity of provisions (and we can assume he was not dismissed for a trifle), this raises the problem of how they were to be transported. The impossibility of transporting large quantities of food overland for long distances has been repeatedly noted in this study, and thus it seems that Arimmas' supplies were to be transported by boat down the Euphrates to Mesopotamia with the army marching alongside, just as the armies of Crassus, Trajan, and Julian were later supplied.[68] That this operation was feasible in Alexander's day is proven by the fact that he later had a fleet built in Phoenicia, disassembled and transported overland to Thapsacus, and then sailed down the Euphrates to Babylon.[69]

65. This is the time it took Darius to cross the Euphrates before the battle of Issus and later to cross the Lycus, see above n. 56; C. 4. 9. 12 wrote that Alexander reached the Euphrates on "the eleventh day." If this is reckoned from Seleucia, about 152 miles from the Euphrates at Carchemish, an 11-day march is indicated. If it was reckoned from Coele Syria, an 11-day march to Thapsacus would originate somewhere between Homs and Hama.

66. A. 3. 6. 8.

67. Military equipment arrived from Greece, even when Alexander was in India (D. 95. 4).

68. Crassus: Plut. *Crassus* 20. 2 for the initial stage of his campaign. Trajan had ships constructed at Nisibis to carry supplies down the Tigris: Dio Cass. 68. 26. 1; Julian: Amm. Marc. 24. 1. 4–24. 1. 15.

69. P. 68. 1; C. 10. 1. 19; Str. 16. 1. 11.

Thus deprived of supplies, Alexander was presented with the choice of marching down the Euphrates Valley to Babylon or marching eastward along the old military highway along the hilly flanks of the Taurus and Zagros mountains, where provisions and fodder were more plentiful and the heat not as intense.[70] To understand the basis of Alexander's strategic decisions before the battle of Gaugamela, the salient facts of fourth-century Mesopotamia's ecology and human geography must be reviewed.

The climate of Mesopotamia changes a great deal between the upper valley and mid to lower valley. Most important for our considerations, the 10-inch (250 mm) isohyet, below which no perennial grasses can grow, crosses east to west below Carchemish, Harran on the Balikh River, Resaina and the upper Khabur, Mosul, and Kirkuk (see map p. 167).[71] Above this line, dry farming can be profitably conducted, and perennial grasses can survive the summer drought. Below this isohyet, however, agriculture can only be conducted by irrigation, and those areas not irrigated remain desert. The average daily high temperature in the mid to lower valley in summer is 120° F.[72] The harvests in the upper, mid, and lower valley take place, then and now, in June.[73] The most significant feature of the human geography of the Euphrates Valley was its cities. In the 558 miles between Thapsacus and Babylon, there were no fewer than eight urban sites in existence in Alexander's day,[74] as well as numerous towns and villages. Although the Euphrates Valley is narrow it is also long, and it has been reliably estimated that the valley between the Khabur and Hit contains over 2,000 square miles of potentially cultivable land. The agricultural resources of the valley between Thapsacus and Hit were adequate to support the armies of Darius on his way to Issus and that of Cyrus the Younger, with its slow, cumbersome, and inef-

70. A. 3. 7. 3.

71. Louis Dillemann, *Haute Mésopotamie orientale et pays adjacents* (Paris, 1962) 64; David Oates, *Studies in the Ancient History of Northern Iraq* (London, 1968) 2–3; Fisher, op. cit., 371f.

72. Martin A. Beek, *Atlas of Mesopotamia* (London, 1962) 16.

73. J. P. N. Galloway, "A Kurdish Village of North East Iraq," *Geo. Journ.* 124 (1958) 362; Russell, op. cit.

74. Beek, op. cit., 47; Directorate General of Antiquities. Iraq, *Map of Ancient Sites of Iraq* (Baghdad, 1954), lists Circesium, Dura, Anat, Thilabus, Is, and Palukat as major urban sites of Iraq occupied in the Achaemenid and Seleucid era. In addition, Sura and Nicephorion were Hellenistic sites in Syria.

ficient logistic system, with the loss of but a few pack animals.[75] If the region supported Darius' and Cyrus' armies, it could also support Alexander's. In contrast, the northern Tigris-Euphrates Valley was a land of open agricultural villages and towns (Nineveh was either deserted or a small village in Alexander's era).[76]

Thus, when Alexander entered the region in the first week of August, he was faced with the following situation. In the south and middle valley, the harvested grain and straw would be stored in the temple and municipal granaries of the cities on the approach of an enemy, and only stubble would remain in the cultivated fields.[77] Those areas not under cultivation in the middle and southern valley would remain desert, and hence no fodder would be available for the horses. In addition, if he wished to obtain provisions, it would be necessary to conduct sieges of the formidable walled cities in the region, as Julian did, an impossibility given the present military situation. There is no evidence from any source that the Euphrates Valley was devastated by Persian troops. Indeed, after the harvest, it is difficult to see what would have been left to devastate. In the north, however, the harvested grain would be easily obtainable from the unwalled towns and villages, and those areas not under cultivation would remain grassy. With these considerations in mind, it is not difficult to understand Alexander's decision to march east instead of south.

Instead of marching through the Euphrates Valley, then, as Darius expected, Alexander drove due east. Fortunately, a bematist's measurement preserves the distance of Alexander's route between Thapsacus and the Tigris where the Macedonians crossed: 2,400 stadia or 276 miles.[78] These bematists' measurements are extremely

75. Sir William Willcocks, "Mesopotamia: Past, Present, and Future," Geo. Journ. 35 (1910) 1–18. For the route of Darius' army: C. 3. 3. 7; C. 3. 7. 1.

76. A. Leo Oppenheim, Mesopotamia: Portrait of a Dead Civilization (Chicago, 1964) 86; Galloway, op. cit., Dillemann, op. cit., 68–126.

77. Darius, unlike Artaxerxes II, had almost two years to prepare for Alexander's approach and to make arrangements for the cities along the Euphrates to resist by having all material that would be of use to the enemy removed from the fields. At harvest time, both the kernels and stalks of grain are removed from the fields. Straw was of vital importance for the Mesopotamian economy, not only for feeding stock, but, more importantly, it was a principal element in the manufacture of mud brick, of which there was always an enormous demand. This was because the cities of the region were under constant repair since their mud brick structures only had a life span of about 12 years.

78. Str. 2. 1. 38.

accurate and provide valuable information on Alexander's routes.[79] The distance indicates that Alexander chose the ancient military route to the Tigris via Harran, Resaina (Ras al-Ain), and Thilapsum (Tell Chagar Bazar), some 276 miles from Thapsacus, since all other routes are longer. Strabo specifically stated Alexander chose the short route between the two locations, which is exactly what one would expect for a forced march.[80] This military highway first receives mention in the Old Babylonian period, and it remained in use until the Roman era. The region through which it passed was, and is, highly fertile and productive, thickly settled with agricultural villages and towns, and the highway crosses the upper Balikh and the Khabur Rivers with their tributaries.[81] Hence, neither water nor grain supplies would present a problem.

The Macedonians marched due east to Harran (Carrhae), and perhaps it was here that Alexander halted the army for a few days to prepare the soldiers physically and mentally for the forced march ahead.[82] It should be noted that even at Harran, the Macedonians were not yet committed to the eastern route: Julian and perhaps Cyrus the Younger both marched to Harran for reasons of supply before turning south down the Balikh and the Euphrates Valley.[83] Darius, then, even at this stage, would not know which direction Alexander would take. From Harran, Alexander ordered a forced march 215 miles to the Tigris, which the Macedonians apparently covered in 14 days.[84] Alexander ordered this march to arrive at the Tigris before any Persian force could stop his cross-

79. See table 8.
80. Alexander force-marched his army along this route: A. 3. 7. 5; C. 4. 9. 13.
81. Dillemann, op. cit., 173; M. E. L. Mallowan, "The Excavations at Tall Chagar Bazar and an Archaeological Survey of the Habur Region, 1934–35," *Iraq* 3 (1936) 2–3; Albrecht Goetze, "An Old Babylonian Itinerary," *JCS* 7 (1953) 51–72; A. Poidebard, *La trace de Rome dans le désert de Syrie* (Paris, 1934) 163f.; Julius Lewy, "Studies in the Historic Geography of the Ancient Near East," *Orientalia* 21 (1952) 1–12, 265–292, 393–425.
82. C. 4. 9. 13. Harran is the next large city east of the Euphrates. It would have taken four days to march the 60-mile distance from Thapsacus to Harran, and with a three-day rest, they would not leave that city until the third or fourth week of August. It is possible that the army halted on the left bank of the Euphrates for a few days instead of Harran. However, it is more likely that it halted near a large city to ease its supply problems for the reasons noted above.
83. Julian: Amm. Marc. 23. 3. 1–7; Cyrus: Xen. *Anab.* 1. 4. 19; Farrell, op cit., 153.
84. C. 4. 9. 14, following the emendation of Kinch. It would have been impossible for any nonmechanized army to march the distance in four days.

ing, which, he learned from captured Persian scouts, was Darius' new strategy.[85] Armies are extremely vulnerable while crossing rivers. By the time word could have reached him at Babylon of the Macedonians' eastward advance, Darius would have no opportunity to march the 367 miles to the Tigris ford at Abu Wijam to prevent their crossing.[86] However, Persian morale and honor demanded that he make the attempt. Even Mazaeus' light cavalry did not have enough time to lay waste completely the east side of the Tigris before the Macedonians had already crossed,[87] a strategy which would have been eminently successful had there been opportunity to implement it thoroughly.[88] As it was, the burning of the village granaries was not complete and was halted by the Macedonians on the third day after the Tigris was crossed.[89] Alexander's speed and surprise tactics had won an important tactical victory.

After the victory at Gaugamela on about September 30, Alexander marched the 287 miles from Arbela to Babylon, a three-week journey with the necessary halts. The army remained at Babylon for 34 days, which they were able to do because the city was supplied by river transport.[90] After this point, no supply problems will have been encountered by the army until the march into Persis in the beginning of February, 330 B.C.

85. A. 3. 7. 4.
86. This reconstruction of the events before the battle of Gaugamela differs somewhat from that in E. W. Marsden, *The Campaign of Gaugamela* (Liverpool, 1964) 11–23, which remains basic for any intelligent discussion of the battle. However, all his distances are too long. He gives an example on p. 23 to check his method of measuring, the distance from Baghdad to Kirkuk, which the *Iraq Directory* (Baghdad, 1936) 41, gives as 301 miles. However, as the map on p. 35 of the Directory shows, the distance measured by the Directory goes from Baghdad to *Kifri* and hence to Kirkuk, while Marsden's map measures the distance from Baghdad to *Tuz Khurmatu* and hence to Kirkuk, a distance of only 285 miles. This Tigris ford is suggested by Aurel Stein, "Notes on Alexander's Crossing of the Tigris and the Battle of Arbela," *Geo. Journ.* 100 (1942) 157, who, however, has apparently put the site of the battlefield in the wrong location. See Marsden, op. cit., 20–21; Streck, *RE* 7 (1910) 861f. It may have taken the Macedonians a considerable time to cross the Tigris, see above, n. 56. Alexander did not even *hear* of the approach of Darius' army until seven days after the Macedonians had completely crossed the Tigris, A. 3. 7. 6–7; C. 4. 9. 25–4. 10. 15.
87. C. 4. 9. 14–15; D. 55. 1–2.
88. As Alexander himself admitted, C. 4. 13. 23.
89. C. 4. 10. 1–15.
90. Hdt. 1. 194. The fertility of Mesopotamia was legendary in antiquity, Hdt. 1. 193; C. 5. 1. 12; above, Introduction, n.16.

4.

Iran and Afghanistan

After a stay of 34 days, the Macedonians left Babylon for a 20-day journey to Susa.[1] When he left the latter city, about the fourth week of December, Alexander approached the Persian heartland of the Niriz Basin. From this point, Alexander can no longer pose as a liberator from Persian rule, and as a consequence, the nature of the opposition he encounters changes. This change is also reflected in the different arrangements for acquiring supplies that he must now use throughout the remainder of his campaign. Up to this point, the Macedonians were generally able to count on local populations to supply them when they surrendered to Alexander before the army marched into their district.[2] Now, however, more often than not, few will voluntarily surrender to him since the local populations are antagonistic toward their new rulers. Under these circumstances, Alexander considered it essential to obtain advance intelligence of the roads, resources, terrain, and climate of the territory he was about to enter.[3] Indeed, he generally

1. A. 3. 16. 7. The army arrived in Babylon about October 21 (see above, p. 70) and stayed there for 34 days (C. 5. 1. 39). Hence, they would leave for Susa about November 25 and arrive in Susa 20 days later at about December 15. The army stayed there for some time (A. 3. 16. 7–11) and perhaps left by the fourth week of December.

2. See above p. 41.

3. In Comisene: A. 3. 21. 7; A. 3. 20. 4; C. 5. 13. 3; in Mesopotamia: A. 3. 7. 3–4; in Cilicia: C. 3. 5. 10; C. 3. 5. 6; D. 32. 2; before Gaugamela: A. 3. 9. 1; C. 4. 9. 11; before the Uxians' territory: A. 3. 17. 2; C. 5. 3. 5–6; before Persis: D. 68. 4–5; in Media: A. 3. 19. 1–5; in Parthia: A. 3. 25. 3; before Sogdiana: A. 3. 29. 6; for Scythia: A. 4. 1. 2; for Chorasmia: A. 4. 15. 4; in India: A. 5. 25. 1; C. 9. 8. 30; C. 9. 9. 5; C. 8. 10. 2; in general: Str. 2. 1. 6. One could add many other examples.

received advance intelligence throughout his campaigns on enemy movements and resources of the country.[4] This is one reason why his campaigns were successful and his army able to successfully cross the same regions in which other armies lost many troops through starvation and dehydration alone. Under these circumstances, however, advance intelligence was more vital than ever before. Alexander would not commit his entire force for a march into a region whose population had not surrendered to him in advance. Instead, the army would be divided into two or more units so that the diminished requirements of each unit could be more easily procured from the countryside. Either the different detachments would take separate routes through the country or the main army would be left at a base well provided with supplies while Alexander advanced alone with light, swift units to subdue the region.[5] In hostile territory, the army would no longer be supplied by gifts, requisitions, or markets but by the pillaging of towns or villages or by foraging teams led by Alexander's most capable lieutenants, such as Philotas, Ptolemy (son of Lagus), Coenus, Hephaistion, or Craterus.[6]

For these reasons, Alexander took only about 17,000 troops with him for the journey into Persis, "a sparse land and rugged," while the main army remained in Susa near the navigable Pasitigris (Karun) River, where supplies were plentiful.[7] The Uxians, through whose territory the Macedonians had to march to reach Persis, did not surrender to Alexander at his approach, but demanded the same tribute they used to receive from the Persian

4. Str. 2. 1. 6, Chapter 2, n. 97. I hope to publish an article on Alexander's intelligence system soon.

5. Separate routes: in Persis: A. 3. 18. 1; in the Oreitans' territory: A. 6. 21. 3–4; C. 9. 10. 6–7; in India: A. 4. 23. 1. Alexander advancing alone with part of his force: before the Uxians and into Persis: below, n. 9; into the interior of Persis in late March or early April, 330: C. 5. 6. 12; before Comisene: A. 3. 20. 1; before entering Sogdia: C. 7. 5. 1. Before entering Persis, both procedures were used.

6. Pillaging: A. 3. 17. 3; C. 4. 9. 8; C. 9. 8. 29; foraging in hostile territory: A. 1. 5. 9; A. 3. 30. 10; A. 4. 24. 8; C. 9. 9. 8; Philotas: A. 1. 5. 9; Ptolemy: A. 4. 24. 8; Coenus: A. 5. 21. 4; Hephaistion: C. 8. 2. 13; Craterus: A. 5. 21. 4. Neither pillaging nor foraging occurs in regions known to have surrendered in advance to Alexander.

7. The Pasitigris is navigable to Susa: Arr. *Ind.* 42. 4–8; supplies were plentiful: D. 65. 2; C. 5. 2. 1. The troops' numbers are given in C. 5. 3. 3. as 13,000 plus 1,000 Agrianians (C. 5. 3. 6), archers, 1,000 mounted bowmen (C. 5. 4. 14), and units of the Companions' cavalry and Thessalian cavalry (A. 3. 18. 1–2). All these probably amounted to about 17,000. Persis is sparse and rugged: Hdt. 9. 122. See map p. 168.

king before they let him through their mountain passes.[8] Alexander first obtained advance intelligence of the region, then attacked their mountain strongholds and pillaged their towns.[9] After their surrender, 30,000 sheep and 500 pack animals were levied from them since they were pastoralists.[10] Another reason for taking only part of the army into Persis was the slender agricultural resources of the region during the Achaemenid era. After an exhaustive and diligent survey, it was found that a total of only 24 tiny villages (average area 2.4 hectares), clustered around Persepolis, were inhabited in the 3,000-square-mile Niriz Basin.[11] It was not possible for these villages to have produced the 22,000 tons of grain necessary to have supported the entire Macedonian army, its followers, and cavalry and pack animals[12] during the four-month stay at Persepolis, especially in the months before the harvest in June.[13]

After defeating Ariobarzanes' forces, who were blocking the Persian Gates (Tang-i Khas), the Macedonians reached Persepolis about the first week of February, 330 and stayed there until the end of May or the beginning of June.[14] Those who wonder why Alexander remained so long at Persepolis have ignored two im-

8. A. 3. 17. 1.

9. A. 3. 17. 3; A. 3. 17. 2; C. 5. 3. 5–6.

10. A. 3. 17. 5.

11. William M. Sumner, *Cultural Development in the Kur River Basin, Iran, an Archaeological Analysis of Settlement Patterns* (Ph.D. Dissertation, University of Pennsylvania, 1972) 265.

12. The Macedonians stayed in Persepolis for four (lunar) months, P. 37. 3. At this time, the army had approximately 87,000 troops, 8,680 cavalry horses (see table 5), and 1,740 baggage animals. Their requirements would be: 87,000 × 3 lb. × c. 120 da. = 31,320,000 lb. = 15,660 tons; 8,680 × 10 lb. × c. 120 da. = 10,416,000 lb. = 5,208 tons; 1,740 × 10 lb. × c. 120 da. = 1,044 tons. 15,660 + 5,208 + 1,044 = 21,912 tons. Sumner, op. cit., 190, 265f., estimates that the total population of the Niriz Basin was about 23,000 in the Achaemenid period at most. It would be impossible, then, for the agricultural resources of the basin to have supported 87,000 personnel and 10,420 animals for four months when it was only adequate to support 23,000 permanent residents. This was especially true in the months before harvest when the residents themselves would be on short rations. Those residents of the area not slain by the Macedonians would also have to be fed for the length of the army's stay.

13. See above p. 27.

14. The Macedonians may have left Susa by the fourth week of December (above, n. 1) and it probably took them 30 days to march the 388 miles between there and Persepolis including the necessary halts. The battle for the Persian Gates also took several days (C. 5. 4. 1–32). Hence, they may have arrived the last week of January or the first week of February. For Alexander's operations against the Persian Gates, see Sir Aurel Stein, "An Archaeological Journey in Western Iran," *Geo. Journ.* 92 (1938) 316f.; John Hansman, "Elamites, Achaemenians, and Anshan," *Iran* 10 (1972) 110.

portant geographical conditions of the Zagros Mountains in winter.[15]

First there is the ice and snow. The only route leading from Persepolis to Media and Ecbatana proceeds through the Deh Bid Pass (8,000 feet) which is often blocked with ice and snowdrifts for many miles until April.[16] It was through this pass that Alexander forced his way in late March or early April for his expedition into the interior of Persis.[17] Curtius describes the severe hardships of the men confronted with the task of forcing the pass by breaking the ice with mattocks:[18]

He had come to a pass blocked with perpetual snows, which the violence of the cold had bound with ice, and the desolation of the landscape and pathless solitudes terrified the exhausted soldiers, who believed that they were beholding the end of the habitable world. In amazement they saw that everything was deserted and without a trace of human cultivation, and they demanded that they should return before even the daylight and the sky should fail them.

This description is no exaggeration, for modern travelers have expressed similar opinions about Deh Bid, and it must have seemed especially ominous to a Mediterranean traveler.[19] If the pass excited such dread at the end of March, a fortiori, conditions would have been much worse earlier in the winter. Although Alexander did force the pass—by flinging himself from his horse and attacking the ice himself with a mattock as an example for his soldiers to follow—he had only 1,000 cavalry and a few light infantry with him. It would have been difficult, indeed, for the rest of the forces at Persepolis to hazard such a journey.

15. There have been many theories analyzing why Alexander remained so long at Persepolis, the most recent by Eugene N. Borza in an extremely useful article, "Fire from Heaven, Alexander at Persepolis," *Classical Philology* 67 (1972) 233-245.

16. Alexander led his expedition over the pass in the fourth week of March, or perhaps a little later (Borza, op. cit., 237), and found it completely blocked by ice and snow (C. 5. 6. 12-14). These upland routes can remain blocked until May or even June, J. V. Harrison, "Some Routes in Southern Iran," *Geo. Journ.* 99 (1941) 117.

17. Borza, op. cit.; for the date, see below, p. 76 for the location.

18. C. 5. 6. 12-14.

19. After a blizzard, the pass can be snowed-in for as long as 40 days, James Morier, *A Journey Through Persia, Armenia, and Asia Minor in the Years 1808 and 1809* (London, 1812) 147. Early travelers, such as Morier, provide the most valuable geographical and climatic information on Alexander's routes available.

But the Deh Bid Pass was nothing compared to the solid fortress of ice and snow, over 200 miles thick from Isfahan to Ecbatana in "frozen, rocky Media." This region has the most severe winters in any part of Persia and as late as March, snow covers the entire area, often to a depth of three or four feet.[20] Stories are told here about the winter wind—as cold as death itself—which can instantly freeze a horse and rider to death. Mountain passes are particularly treacherous since they are often blocked by snow drifts to a depth of ten feet or more and one can easily lose the track and vanish. Until relatively recently, the entire area was isolated from Isfahan from November to March.[21] Obviously, it would be impossible for a large army with followers, including women and children, and clumsy wagons to cross such terrain in winter. Indeed, Antiochus Sidetes' army was trapped at Ecbatana for the winter of 130/129, a delay that caused the destruction of his entire force.[22] Darius was likewise immobilized at Ecbatana: he had every reason to put as much mileage between himself and Alexander as possible, to advance beyond Parthia into Bactria, laying waste to the land as he went to prevent Alexander from following, as was his original intention.[23] But if he was immobilized, he was also protected, for no one could penetrate the icy ramparts of Media in winter.

Climate, however, was only part of the reason the army delayed at Persepolis until May or June. A much more serious problem was the lack of supplies available in Persis for the 514-mile journey to Ecbatana. Persis, as Herodotus notes, was "a sparse land and rugged," and although it contained "cities," such as Pasargadae and Persepolis, which might lead to the mistaken conclusion that the

20. Conolly, op. cit., 194; Naval Intelligence Division, Great Britain, *Persia* (1945) 157, 185–186; Special Operations Research Office, U. S. Army, *Area Handbook: Iran* (Washington, 1963) 55; Harrison, op. cit., 117; W. B. Fisher, ed., *Cambridge History of Iran*, Vol. 1 (Cambridge, 1968) 221–223; Gen. A. Houtum-Schindler, *Eastern Persian Irak* (London, 1896) 22.

21. Sir Robert Ker Porter, *Travels in Georgia, Persia, Armenia, Ancient Babylonia*, Vol. 2 (London, 1822) 79f.

22. J. 38. 10. 8; E. R. Bevan, *The House of Seleucus*, Vol. 2 (London, 1902) 243f. The severity of the winter, the lack of provisions, and the consequent problems of distribution (see above, p. 61) caused Antiochus' army to scatter in winter quarters throughout the Median Plain. By early spring, his forces were demoralized, weakened, and unorganized, and fell easy prey to Phraates and the Parthian army. The fate of Antiochus Sidetes, a brave and able commander, shows the foresight of Alexander in leaving the bulk of his forces at Susa where supplies were adequate.

23. A. 3. 19. 1; C. 5. 8. 1.

region was capable of supporting a large population, one must remember that except for their garrisons these sites were uninhabited for the greater part of the year.[24] The reason for this, as we have seen, was the limited area of cultivation in the Niriz Basin which was inadequate to support a large population all year long. Moreover, because of the limitations of overland transport in antiquity, supplies were only obtainable within a 60 to 80-mile radius from the center of consumption.[25] The region between Persepolis and Deh Bid is particularly desolate:

He [the Khan of the region] had himself often experienced the severities of the country, and he, better than anyone, knew the distress which the detention of two or three hundred men in a spot so destitute and insulated [the Deh Bid Pass] would occasion. He had provided sustenance for ourselves and our cattle for one night only, and this he had transported with great trouble from Mourgh-aub [near Pasargadae] and other villages. Indeed, through the whole of our march great and early were the preparations made by the chiefs of the country for our reception. If these were the difficulties of our passage, the march of an army could not be easily conducted. The country in its present state could not complete magazines of provisions, even when required by its own government. It must however always be recollected, that this is the least fertile province of the kingdom.[26]

Clearly, the Macedonian forces at Persepolis, like Morier's expedition, needed magazines of supplies along the route if they were to proceed north to Ecbatana, and to make arrangements for these magazines was undoubtedly one of the reasons Alexander launched his minor campaign along this route in late March, "capturing some of the towns by storm and winning over others by his own fair dealing."[27] By the process of elimination it can be determined that Alexander's campaign was indeed directed against the towns along the route the Macedonians would follow to the Median capital in late May or early June. Since the Niriz Basin, except for the cluster of villages around Persepolis, was uninhabited in Alexander's era, no campaign would be conducted here. As was noted above, there is only one route out of the Persepolis–Pasargadae

24. Hansman, op. cit., 110; Arthur Upham Pope, "Persepolis as a Ritual City," *Archaeology* 10 (1957) 123–130.
25. See above p. 56.
26. Morier, op. cit., 148.   27. D. 73. 1.

region to the rest of Persis and beyond, and this passes eastward through Deh Bid. Once past Deh Bid, Alexander would have the choice of either proceeding south, where the land is only suitable for upland (summer) pasture, or north along the Royal Road to Ecbatana, where there were several towns surrounded by arable land.[28] Both Diodorus and Curtius spoke of towns and cultivation,[29] and hence it is certain that Alexander's expedition was indeed directed against the towns along the Royal Road. Once again, it should be remembered that even if sufficient supplies could have been collected from the Persepolis region, the expedition could only carry a 14-day ration of grain with them at most, for by that day the pack animals and personnel will have consumed all the provisions they were carrying.[30] If the inhabitants of the villages along the Royal Road to the Median capital (514 miles from Persepolis) fired their fields and granaries and dispersed their flocks before the approach of the Macedonians, it would have been fatal to the progress of the army.

Why could not Alexander march through the lands of the Uxians to Susa and hence to Ecbatana? North of Susa, the ice and snow would be just as much a problem; also, the Uxians were severely handled by the Macedonians as they proceeded to Persis, and many of their villages were pillaged and the inhabitants slain.[31] It is most unlikely that their villages would still contain many sheep or grain from the previous year's harvest, and the present year's harvest would not begin until June or July.[32]

28. For the region south of the Deh Bid Pass see, Sir Aurel Stein, "An Archaeological Tour in the Ancient Persis," *Geo. Journ.* 86 (1935) 496; Morier, op. cit., 150f. No remains of *qanats* (underground irrigation tunnels) or ancient settlements have been found here, and there is only a limited amount of cultivable land and water resources. In the region north of Deh Bid, remains of fire temples have been found at Yezd-i-Khast, Naisar, and a large, important temple complex near Isfahan, *Arch. Mitt. aus Iran* 6 (1973), map opposite p. 66; *Iranica Antiqua* 5 (1965) 39–82. The latter town was the Achaemenid Gabae, J. Marquart, "Untersuchung zur Geschichte von Eran," *Philologus Suppl.* 10 (1907) 32; *Klio* 8 (1908) 13–20; A. V. William Jackson, *Persia: Past and Present* (New York, 1966) 264; Hans Treidler, *RE Suppl.* 10 (1965) s.v. Paraetacene, 478–482. There is also an Achaemenid site at Tepe Nush-i Jan, *Iran* 7 (1969) 19. There are traditions of Achaemenid settlements at Isfahan, Gulpaigan, and Vaneshan, (Jackson, 248–264). All these sites are on or near the natural route of communication from Persis to Ecbatana.

29. D. 73. 1; C. 5. 6. 15.

30. See above, Chapter 1, n. 27.

31. A. 3. 17. 3.

32. Sir Arnold T. Wilson, *Persia* (London, 1932) 54; Porter, op. cit., Vol. 1, 456.

This brings us to the reason for the timing of Alexander's departure in late May or early June. The towns of Persis would be on short rations just before the harvest,[33] and undoubtedly much of their surplus from the previous year's harvest was used to provision Ariobarzanes and his 25,000 troops. Since the harvests occur here in late June or early July, the earliest date the Macedonians could utilize the milkripe ears of grain was in late May or early June.[34] Thus, far from dallying at Persepolis for four months, Alexander left at the earliest possible moment. Darius also left Ecbatana shortly after Alexander's departure,[35] doubtless for the same reasons, but Alexander's swiftness caught him unprepared. No matter where Alexander spent the winter of 331/330, the fact remains that no army could march across the Zagros Mountains in winter.

Now there occurs an extraordinary series of marches. Alexander and the forces with him marched a total of about 950 miles from Persepolis to Hecatompylos in Parthia from early June to July of 330. It must be remembered that at no time did Alexander march with his entire army from Persepolis to Parthia, but only with its lightest, swiftest units. The entire Macedonian army did not reassemble again for *marching* until Alexander reached Sousia in Areia.[36]

When Alexander left Persepolis with his 17,000 troops for the Royal Road into Media, the army would find small areas of cultivable land at Surmaq; Abadeh, 16 miles distant; Yezd-i-Khast, an-

33. See above, p. 27. Although Arrian (3. 19. 1) wrote that Alexander left for Media (for he had heard that Darius was there), surely, this does not mean that he waited at Persepolis for four months until he learned where Darius was located. Alexander knew where Darius was headed after Gaugamela (A. 3. 16. 1–2), and, at any rate, ignorance of Darius' whereabouts would not be a sufficient reason for his delay at Persepolis for four months. Alexander would not have pined away at Persepolis indefinitely waiting to hear about Darius, but would strike out as soon as possible in the direction he knew Darius was headed after Gaugamela. The very least Alexander knew was that Darius was not in Babylon, Egypt, Syria, Anatolia, Susa, or Persis, and there was only one place he could have been: northern Persia. Arrian's statement gives the reason for the direction of Alexander's march and not the reason for the delay at Persepolis.

34. See above, p. 27.

35. A. 3. 19. 5.

36. A. 3. 25. 4. Ἀλέξανδρος δὲ ὁμοῦ ἤδη ἔχων τὴν πᾶσαν δύναμιν at Sousia, Except for the troops with Parmenio, guarding the treasure, who returned in Arachosia (C. 7. 3. 4).

other 36 miles; Shah Riza, 43 miles away; and Isfahan (Gabae), 45 miles away.[37] Water could also be obtained at each of these locations. Except for Isfahan, the cultivable areas are not extensive, but they could probably produce sufficient grain for Alexander's small force. The extensive tract of cultivable land surrounding Isfahan is extremely productive, and no doubt the force carried supplies obtained here for the 262-mile journey across the Zagros Plateau to Ecbatana. Perhaps the army followed the route past Gulpaigan, Kumain, and Sultanabad, where their supplies could be supplemented before reaching the extensive plains surrounding the Median capital. It was perhaps near Gabae that Alexander heard of Darius' decision to retreat to Parthia and Bactria.[38] There is no evidence that the rest of the Macedonian army joined the king at any point along the march from Persepolis to Ecbatana. Indeed, it would make no sense for them to have done so considering the scarcity of supplies along the route and the need for haste. The whole army seems to have regrouped once again at the Median capital after the forces at Susa marched directly to Ecbatana, some 263 miles away. After he learned that Darius was in retreat toward Parthia, Hyrcania, and Bactria, laying waste to the land as he went, Alexander set off in pursuit from Ecbatana, taking only the Companion cavalry, the mounted scouts, the mercenary horse, the part of the phalanx not detailed to guard the treasure at Ecbatana, the Agrianians, and the archers.[39]

Parmenio was ordered to transport the 7,290 tons of gold and silver stored at Persepolis, Susa, and Pasargadae to Ecbatana with 20,000 mules and 5,000 camels, an extraordinary problem in logistics.[40] When he had finished this task, he was ordered to take the mercenaries, Thracians, and all the cavalry except the Companions and subdue the Cadusians, who dwelt between the Amardus (Safid Rud) and Cyrus (Kura) rivers, and to march into Hyrcania.[41]

37. Morier, op. cit., 150f.
38. A. 3. 19. 4; C. 5. 13. 2. Alexander apparently reached the town in 12 days from Persepolis with a march rate of 21 miles per day. Curtius mistakenly calls the town Tabae.
39. A. 3. 19. 1; A. 3. 20. 1. The phalanx was among the lightest equipped of Alexander's troops, wearing only greaves, a helmet, leather breastplate, and a light shield as armor; hence their use in hot pursuits, Snodgrass, op. cit., 117.
40. D. 71. 1–2; P. 37. 2; Str. 15. 3. 9. The weight is only approximate, based on the weight of a silver talent.
41. A. 3. 19. 7.

The reason for this order was not only to subdue the Cadusians but also to alleviate the army's supply problems in Parthia. The entire army could not, and did not, follow Alexander to Rhagae through the Southern Caspian Gates to Hecatompylos because of the insufficient supply of water along the route in July and because the area's slender agricultural resources had already been taxed to the limit by the passage of two armies.[42] When Alexander reached Hyrcania, there were only 20,000 infantrymen and 7,000 cavalry with him,[43] that is, only the forces he took from Ecbatana. The rest of the army left the Median capital and marched north, probably via the Qazvin Plain and the Safid Rud to the vicinity of Resht and hence through Hyrcania and into Areia where they regrouped at Sousia.[44] Parmenio himself remained behind at Ecbatana as the governor of Media, and he was initially in charge of the treasure of 180,000 talents stored there.[45] As was already noted, Parmenio's achievements are constantly underrated or ignored by the sources, and the reporting of this expedition is yet another example.[46] No doubt, too, the old general did not have time to write his memoirs before he was killed a few months later.

Alexander, meanwhile, ordered a forced march from the Median capital to Rhagae in pursuit of Darius, and the army covered the distance in 11 days.[47] There were essentially two routes the Macedonians could have taken. The first runs northeast via Qazvin and hence southeast to Rhagae, a distance of 240 miles; the second, southeast from Ecbatana via Arak and hence northeast to Qum or Zarand, a distance of about 257 miles.[48] The first route is

42. A. 3. 20. 4; A. F. von Stahl, "Notes on the March of Alexander the Great from Ecbatana to Hyrcania," *Geo. Journ.* 64 (1924) 320–325, for the terrain.

43. P. 47. 1.

44. A. 3. 25. 4.

45. D. 80. 3; C. 6. 8. 18.

46. Parmenio was responsible for Alexander's successful strategy at the Granicus (Green, 495–508) and perhaps at Issus (above, Chapter 2, n. 137), yet scarcely a trace of this achievement appears in the sources.

47. A. 3. 20. 2.

48. The second route is suggested by von Stahl, op. cit., 319–320. The first route is suggested by G. Radet, "La dernière campagne d'Alexandre contre Darius," *Mélanges Gustave Glotz*, Vol. 2 (Paris, 1932) 765–778. The caravan route between the two towns, 210 miles via Nowbaran and Zarand, does not contain adequate resources for a military route (C. 5. 8. 5) and would be too short a distance for a forced march of 11 days. It would give an average march rate of only 19 miles per day, which is slow for the few fast, light units with Alexander, as is shown by their subsequent performance.

somewhat shorter and thus is the more likely one for an army in a hurry; it is also better supplied with fresh water and cultivable land. The second route traverses a section of the Great Salt Desert between Qum (or Saveh) and Rhagae, and the small streams here are saturated with salt even during the rainy season, which had now passed.[49] The first route was also thickly settled in antiquity, although the precise dates of the settlements have not yet been established.[50] It is difficult to determine to what extent the route was laid waste by Darius, since the speed of the Macedonians' pursuit may have prevented the Persians from doing the job thoroughly. Although many soldiers were left behind and many horses died along the route, this was because of exhaustion and because the speed of the march prevented the horses from grazing, not from lack of supplies.[51] At Rhagae, Alexander received intelligence that Darius had passed through the area a considerable time earlier, and believing that he could no longer catch him by hot pursuit, he gave his troops a much-needed rest for five days before proceeding to the Southern Caspian Gates—the Tang-i Sar Darrah.[52]

There has been some discussion of Alexander's march rates here,[53] but there is no real problem. Arrian stated that the Caspian

49. For the terrain of the first route, see Porter, op. cit., Vol. 1, 296f.; Morier, op. cit., 249–253. For the second route: Porter, op. cit., Vol. 1, 370–373; Morier, 180–183; A. H. Mounsey, *A Journey through the Caucasus and the Interior of Persia* (London, 1872) 172. See now the map in Von Hagen, op. cit., 279. Significantly, one of the more desolate valleys of the second route is called the Malek-el-Moat-dareh, the Valley of the Angel of Death.

50. *Arch. Mitt. aus Iran* 6 (1973), maps opposite pp. 7, 38. Cf. Morier, op cit., 251–252; Porter, op. cit., 296.

51. A. 3. 20. 1. The region surrounding Rhagae is a major producer of Iran's wheat and barley, and it was equally productive in antiquity, Naval Intelligence Division, *Persia*, 451; Fisher, *Iran*, 292; Special Operations Research Office, op. cit., 430; Str. 11. 13. 6.

52. A. 3. 20. 3. For the identification of the Gates, see A. V. Williams Jackson, *Constantinople to the Home of Omar Khayyam: Travels in Transcaucasia and Northern Persia for Historic and Literary Research* (New York, 1911) 127–128; John Hansman, "The Problems of Qūmis," *JRAS* 100 (1968) 111–139. There are two Caspian Gates, the southern one followed here by Alexander in his pursuit of Darius, and the northern Gates piercing the Elburz Mountains past Mt. Demavend by the Imamzadeh Pass, which were described by Strabo (11. 13. 6–7) as being 500 stadia north of Rhagae.

53. By R. D. Milns, "Alexander's Pursuit of Darius through Iran," *Historia* 15 (1966) 256; and C. Neumann, "A Note on Alexander's March Rates," *Historia* 20 (1971) 196–198. Neither understands that an army's march rate is inversely proportional to the number of troops; see table 7.

Gates were one day's march from Rhagae, 42 miles away, "for anyone marching as Alexander did."[54] There are two questions presented by this passage. The first is hypothetical: Could Alexander's
divisions have reached the Caspian Gates from Rhagae in one day,
marching as they did? How did they march? The fast, light units
marched all night long until noon of the next day, that is, in 16-
hour stretches,[55] a common procedure in desert marches. Although
the terrain here is desolate, it is flat and smooth and would offer
no obstacle for an average march rate of 2.6 mph, even with the
necessary halts. The second question is: How far did Alexander
actually march the first day from Rhagae, when he encamped "by
the Gaspian Gates"?[56] One does not conclude from this statement
that Alexander encamped on the very spot where the Caspian
Gates began; like any competent general, he will have encamped
where strategic and logistic requirements could be best fulfilled.
His camp was certainly at Airan Kief, 34 miles from Rhagae and 8
miles from the Gates.[57] This location possesses the only source of
water until the village of Aradan, 24 miles further away. Considering the enormous water requirements of an army and its horses,[58]
Alexander would have been foolish to have encamped anywhere
else. He was about to skirt one of the most inhospitable regions of
the world, the Dasht-i-Kavir—the Desert of Salt—and water supply
would have been of paramount importance.

On the second day, the divisions probably encamped near Aradan where there are springs and some cultivation. Here, Alexander
learned through advance intelligence that the country beyond was
desert, and he sent Coenus, one of his most trusted lieutenants, to
collect supplies for the journey ahead.[59] However, on learning of

54. A. 3. 20. 2.
55. A. 3. 21. 3–9.
56. A. 3. 20. 4, Καὶ τῇ μὲν πρώτῃ πρὸς ταῖς Κασπίαις πύλαις ἐστρατόπεδευσε.
57. Jackson, *Constantinople*, 123; von Stahl, op. cit., 319.
58. See Appendix 1.
59. A. 3. 20. 4. We follow the reconstruction of von Stahl, op. cit., 319–320, with
the final capture occurring near Damghan, rather than Radet, op. cit., 772–776, who
has the capture near Shahrud. The latter distance, about 267 miles, is far too long
for a force consisting mainly of infantry (A. 3. 20. 1) to cover in six days. The average
march rate would be 45 mpd, while he only covered 34 miles the first day (above, n. 57)
and only covered 46 miles with a force consisting *entirely* of cavalry, led at full speed,
on the last day (A. 3. 21. 7–9).

Darius' arrest by Bessus and Barsaentes, Alexander did not even wait for Coenus to return with supplies but immediately set out in pursuit, taking *only* the Companions, the mounted scouts, the lightest infantry, and two days' rations. After marching all night till noon the next day, the brigades rested and then at twilight traveled again all night till dawn when they reached the abandoned Persian camp, probably southwest of Samnan. Marching the next night to the following noon, the Macedonians reached the village where Darius' captors had encamped the night before, near the Rion River. Advance intelligence informed the king that the Persians had abandoned their tradition of not making night marches and had pressed onward. He also learned that there was a shorter route than the one the fugitives had followed, which, however, was devoid of water. The route was shorter because, unlike the main road, it did not proceed through the mountain pass that separates Samnan and Ahuvan. Alexander now dismounted the cavalry and ordered 500 infantrymen to mount the horses. Starting at dusk, the brigade traveled 42 miles over the desert through the night, reaching the Persians at dawn near Damghan. The Macedonians had achieved a march of almost 200 miles over difficult terrain in six days with an average daily march of 33 miles.

At Hecatompylos the army rested, and the stragglers left behind in the pursuit were given time to regroup. Supplies were also brought in from the surrounding territory.[60] The site of Hecatompylos was located long ago at Sahr-i Qumis, 32 km. southwest of Damghan, just south of the village of Qusheh. The site is a two-day march from the border of Hyrcania and is about 125 miles from the Caspian Gates.[61]

After regrouping at Hecatompylos, the Macedonians crossed the Shemshir-cur Pass and marched into Hyrcania, whose fertility was

60. C. 6. 2. 15; D. 75. 1.
61. The site was first identified by A. Houtum-Schindler, "Notes on some Antiquities Found in a Mound Near Damghan," *JRAS* 9 (1877) 425–427; later by Jackson, *Constantinople*, 162–176; and most recently by Hansman, "Qūmis," 111–139. Hansman is incorrect, however, in stating that Strabo's measurement from the Caspian Gates to Rhagae was measured to the Tang-i Sar Darrah. Strabo's Caspian Gates are the northern Gates, 500 stadia north of Rhagae, Str. 11. 9. 1; 11. 13. 6. Fortunately for Hansman, the distance between the two passes is similar. For an analysis of the bematist's measurements given in Pliny 6. 61–62 and the distances in Str. 11. 8. 9, see table 8.

legendary.[62] At the Macedonians' first camp near Gurgan (Astarabad) Bay, Phrataphernes, the satrap of Hyrcania and Parthia, through whose territory the army would proceed, made his submission to Alexander.[63] From here, Alexander advanced westward along the coast for an expedition against the Mardians and halted at Zadracarta, which is certainly to be identified with the modern Sari.[64] Almost every step of the Macedonians' route in Hyrcania can be reconstructed, thanks to the abundant and accurate geographical information provided by Curtius. One may be tempted to dismiss Curtius' description of Hyrcania as a fairyland, but every detail of his account had been verified by geographical and botanical studies of the country.[65] Even the honey dripping from the trees is accurate. The honey—called *gaz* by the Persians—is collected from the Caspian Honey Locust in the region and is used to make candy. Indeed, the product has given its name to Bandar-i-Gaz (the modern Bandar-i-Shah). Curtius' description of the famous Hyrcanian forests with their junglelike tangle of vines and branches is also accurate and must have made a striking impression on an observer used to the light, coniferous forests of the Mediterranean. The region is "so abundantly clothed with trees of the forest, that often a pathway can scarcely be forced through the intricate jungle, so riotous in colour that the traveller can almost awake with the belief that he has been transported in sleep to some tropical clime."[66] It is difficult not to be impressed by Curtius' remarkable geographical knowledge of Alexander's route.[67]

62. For the route: von Stahl, op. cit., 324–326; P. Pédech, "Deux campagnes d'Antiochus III chez Polybe," *REA* 60 (1958) 75–76; from the accurate description in C. 6. 4. 3–7. For the fertility of the region: D. 75. 4–7; C. 6. 4. 20–22; Naval Intelligence Division, *Persia*, 35f.

63. A. 3. 23. 4. For the logistic significance of these surrenders, see above, p. 41.

64. The site has sometimes been identified with Astarabad, but since this town was founded about 720 A.D. by the Arab commander Yazid b. Muhllab, the deputy of the seventh Umayyad caliph Sulayman, this identification can hardly be correct, Lord George N. Curzon, *Persia and the Persian Question*, Vol. 1 (London, 1966) 356. While traditions concerning Astarabad do not antedate 720 A.D., there are traditions of an Achaemenid settlement at Sari. Sari fits perfectly the geographical information in Curtius, Arrian, and Diodorus, and there can be no doubt about its identity, von Stahl, op. cit., 328. Its ancient name would seem to be preserved in its present name, Zerd-Karta or Sari-Karta, which means chief town. The site has not yet been excavated.

65. Von Stahl, op. cit., 325–328; Naval Intelligence Division, *Persia*, 35f.

66. Naval Intelligence Division, *Persia*, 35.

67. The sources' description of the Caspian Honey Locust is not a "misunderstanding," as it was described by Truesdell S. Brown, *Onesicritus: A Study in Hellenis-*

After Alexander received the submission of several Persian dignitaries at Zadracarta and conducted a campaign against the Mardians, the army marched eastward through Parthia to Sousia (Tus)[68] on the border of Areia, where the satrap Satibarzanes made his submission. The route the Macedonians followed from Hyrcania across Parthia to Sousia was in all probability the ancient Silk Route, which proceeded from Shahrud to Maiameh, Abbasabad, Sebzewar, and Nishapur. This route is indicated once again by a bematist's measurement of 4,530 *stadia* (521 miles) or 565 Roman miles (520 miles) from Hecatompylos (Sahr-i Qumis) to Alexandria Areion (Herat).[69] The accuracy of these measurements is established in table 8, and they provide valuable information on Alexander's routes. Since Alexander's bematists' measurements are accurate between the Caspian Gates and Hecatompylos, between Alexandria Areion and Alexandria ad Caucasum, between the latter city and Peucolatis, between Peucolatis and Taxila, and between Taxila and the Jhelum, in all probability they accurately measure the distance of Alexander's route here also. By the process of elimination, the only route which corresponds to the bematists' measurement is the ancient Silk Route, since all other possible routes are longer.[70] This corridor of land has adequate water and

---

tic Historiography (Berkeley, 1949) 89, but an accurate description of the tree. Curtius' geographical accuracy has been verified by others, e.g., Sir Aurel Stein, *On Alexander's Track to the Indus* (London, 1929) 137f.; von Stahl, op. cit., 325–328; Pédech, op. cit., 75–76. His descriptions are arranged in a series of vignettes, occurring whenever something unusual or remarkable attracts his attention, and are found in no other author except on three occasions in Diodorus (concerning the Oasis of Siwah, D. 50, C. 4. 7. 10–12; Hyrcania, C. 6. 4. 16–5. 21, D. 75; and the Parapanisadae, C. 7. 3. 6–18; D. 82). Onesicritus is the ultimate origin for many of his descriptions, Brown, 91, 115, especially in India. Arrian did not think well of Onesicritus as a source (A. 6. 2. 3), which may explain why almost none of the information preserved in Curtius from this source is repeated in Arrian.

68. There are traditions of an Achaemenid settlement at Tus (or Tos), and although no excavations have yet been undertaken here, its present name seems to have been derived from *Tausa, and ultimately from *Tausia. E. Herzfeld, "Sakastan," *Arch. Mitt. aus Iran* 4 (1932) 38; *Arch. Mitt. aus Iran* 1 (1929–30) 106; Jackson, *Constantinople*, 278; Marquart, op. cit., 65.

69. For the bematists' measurements, see table 8. For the generally accepted identification of Alexandria Areion with Herat, see H. H. Wilson, *Ariana Antiqua* (London, 1841) 151; V. Tscherikower, "Die hellenistischen Städtgrundüngen von Alexander dem Grossen bis auf die Römerzeit," *Philologus Suppl.* 19.1 (1927) 102.

70. Most maps of Alexander's route following Marquart, op. cit., 65, have him go through the Atrek Valley, a distance of some 660 miles from Sahr-i Qumis to Herat. The route of the modern railroad is about 546 miles.

agricultural resources to support a large army, and strong Zoroastrian traditions indicate that it was the most densely populated region of Khorasan in the Achaemenid era.[71] Doubtless, a thorough archeological survey of the region would also support this conclusion and there are numerous pre-Islamic remains along the route.[72] Such a survey, however, has never been undertaken in Khorasan. One urgently needs to be conducted and would no doubt more than repay the effort by increasing our understanding of this vital area of ancient Persia.

At Sousia, certain Persians reported to Alexander that Bessus was wearing his cap in royal fashion, donning imperial robes, and calling himself Artaxerxes the king of Asia.[73] Alexander made immediate preparations for a campaign into Bactria against Bessus. Since the initial stage of his route was to pass through an uncultivated and sparsely settled region,[74] one of Alexander's first orders was that all excess baggage, wagons, and personal possessions were to be burned, beginning with his own.[75] Xenophon followed a similar procedure before making a winter march into eastern Anatolia and noted that it saved half the army's supplies.[76] Although the section of Turkmenistan through which Alexander

71. During the 1830s when the route was thoroughly ruined and devastated by Turkomen raids, it still supported 60,000 pilgrims per year on the journey from Shahrud to Meshed from the months of April to November, Conolly, op. cit., 188. Wheeled vehicles were not used in Persia even until the nineteenth century because of its rugged topography, James Morier, *A Second Journey through Persia in the Years 1810 and 1816* (London, 1818) 197, but all goods were transported by pack animals, as in Alexander's day. When continuous historical traditions of the region begin in the eighth century A.D., the Silk Route is the most important in Khorasan, Brian Spooner, "Arghiyān: the Area of Jārjam in Western Khurāsān," *Iran* 3 (1965) 100. For the Achaemenid traditions see Jackson, *Constantinople*, 204–248.

72. Jackson, *Constantinople*, 204–248.

73. A. 3. 25. 3.

74. See below, p. 89.

75. C. 6. 6. 15–16.

76. Xen. *Anab.* 4. 1. 12–13. Bonaparte, retreating from Russia, followed the same procedure for the same reasons. J. R. Hamilton, *Plutarch Alexander: A Commentary* (London, 1969) 157, doubts this Curtius passage on the basis of P. 57. 1–2, who placed the incident before the entry into India. It makes better sense for Alexander to have burned his wagons before entering the Kara Kum than before entering rich, fertile India. Moreover, Curtius' geography is accurate until Sogdia, whereas Plutarch becomes confused after Ecbatana. One would not expect Curtius to mistake Bactria for India, whereas such confusion is natural for Plutarch. Indeed, Plutarch discusses events in *Bactria* and *Sogdia* after this "India" passage.

was to proceed was intensively settled and agriculturally productive in Alexander's era,[77] supplies were scarce along the initial part of the route from Sousia across the Kuh-i-Hazar Masjed range. No doubt Satibarzanes, who surrendered to Alexander at Sousia, was to oversee the establishment of magazines along the route. A small garrison was established in Areia to prevent the Macedonians from unwarranted pillaging[78] and perhaps to insure that Satibarzanes would fulfill his obligations to Alexander.

On his way into Bactria, Alexander received news that Satibarzanes had revolted, massacring the garrison. Alexander left Craterus in command of the rest of the army, while he himself turned back; and taking *only* the Companions, mounted javelin men, the archers, Agrianians, and the brigades of Amyntas and Coenus, he advanced 600 *stadia* (69 miles) from where he left Craterus to Artacoana.[79] Where did Alexander leave Craterus and the rest of the army? Curtius provides the answer:[80] it was near a large flat-topped mountain, extremely steep on its western side but sloping more gently toward the east. On its summit there was an extensive grass-covered plain with a spring of abundant water. The Areians ordered those not fit for war to seek refuge there, and the natural fortress was manned by 13,000 troops. Alexander left virtually the entire army to besiege the place, and although the western end of the fortress was steeper, the Macedonians attacked from this direction. They were able to climb part of the way up the cliffs but were stopped by impassible precipices. The mountain stronghold was so formidable that for the first and only time in his career, Alexander was at a loss how to capture his objective. Finally, the army built a ramp of felled trees up the west end. This accidentally caught fire, and the blaze, fanned by a powerful west wind, spread to the entire mountain, killing almost all the Areians inside the stronghold.

The site of this mountain stronghold has not been previously identified, but it is beyond all question the famous Kalat-i-Nadiri: "One of the most extraordinary natural phenomena in the world, and famous even in this land of mountain fastness and impregna-

---

77. See n. 85.
78. A. 3. 25. 2.
79. A. 3. 25. 6.
80. C. 6. 6. 25; 6. 6. 23–32.

ble defiles for its inaccessibility and amazing natural strength."[81] This stupendous natural fortress is about 44 miles north of Sousia and has walls 1,500 feet high on the south precipice and 2,000 feet high on the west, while the eastern walls are lower. Although the western end is steeper, it is also less inaccessible than the other sides—hence the Macedonian assault from this end. In its interior, there is a grassy plain some four or five miles in circumference, with a large pool fed by perennial springs. From here one can see the natural walls of the perimeter towering 500 feet over the plain. On the exterior, the first half of the walled perimeter has a moderate slope and can be climbed, but the higher half rises in a sheer vertical cliff. The walls crest in a basaltic wedge so narrow that it is impossible to walk along it. A fierce west wind blows here from June to September and is called, appropriately, the Wind of One Hundred and Twenty Days (Bad-i-Sad-o-bist roz). This fortress has served as a place of refuge throughout Persian history from nomad invaders from the steppe. It is indeed the most famous stronghold in the Near East, the "Gibraltar" of Persia, and the

81. Curzon, op. cit., Vol. 1, 113. For the Kalat-i-Nadiri, see P. M. Sykes, "A Fifth Journey in Persia," *Geo. Journ.* 28 (1906) 569f.; Capt. G. Napier, "Extracts from a Diary of a Tour in Khorassan and Notes on the Eastern Alburz Tract," *JRGS* 46 (1876) 74–79, who also gives the topography of the route between Sousia and the fort. Sykes' description is the most accurate and detailed, and we follow him in our account. Curtius (6. 6. 23) gave the perimeter of the fortress as 32 stadia, or about four miles. Presumably, this is the perimeter of the interior plain, which another traveler to the Kalat, a Greek named Basil Batatzes, gave as 40 to 50 stadia, Ch. Schaefer, *Nouveaux Mélanges Orientaux* (Publications de l'Ecole des Langues Orientales Vivantes, Paris 1886). I have not been able to find a subsequent measurement for the interior perimeter since Basil's in 1728. My identification has been accepted by Green, 337.

It is possible that local legends have preserved a memory of Alexander's siege. In Firdusi's tenth-century epic *Shah Nama* (Arthur George Warner and Edmond Warner, trans., *The Shahnama of Firdausi*, Vol. 3 [London, 1908] 38ff.; Sykes, 570–571), the semilegendary king of Persia, Kei Khusru, sent his commander Tus to invade Turan, or central Asia, giving him specific instructions to avoid passing Kalat, which was held by his half-brother Farud. Tus, however, on finding that all other routes into central Asia led through deserts, marched toward the fortress. Farud, seeing the approach of a mighty host, sallied from the fort with its garrison, and Tus, ignoring the fact that Farud was the king's brother, engaged in battle. After a heroic struggle in which many Persian champions perished, Farud received a mortal wound and with difficulty returned to the stronghold, where he was received by his mother who set fire to the whole fortress and hamstrung the horses. The women committed suicide by hurling themselves from the precipices, and Farud and the remaining soldiers killed themselves. The whole incident, with a king invading central Asia via the Kalat because the alternative routes passed through desert, and especially the end of the siege, resembles the account in C. 6. 6. 23–32.

only fortress that successfully withstood a siege by Tamerlane. There is no other geological formation in this area, or indeed the entire Near East, that corresponds to Curtius' detailed description, and there can be no doubt about its identity.

The location of this fortress provides a great deal of information concerning Alexander's planned route into Bactria and the location of Artacoana, a section of Alexander's route that has heretofore been blank.

First, the route into Bactria. It is obvious that the initial stage of Alexander's Bactrian campaign followed the route from Sousia north to the Kalat and not eastward, as Marquart thought.[82] The language of Curtius and Arrian is clear on this point.[83] Alexander *left* Craterus and the army to besiege Kalat, while he himself marched on Artacoana. Now, if Alexander's route were eastward from Sousia, he would not *leave* the army behind to besiege the stronghold, but would rather order the army northwest to besiege it.

The initial stage of the march shows that Alexander attempted to enter Bactria by the traditional invasion route (used by Genghis Khan, Tamerlane, Tus, the Sacae) from northeastern Persia to the Tejend Valley past the Merv Oasis to the Royal Road from Merv to Bactra,[84] or to another destination he thought suitable. Today, this route would impose great difficulties for an army traveling as the Macedonians did without modern methods of transport since it is only sparsely inhabited. However, once again we find that the ancient region was densely settled and crisscrossed with numerous irrigation canals (one barrage, incidentally is named after Alexander), whereas in modern times, until recent Soviet irrigation projects, the area was a deserted wasteland. Ruined sites and abandoned irrigation works are densely clustered from Dushak

82. Marquart, op. cit., 67. Besides other difficulties with his route, it proceeds some 84 miles through unbroken desert from Pole-Khatun to Bala Murghab.

83. C. 6. 6. 25, *relicto*; A. 3. 25. 6, καταλιπών.

84. This Royal Road (Shah-Rah or military road) was always important as a trade and communications route, K. DeB. Cordington, "A Geographical Introduction to the History of Central Asia," *Geo. Journ.* 104 (1944) 73–74. It was followed by Isidore of Charax, *GGM* 1, 252–253. Cf. R. Ghirshman, *Iran* (Baltimore, 1954) 249; *Bibl. Geog. Arab.* 1, 270–271; 3, 298, 347; Charles Marvin, *Colonel Grodelcoff's Ride from Samarcand to Herat through the Uzbek States of Afghan Turkestan* (London, 1880); C. Sykes, "Some Notes on a Recent Journey in Afghanistan," *Geo. Journ.* 84 (1934) 327–336.

across the Tejend Oasis to the Merv Oasis. Until their destruction by Turkomen raids (from the seventeenth to nineteenth centuries), a system of irrigation canals linked the Tejend and the Murghab, thus facilitating travel.[85] Alexander, then, planned to invade Bactria by a flank attack from Merv (Margiana, a district of Bactria). His later Bactrian campaign was also directed from the flank, this time from the Eastern Hindu Kush. Alexander deliberately avoided entering the center of the country from the main road through Bamian for strategic reasons.[86] His first strategy, attacking from Margiana, was probably intended to sweep the opposition eastward against the Hindu Kush and the Pamirs so that he would only have to fight on one front. His second strategy, attacking from the Hindu Kush, was intended to drive Bessus and his allies into the deserts of Chorasmia, where they would have to make a stand and fight. If he invaded Bactria from the center, from Bamian, Alexander would have to fight on two fronts, both east and west. We may also see in this strategy an example of Alexander keeping his enemy off balance by doing the unexpected.

Now for the location of Artacoana. The sequence of events for Alexander's return into Areia is clearly given by Arrian.[87] When he heard of Satibarzanes' tergiversation, the king took a light armed force, and leaving Craterus at Kalat (the location is provided by C. 6. 6. 25), he advanced 600 *stadia* (69 miles) to Arta-

---

85. E. Ehlers, "Klimageschichte und siedlungsgang in vor und frühgeschichtlicher Zeit in der Turkmensteppe Nordpersiens," *Arch. Mitt. Iran* 4 (1971) 7–21; L. I. Hlopina, "Southern Turkmenia in the Late Bronze Age," *EW* 22 (1972) 199–214; Grégoire Frumkin, *Archaeology in Soviet Central Asia* (Leiden, 1970) 141–146; *Iranica Antiqua* 4 (1964) 69–84; M. P. M. Lessar, "M. P. M. Lessar's Journey from Askabad to Sarakhs," *PRGS* 4 (1882) 486f.; M. P. M. Lessar, "M. P. M. Lessar's Second Journey in the Turkomen Country, Askabad to Ghurian near Herat," *PRGS* 5 (1883) 1–23; Edmond O'Donovan, "Merv and its Surroudings," *PRGS* 4 (1882) 345–358; Lt. Col. C. E. Stewart, "The Country of the Tekke Turkomans and the Tejand and Murghab Rivers," *PRGS* 3 (1881) 538–543. One site given on the map facing p. 56 in *PRGS* 5 (1883) has the intriguing name of Arti-Kala. E. Atagarryev and O. Berdyev, "The Archaeological Exploration of Turkmenistan in the Years of Soviet Power," *EW* 20 (1970) 285–306; Robert A. Lewis, "Early Irrigation in West Turkestan," *AAAG* 56 (1966) 472f.

86. The route through Bamian (Bamyan or Bamiyan) was one of the principal entrances into Bactria: it follows the lowest passes and is open for longer periods in winter, A. Foucher and E. Bazin-Foucher, *La vieille route de l'Inde de Bactres à Taxila*, Vol. 1, *MDAFA* 1 (1942) 24–27, 203. One of the reasons Alexander may have taken the road via Merv was to avoid the difficulties of crossing a mountain pass held by an enemy, see Appendix 2.

87. A. 3. 25. 6.

coana. This is the obvious interpretation of events. Now, Satibarzanes had advanced to Artacoana, wishing to attack Alexander on his march into Bactria with the cooperation of Bessus and his forces.[88] Thus, the site of the city will be rather to the north and east of Sousia than to the south or west, since this was the direction of the Macedonian march and also the location of Bessus and his cohorts. The region 70 miles north to east of Kalat is strewn with scores of ruined sites and abandoned irrigation works, in both the Soviet Union and Iran.[89] If Artacoana is located in the Soviet Union, it will only be a matter of time before the intensive excavations and survey work undertaken in Turkmenistan will uncover it. Khorasan in Iran, as was noted, has not yet received adequate attention from archaeologists, and if the city is located here, we will have to wait a good deal longer for its discovery.

After Alexander captured the Kalat-i-Nadiri and subdued the rest of Areia, he did not continue the march into Bactria by his former, northern route, since the meager agricultural resources of its initial section had no doubt been exhausted by the army's earlier advance and return into Areia. Furthermore, winter was now approaching and the army would need to remain in an extensively cultivated region for a considerable period. Therefore, he marched southeast through the fertile Jam and Heri Rud valleys to Herat and hence south to the Lake Seistan area—the ancient Zarangaea. Few regions on earth are more inhospitable than Seistan. The Wind of One Hundred and Twenty Days reaches its full fury here from June to September, often reaching hurricane force. "It creates a pandemonium of noise, sand, and dust, but although hot and parching, it mitigates the summer heat and blows away the insects which from April to June make life in Seistan a purgatory."[90] However, plagues of midges, mosquitoes, horseflies, and poisonous snakes and hurricane-force winds are only mild irrita-

88. A. 3. 25. 5.

89. Stewart, op. cit., 513–546; Lessar, "Second Journey," 1–23. The ancient geographical references to the site tell us only that it was located in Areia, Pliny *NH* 6. 93; Str. 11. 10. 1; Isidore of Charax, *GGM* 1, 252–253; or perhaps in Parthia: Ptol. *Geo.* 6. 5; Amm. Marc. 23. 6. 43. It is certainly not the same as Alexandria Areion, since both cities are named distinctly in our sources.

90. Naval Intelligence Division, *Persia*, 162; William Trousdale, "The Homeland of Rustam," *ILN* (December 1975) 91–93.

tions next to the blowing sand. It not only sandblasts all the buildings (and people) in the region, giving them a short life span, but
also heaps up masses of large, rapidly moving sand dunes that
can overwhelm fields, buildings, and indeed entire towns in a matter of months. For these reasons, all towns and buildings—ancient
and modern—not only have their backs against the northwest
wind but often project only their northwest corners in this direction. In addition, there is the unpredictable behavior of the
lake and the lower Helmand River itself. The river frequently
changes its bed, and after heavy precipitation in Afghanistan, the
lake will often expand to two or three times its normal size, wreck-
ing painfully constructed irrigation complexes and submerging
towns and villages. Alternatively, the changing course of the river
can leave former irrigation works high and dry.

Yet, despite all these serious disabilities, the region was one of
the most densely settled and agriculturally productive regions of
the Near East, as is proven not only by the many ruined irrigation complexes (the earliest dating to the second millennium
B.C.), but also by the fact that there are over a hundred ruined
urban sites here—one of the largest concentrations of urban centers anywhere in the world. The ancient inhabitants were able to
successfully combat the sand, wind, and the changing course of
the river, problems that baffle their modern descendants. Recent
excavations have proven that it was a major region of human
settlement in the Achaemenid era,[91] and undoubtedly it was more

91. Umberto Scerrato, "A Probable Achaemenid Zone in Persian Sistan," *EW* 13
(1962) 186–197; Umberto Scerrato, "Excavations at Dahn-i Ghulaman (Seistan-Iran):
First Preliminary Report (1962–3)," *EW* 16 (1966) 9–30; Walter A. Fairservis, Jr.,
"Archaeological Studies in the Seistan Basin of South Western Afghanistan and Eastern Iran," *Anthropological Papers of the American Museum of Natural History* 48.1
(1961). The excavations confirm the Persian traditions that make Seistan a prominent
center in the formation of ancient Persia. The site of the capital of Zarangaea in
Alexander's time may have been Dahn-i Ghulaman (although it seems to have been
deserted after the fifth century B.C.). The capital of Zarangaea may or may not have
been the same city as Alexandria Prophthasia. Conditions for excavation (excluding
the wretched climate) are extremely difficult because the cities were built of mud
brick which dissolves, or rather melts, back into its original element, mud. Hellenistic
or Achaemenid mud cannot be told apart from Islamic or modern mud. Thus, trying
to find which of the 100 ruined sites was Prophthasia is an exercise in futility. Stratigraphy is difficult to determine and buildings are rarely preserved. The depth of
the mud deposits is often 20 to 30 meters thick, and the extensive areas of some of
the cities—which often cover many square miles—makes the location of Hellenistic
or Achaemenid strata difficult. Given these problems and the fact that several sites

than capable of supplying the Macedonian army for part of the winter of 330–329.[92] It was also near the navigable Helmand River, which allowed imports from its fertile valley.

In January or February, the Macedonians left Seistan for a 60-day journey through the territory of the Arimaspi, or Euergetae as they were later called, who dwelt along the lower Helmand Valley, an intensively settled and cultivated region in the Achaemenid and Hellenistic eras.[93] By late March or early April, the army began crossing the region of the Parapanisadae, an Indian tribe dwelling in the uplands between Ghazni and the Hindu Kush.[94] Once again, Alexander seems to have waited for the winter wheat and barley harvest, which occur in the lower Helmand Valley in April or May, before advancing through the Parapanisus.[95] Although the army probably carried a 14-day grain supply for the journey—the maximum amount of provisions they were capable of carrying—this was not adequate to last throughout the four-week journey of 325 miles between Kandahar and the Kabul Valley. The area under cultivation declines as one travels north from the former city since the cultivable areas become restricted to

were occupied simultaneously in Alexander's day, it is a safe assumption that, barring the find of an inscription (which seems extremely improbable), the site of Prophthasia will never be securely located. The region contains over 100 archaeological sites, and new ones are being discovered frequently.

92. We follow the generally accepted chronology of T. B. Jones, "Alexander and the Winter of 330–329 B.C.", *CW* 28 (1935) 124–125. It was impossible for the Macedonians to have marched 1,300 miles from Hecatompylos to Ghazni from July to late October or early November, as well as undertake a major campaign in Hyrcania and Mardia, remain 15 days at Zadracarta (A. 3. 25. 1), organize and conduct a march into Bactria, return from the march and subdue the Areians, and conduct the trial of Philotas.

93. C. 7. 3. 1–4; A. 3. 27. 4–5; D. 81. 1–2. Isidore of Charax also followed this route, *GGM* 1, 253–254. Norman Hammond, "An Archaeological Reconnaissance in the Helmand Valley, South Afghanistan," *EW* 20 (1970) 437–459; Klaus Fischer, "Historical, Geographical, and Philological Studies in Seistan by Bosworth, Daffinà, and Gnoli in the Light of Recent Archaeological Field Surveys," *EW* 21 (1971) 45–51. Cf. Henry Walter Bellew, *From the Indus to the Tigris* (London, 1874) 155–198. Bellew (219) noted that the insects were intolerable in Seistan in early March, yet another reason for Alexander to have left early.

94. For the date of the crossing during the cosmical setting of the Pleiades: Str. 15. 2. 10; Borza, op. cit., 237. For the location of the Parapanisadae between Ghazni and Kabul see: Alessio Bombaci, "Ghazni," *EW* 8 (1957) 247–257; *EW* 9 (1958) 156; A. K. Narain, *The Indo-Greeks* (Oxford, 1957) 28.

95. Naval Intelligence Division, *Persia*, 434; Bellew, op. cit., 189–192; W. Kraus, ed. *Afghanistan* (Tuebingen, 1972) 244.

mountain valleys where the harvests do not occur until August.[96] For these reasons, the Macedonians experienced a supply shortage in this region.[97]

The ancient route between Kandahar and Kabul has been extensively treated by others,[98] so there is no need to discuss it in detail here. Snowfall in the northern section is heavy, and the passes cannot be crossed until late spring (although the Macedonians forced them somewhat earlier). Until then, "there is risk of being lost in deep snow drifts, and, between Ghazni and Kabul especially, they say winds blow which are sharp enough to 'cut the life out of a man.' "[99] Little wonder the army suffered here from the cold and snow.[100] The territory of the Parapanisadae is now occupied by the Hazaras, who build the same type of dwellings seen by Alexander's men.[101]

The army remained some days in the rich Kabul Valley, allowing stragglers to catch up and to make preparations for crossing the Hindu Kush. The Macedonians undoubtedly used the Khawak

96. Wilfred Thesiger, "The Hazaras of Central Afghanistan," *Geo. Journ.* 121 (1955) 312–319; Arnold J. Toynbee, *Between Oxus and Jumna* (Oxford, 1961) 54–55; James Atkinson, *Expedition into Afghanistan* (London, 1842) 181–270.

97. A. 3. 28. 1.

98. Bombaci, op. cit., Klaus Fischer, "Zur Lage von Kandahar an Landverbindungen zwischen Iran und Indien," *Bonner Jahrbucher* 167 (1967) 129–232. This is the best and most thoroughly documented study on this route, but, unfortunately, it shows how little is yet known about the locations of the various towns Alexander passed through here. Kaitul (near Kandahar) was undoubtedly one of them, perhaps Alexandria of the Arachosians. An intriguing bilingual Aramaic-Greek inscription of king Asoka was found here, *EW* 10 (1959) 243–260. However, the name Kandahar is not derived from the name of Alexander, for the town was called Kandara in the Persepolis Fortification Tablets dating to 509–494 B.C. R. T. Hallock, *Persepolis Fortification Tablets*, University of Chicago Oriental Institute Publications, 92 (Chicago, 1969) 708 s.v. Kandara. Mir Zakeh (which Fox, op. cit., 293, mistakenly calls Gardez), 53 km. east northeast of Gardez was once a Greek town, *MDAFA* 14 (1953) 65; *MDAFA* 20 (1965) 62, but this mountain outpost has nothing to do with the route between Kandahar and Kabul. Fox's route (281) in Afghanistan has the Macedonians march 150 miles through the Dasht-i-Margo—the Desert of Death—between the border of Seistan and Kandahar, a truly astonishing reconstruction. The army made a similar march through the Gedrosian Desert and lost three-quarters of its troops; see below, p. 115f.

99. Conolly, op. cit., Vol. 2, 55.

100. C. 7. 3. 13.

101. C. 7. 3. 8–10, D. 82. 2; Thesiger, op. cit., 314. While archaeology has not yet confirmed Curtius' and Diodorus' descriptions of the dwellings of the Parapanisadae, a vaulted roof of brick is the obvious solution for roof construction in areas which receive heavy snowfall but possess no timber, as the modern houses testify.

Pass (11,650 feet) for their crossing, for although it is one of the longest passes over the range (47 miles), it is also the lowest, the best provided with forage, and the most suitable for a late spring crossing.[102] The crossing took 16 or 17 days, not the usual four days, since the army encountered the same problems of moving large numbers of men and animals through narrow spaces that we have noted before.[103] Since the narrowest part of the pass would not allow more than sections of three infantrymen to pass abreast, the infantry probably crossed in double file and the cavalry horses in single file with the baggage animals forming another file beside them: the best way for an army to utilize supplies in a narrow space.[104] By the time they started to cross (probably in May or June), no snow would lie below 8,000 feet on the pass.

The army's known crossing time of the Hindu Kush raises an interesting possibility of determining the numbers of the Macedonian army at this time. Suppose each part of the army's column was able to travel 12 miles on the first day while marching to the steep ascent to the crest.[105] Each part of the column should have been able to cross in four days, the usual time for crossing the pass. As Maurice has demonstrated, in a double file, 10,000 soldiers occupy a space of 12 miles, and 4,224 cavalry horses in single file also occupy a space of 12 miles.[106] Since everyone had crossed the

102. Felix Howland, "Crossing the Hindu Kush," *Geo. Rev.* 30 (1940) 276. The pass Alexander took returning from Bactria into India, which was different from the Khawak Pass, is usually given as the Kaoshan (Kushan) Pass (14,600 ft.). However, this precipitous and treacherous pass is seldom used. Foucher, op. cit., 26, remarking on the suffering of Wood's Indian attendants while crossing this pass remarked, "Well might it be called the Hindu Kush, the Killer of the Hindus!" It would have been unwise for Alexander to have used this pass when he could have taken the Salang Pass (12,000 ft.) which is equally as fast and much less dangerous. The Salang is often used by armies in a hurry.

103. For the length of the crossing: D. 83. 1; C. 7. 3. 21. See also above Chapter 3, n. 56.

104. Maurice, 225; Anderson, op. cit., 45; Xen. *Cyrop.* 6. 3. 3. From the photograph of the pass in Frank and Helen Schreider, "The World of Alexander," in National Geographic Society, *Greece and Rome: Builders of Our World* (Washington, 1968) 229, it is obvious that no more than three abreast can be accommodated on the pass.

105. Schreider, op. cit., 228, expected to make 10 miles on the first day, but they only made three. Hopefully, the Macedonians were in better condition than they.

106. Maurice, 229. He has allowed for the greater interval needed by ancient soldiers carrying spears than for modern soldiers carrying rifles. The followers, who did not carry spears, would need a lesser interval, but doubtless they did not main-

pass on the sixteenth day, no one would leave to cross the pass after the thirteenth day, that is, the last section of the army's column began crossing the pass on the thirteenth day. At two abreast, with the pack and baggage animals forming another file alongside, about 100,000 troops and followers and 12,672 cavalry horses in single file could cross the pass in 16 days. It would have taken 3 days for 12,672 cavalry horses to enter the pass and 10 days for 100,000 personnel. We estimated that by the time Alexander crossed the Hindu Kush, he had approximately 64,000 troops and 10,000 cavalry horses. The remaining 36,000 that crossed may have been followers, who by this time totaled about one-half the number of combatants.[107] If the soldiers marched in single file, only 50,000 personnel could have crossed the pass in 13 days, which is too few. From the photographs of the pass, it is clearly impossible for more than two soldiers and a pack animal or a cavalry horse and a pack animal passing abreast to be accommodated at its narrowest part. Like water in a funnel, it is the narrowest part that determines the rate of crossing. While this process obviously yields only an estimate for the troop and cavalry numbers, the space occupied by 10,000 troops and 2,224 cavalry cannot have differed greatly from Maurice's figures, nor can more than three abreast be accommodated on the pass, nor can the distance the Macedonians traveled on the first day of crossing have differed significantly from 12 miles, given the steep and difficult ascent.

Once again, the Macedonians experienced difficulties with snow and cold crossing the pass, and there was a supply shortage.[108] What probably happened was that although the army carried 10 days' rations over the pass with them, the first sections of the column to cross the pass had to wait almost two weeks in devastated territory for the rest of the army to cross.

The region of Bactria north of the Hindu Kush does not re-

tain as good a march discipline as the troops and their column would inevitably stretch out. This interval, about 12.5 feet, is only slightly greater than in a modern army, 11 feet. Doubtless, the cavalrymen dismounted their horses on the ascent, common procedure, and they would walk between their mounts. The intervals, however, would still be maintained.

107. For the approximate numbers of troops in the army, see table 6. See also below, p. 137 for the followers.

108. A. 3. 28. 9; C. 7. 4. 22.

ceive sufficient rainfall for the production of crops by dry farming techniques, and all agriculture must occur where the rivers debouching from the mountains enter the Bactrian plain, allowing irrigation. Once across the mountains, the army proceeded down the Kunduz River valley, a rich, productive agricultural region when irrigated properly.[109] But part of the land here had been devastated by Bessus' cohorts, and initially the Macedonians were forced to eat their pack animals and fish from the river.[110] The army first reached Drapsaca (Kunduz?)[111] and rested, which shows that the devastation of the country was not complete and that the site must have been located in a river valley. From here, they marched west to Aornos (Shahr-i-Banu?),[112] where Alexander left a guard. Once again, this town must have been located on a river since in this region all agricultural production and human settlements of any size cannot occur anywhere else. Undoubtedly this

109. Kraus, op. cit., 35; Toynbee, op. cit., 93; Johannes Humulum, *La Géographie de l'Afghanistan* (Gyldendal, 1959) 112, 210–211; C. Sykes, op. cit., 327–336.

110. C. 7. 4. 22; A. 3. 28. 8; C. 7. 4. 24–25. Once again, Alexander deliberately avoided using the main pass into Bactria through Bamian for the reasons noted above, p. 90f.

111. Alexander passed through two Bactrian towns before reaching the capital: Drapsaca and Aornos. There are two sites thus far which have yielded Hellenistic remains and are located between the Hindu Kush and Balkh: Kunduz on the Kunduz River and Shahr-i-Banu, near Khulm. Both of these sites are along the route we have suggested Alexander followed. From the former have been found numerous Greco-Bactrian coin hoards and a series of Greek Ionic (or Corinthian) column bases with a cyma reversa instead of an upper torus like the Corinthian column base at the temple of Apollo at Bassae, dating to the late fifth century or early fourth century B.C., and those found at Emporio, Chios, dating to the Hellenistic period. The bases are illustrated in Evert Barger, "Exploration of Ancient Sites in Northern Afghanistan," *Geo. Journ.* 93 (1939), photograph facing p. 383; cf. Klaus Fischer, "Preliminary Notes on some Ancient Remains at Kunduz," *Afghanistan* 1 (1961) 12–13; *MDAFA* 20 (1965). At Shahr-i-Banu, Hellenistic pottery was found, virtually the only such pottery found in Bactria, *MDAFA* 8 (1958) 59–73.

I cannot omit a reference to the Hellenistic city at Ai Khanoum at the confluence of the Kokcha and Amu Darya, which has certainly been one of the most important archaeological discoveries of the last decade. This is the only single-level Greek site yet discovered in Bactria; an entire Hellenistic city, with gymnasia, a Heroon, perhaps dedicated to the founder of the city (a certain Kineas), porticos with exquisite Corinthian columns, herms, inscriptions containing Greek lyric poetry, and a precept from the Delphic Oracle, 3,500 miles away. The abundance of Greek remains becomes all the more impressive when one remembers that at Bactra itself, the capital of the empire, only two Hellenistic potsherds have been found (as of 1955) beneath heavy Sassanid and Islamic deposits. Paul Bernard, *CRAI* (1970) 301–349. It is, however, too far to the northeast to have been Drapsaca or Aornos.

112. See n. 111.

river was the Khulm, the only river between the Kunduz and the Bactrus. Finally, the Macedonians reached the capital Bactra (Balkh)[113] on the Bactrus (Balkh) River, the largest oasis of the region.

113. While finds other than coins have been rare for Hellenistic Bactra, the identity of the site rests on the corruption of its name through New Persian and Arabic to Balkh, Tomaschek, "Bactra," *RE* 2.2 (1895) 804–805. The site also fulfills the geographic information provided by Greek sources, W. W. Tarn, *The Greeks in Bactria and India* (London, 1938) 114f. The walls one sees here now are Islamic, perhaps Timurid in date, and rest on earlier walls of the Sassanid era, Rodney S. Young, "The South Wall of Balkh-Bactra," *AJA* 59 (1955) 267–276; *MDAFA* 19 (1964) 61–105.

5.

Uzbekistan, Tadzhikistan, Turkmenistan, Pakistan, and Southern Iran

Leaving the city of Bactra for the Oxus (Amu Darya), the Macedonians were about to enter a different world, which even now is imperfectly understood. No site Alexander visited in Sogdia can be identified with certainty. Even the identification of Maracanda with Samarcand, which once seemed to reflect the only genuine tradition of Alexander's campaigns in this region, has been shaken by recent archaeological research.[1] It is doubtful whether the sites of Nautaca, Alexandria Eschate, Bagae, or Bazira will ever be securely located. The traditions of settlement continuity that enable us to correctly identify Tyre, Tarsus, Ancyra, and Arbela, are almost entirely lacking for Sogdia until the seventh century A.D. The identifications that von Schwarz made in the last century, while quaint and picturesque, can no longer be seriously considered.[2]

1. Grégoire Frumkin, *Archaeology in Soviet Central Asia* (Leiden, 1970) 128. But see below, n. 16.

2. Franz von Schwarz, *Alexander des Grossen Feldzüg in Turkestan* (Munich, 1893). E.g., p. 27: Aornus must be Khulm because the Greeks used the term Aornos for locations on heights and Khulm is on a hill. Leaving aside the fact that virtually every site in Afghanistan is on a hill or mound, no archaeological evidence from Khulm indicates that it was inhabited in the Achaemenid or Hellenistic eras. P. 37: The Branchidae must have lived at Kilif because when they lived in Ionia they were seafaring folk, and since the inhabitants of Kilif were engaged in ferry operations in the 1890s, naturally the Branchidae lived here. Leaving aside the fact that after exhaustive surveys and excavations in Uzbekistan, no trace of habitation has been found at Kilif for the Achaemenid or Hellenistic eras, the episode of the Branchidae is most improbable, coming as it does in the midst of Alexander's hot pursuit of Bessus. P. 40: Schwarz mistakes the Kashka for the Jaxartes, see below, n. 18. One could add

Naturally, since the sites themselves are unknown, Alexander's routes between them cannot be restored with certainty. Hence, any reconstruction of the Macedonian's operations in Sogdia can only be tentative and must be based on the general principles of the army's motion and logistic system, as well as the human geography of the region.

Rainfall in Sogdia is inadequate for the cultivation of crops by dry farming, and all agricultural production and human settlement is now, and has always been, along the river valleys where irrigation is possible.[3] The river valleys of the Zeravshan, Kashka, Shirabad, Surkhan, Kafirnahan, and Wakhsh are extremely fertile because of their rich loess soils and the fertile silts the rivers deposit on the land in spring. The immense importance of irrigation for settled human life in Sogdia can best be seen in the Zeravshan Valley. The name of the river itself, "Scatterer of Gold," does not refer to any particles of that metal it carries, but to the extraordinary value of its yellow, silt-laden water in fertilizing its valley.[4] The river's importance for irrigation is also reflected in its Greek name, Polytimetus, or "Very Precious," and there is evidence that the river was worshiped as a deity in antiquity for this reason.[5] As in Egypt, the difference between irrigated and nonirrigated land is not subtle or gradual but sudden and dramatic. Although much of Sogdia's soil is rich loess, without irrigation it is only capable of supporting an ephemeral desert vegetation in early spring. Further away from the river valleys toward the east, the land becomes sandy desert penetrated by only a few caravan trails, while toward the west, it is dominated by the sterile foothills of the Pamirs. All travelers are struck by the contrast between the yellow steppe surrounding the lush, green oases along the river valleys. All settled human life in Sogdia is dependent on these rivers, and they were vitally important to the Macedonians for provisioning and communications routes.

---

many other examples. This is not to say that there is not much valuable information on travel, routes, and ethnography, but his identifications, made as they were before the inception of scientific excavations and surveys, cannot now be accepted. The book is out of date.

3. Lewis, op. cit., 471; O. Olufsen, *The Emir of Bukhara and his Country* (Copenhagen, 1911) 170, 486.

4. Olufsen, op. cit., 141; Frumkin, op. cit., 78; Tarn, *Bactria and India*, 104.

5. Frumkin, op. cit., 78.

In the early summer of 329, Alexander left Bactra for the Oxus with detachments of light-armed troops.[6] Since the Sogdians had not surrendered to him, the main army and the heavy baggage were left at Bactra near the navigable Oxus where supplies were plentiful. Although the army only traveled 46 miles from Bactra to the Oxus opposite the Sogdian stronghold of Termez, the army suffered frightfully from the heat and aridity.[7] Once again, one may be tempted to dismiss Curtius' account of this march as overly melodramatic, if it were not for the fact that modern travelers have experienced precisely the same difficulties traveling here in summer:

The sand burned through one's boots and a breath of wind from the burning hot drift-sand hills struck the face like flames from a fire. Gun barrels and all metallic objects were heated to such a degree that they could not be touched and even the water of the Amu-Darya was heated in July and August to 28° C [86° F]. . . . The fine dust particles are everywhere, and in connection with the heat and the drought it occasions a terrible thirst which is not easily satisfied.[8]

Because of the intense heat and extremely low humidity of the region, human life becomes almost dormant in summer, and the high evaporation causes the skin to chap and develop sores so that ex-

6. C. 7. 5. 1.

7.Termez: W. W. Tarn, "Two Notes on Seleucid History: Tarmita," *JHS* 60 (1940) 89–94; W. Barthold, *Turkestan Down to the Mongol Invasion* (London, 1968) 76; A. Foucher, "Notes sur l'itinéraire de Hiun-Tsang en Afghanistan," *Etudes asiatiques publiées à l'occasion du 25e anniversaire de l'Ecole française d'Extrême Orient*, Vol. 1 (Paris, 1925) 278: L. I. Albaum and B. Brentijes, *Wächter des Goldes, zur Geschichte und Kultur mittelasiatischer Völker vor dem Islam* (Berlin, 1972) 81; Aleksander Belenitsky, *Central Asia* (Cleveland, 1968) 74; Frumkin, op. cit., 110–111; Boris J. Staviskij, "The Capitals of Ancient Bactria," *EW* 23 (1973) 265. Tarn originally identified the town as Alexandria on the Oxus, which was later refounded by Demetrius I as Demetria. This view was rejected by Narain, op. cit., 41, but is accepted by Soviet archaeologists in the light of recent excavations. Von Schwarz identified Alexander's crossing as Kilif, but no evidence supports the view that it was occupied in Alexander's era. The distance between Bactra and the Oxus across from Termez is about 46 miles, which is the distance in C. 7. 5. 1–13 between Bactra and the Oxus traveled by the army. It is about 80 miles between Bactra and Kilif. Termez was in ancient times the major ford across the Oxus, since there is a large island in the middle of the river here. It was directly opposite Bactra on the river and was a strategic town as long as Bactra retained its importance. For the suffering of the army on the journey to the river: C. 7. 5. 1–13.

8. Olufsen, op. cit., 258, 260.

posed areas must be smeared with oil. Blindness by reflected sunlight is frequently a problem and the 120–130-degree heat is so unbearable that it is literally impossible for even the natives to be out of doors after 7:00 A.M.[9] Hence, all travel in summer must be conducted at night wherever possible, when temperatures are cooler.

After Alexander's light force crossed the Oxus on floats made from tent skins, which took them five days,[10] messengers arrived from Spitamenes and Dataphernes informing Alexander that Bessus was under arrest[11] at Nautaca, a town probably located on the Kashka River.[12] Alexander then sent Ptolemy with a few light detachments to capture Bessus, and they advanced about 170 miles up the Shirabad River valley through the Iron Gate at Derbent to the town, covering the distance in only four days.[13] At Nautaca, the Macedonians replaced their horses for those of the country, since a great many had been worn out by the forced march from the Hindu Kush to the Oxus and hence to the town.[14] If the same distinction between breeds existed in antiquity as today, these Turkmen horses—the blood-sweating Heavenly Horses of ancient Chinese sources—had somewhat less speed than European or Arabian breeds but more strength and endurance—important considerations for the campaigns Alexander was about to conduct.[15] Alexander's

9. Ibid., 258.
10. C. 7. 5. 18; A. 3. 29. 4.
11. A. 3. 29. 6.
12. Bessus is located at Nautaca, A. 3. 28. 9, which is between the Oxus and the Zeravshan, A. 3. 29. 4–30. 6, and about 150–170 miles—about a 10-day march (A. 3. 29. 7)—from the right bank of the Oxus. This indicates a site on the Kashka Darya which was intensively settled in Alexander's era (Lewis, op. cit., 479f.), but there is no indication which site was Nautaca. Cf. von Schwarz, op. cit., 74, who placed Nautaca at Karshi (the ancient Nakhshab) on the Kashka.
13. This was always the major route between Termez and the Kashka because of its water and agricultural resources, Barthold, op. cit., 138–139. Von Schwarz believed that the Macedonians traveled directly from Kilif to Karshi on the Kashka Darya over the steppe. Even if the army crossed at Kilif, which is doubtful, there is no justification whatsoever for such a route. The route travels 136 miles over unbroken steppe and desert, and the detailed map for the route given for *RGS Suppl. Papers* 1 (1886) 203–263 lists only five small wells along its length. Well water in this region often becomes too brackish to drink in the summer (Olufsen, op cit., 260). Given the huge water requirements of an army and its horses (see Appendix 1) and the difficulties of distributing water from single wells (see above, p. 57), it would have been impossible for an army to have used this route, especially in summer.
14. A. 3. 30. 6.
15. Naval Intelligence Division, *Persia*, 449.

next objective was Maracanda (Afrasiab?),[16] a populous oasis on the Polytimetus River, and from here the army advanced to the Jaxartes (Syr Darya) via the Gates of Tamerlane, Jizak, and Uratube.[17] It was near this river, not the Kashka Darya near Karshi, that Macedonian foraging teams, while scattered in the fields, were attacked by the inhabitants of a mountain stronghold in the vicinity.[18] Near the Jaxartes, Alexander founded another city, Alexandria Eschate (Corsu Gozien?)[19] as a bastion against nomad incursions from across the river. The circumference of its walls, 5.5 miles, was taken from the area occupied by the Macedonian camp—a reminder of the huge area needed by an encamped army.

While laying out plans for his new city, the king learned of the general revolt of Sogdia behind him, and he immediately advanced to subdue the rebels. He first captured seven cities in the vicinity that had revolted, the largest of which, Cyropolis (Kurkath),[20] was founded by Cyrus the Great. It is significant in considering the survival of traditions in this area that this same region is still called Jety-asar, or "the Seven Fortresses" in modern Kazak, even though the region is littered with forts, over 400 by one count. Next, Alexander sent a force of 2,000 foot soldiers and 300 cavalry under Andromachus to Maracanda, where the Macedonian garrison was being besieged by Spitamenes, while he himself conducted a brilliant operation against the Scythians across the Jaxartes. Here the army saw heaps of stones set up to commemorate the burial places

16. Afrasiab is the old Samarcand, about one mile north of the new city. Local traditions state that it was founded by Alexander (Barthold, op. cit., 84). Although Achaemenid pottery had been found at the site (*MDAFA* 15 [1957] 93; *EW* 16 [1966] 30), it has not yielded any remains from the Hellenistic era. Perhaps it was destroyed in a revolt shortly after it was occupied by its garrison. The region around Samarcand was densely populated in Alexander's era.

17. Von Schwarz, op. cit., 45–46, the only feasible route between the Zeravshan Valley and the Syr Darya.

18. Both Curtius, 7. 5. 36–7. 6. 6, and Arrian, 3. 30. 6–11, place this incident near the Jaxartes, not between the Oxus and Samarcand. Curtius (7. 6. 10) has mistakenly placed Maracanda on the Jaxartes (or Tanais, as he calls it), one of the few geographical errors Curtius makes in Book 7.

19. B. A. Litvinskij and N. O. Tursunov, "The Leningrad Krater and the Louvre Sosibios Vase (Neo-Attic Art and Central Asia)," *EW* 24 (1974) 89. The site is 4 km. south of Leninabad. After 15 years of excavation, the director of the Khodzent (Leninabad) excavations has concluded that the site of Alexandria Eschate does not lie here. For the circumference of the walls: J. 11. 5; C. 7. 6. 25.

20. E. Beneviste, "La ville de Cyreschata," *Journal Asiatique* 234 (1943–45) 163–166. The site has not been excavated.

of Scythian chieftains—*kurgans*—which the men believed were boundary markers set up by Dionysos himself.[21]

When Alexander returned, he learned of the destruction of Andromachus' force—the most severe loss ever experienced by the Macedonians in battle—and taking only one-half the Companion cavalry, the archers, Agrianians, and the lightest armed of the phalanx, he advanced to Maracanda, covering the 1,500-*stadia* distance in three or four days.[22] The distance, 1,500 *stadia* or 172 miles, closely approximates the distance between Corsu Gozien and Afrasiab by the main trunk road, some 177 miles. The king, however, was not able to capture Spitamenes, who disappeared into the desert with his allies, perhaps to Margiana or the Amu Valley. Apparently, Alexander was not able to get intelligence concerning the desert routes through the sand dunes followed by the rebels—probably they were known only to the Scythians themselves—and without this intelligence no pursuit was possible. It is a testimony to the productivity of Sogdiana in the fourth century B.C. that at no time in the entire campaign did a supply shortage occur.[23]

In the spring of 328, when the wheat and barley in the irrigated fields began to ripen and the ice floes on the Oxus began breaking up—making it passable once more by boats—Alexander crossed the river once again with his forces from Bactra. He divided the army into five units to subdue the various mountain strongholds in the region still holding out—a difficult task, since there is scarcely a hill in eastern Sogdia without a fortress perched menacingly atop.[24] From Maracanda, Alexander advanced with his unit to those parts of Sogdia that had not yet submitted, and won them over. Alexander's expedition into Margiana was also included in this campaign.[25] After crossing the Kashka and the Amu, the king proceeded

---

21. C. 7. 9. 15; Frumkin, op. cit., 30, 31, 47.

22. A. 4. 6. 4; C. 7. 9. 21.

23. Except for Andromachus' cavalry division (A. 4. 5. 5), which was due, however, to a forced march, giving the horses no time to graze or be fed.

24. Sir Aurel Stein, *Innermost Asia*, Vol. 2 (London, 1928) 867f.

25. C. 7. 10. 15; cf. A. 4. 16. 3. Both authors are discussing the king's activities in the spring of 328 after Alexander had crossed the Oxus into Sogdiana, and the army saw the oil portent near the king's tent (C. 7. 10. 14; A. 4. 15. 7). Curtius' geographical sequence of Macedonian operations in Sogdiana, the sequence of marches, battles, and the locations of halts, is identical to that of Arrian, except for the misplacing of Maracanda (C. 7. 6. 10., although the manuscripts read *Marupenta* here and not Maracanda), and the placing of the capture of the Rocks of Sogdiana (C. 7.

to Margiana via Balkh, Maimana, and Bala Mourghab.[26] In the oasis of Merv at Giaur Kala, Alexander founded another city, which had a long and rich history until its sack and destruction by Genghis Khan. Naturally, Alexander himself went to Margiana, not one of his subordinates. The king personally inspected each site of the cities he founded, including this one.[27]

Curtius' account of the Margiana expedition provides information on the mysterious and elusive Ochus River. From Maracanda, Alexander proceeded south and crossed the Ochus and Oxus rivers, in that order, and advanced to the oasis.[28] Tarn identified this river with the lower Arius or Tejend. However, this contradicts Arrian, who specifically states that the Arius, that is the lower Arius, disappears into the sand.[29] Besides, one cannot cross the Arius before crossing the Oxus to enter Margiana. Only the Kashka Darya can fulfill the topographical information provided by Curtius.

Spitamenes' mobility was becoming increasingly restricted by the establishment of garrisons and the mobile Macedonian cavalry detachments stationed around the country. One of these local cavalry detachments would be within close striking range wherever Spitamenes made an attack from the desert. In this way, responses to Spitamenes' attacks could be made more quickly than if the entire Macedonian force was concentrated in one location, since the time and distances required for a counterattack were reduced. Like the Turkomen raiders of later eras, Spitamenes' forces were never large since their bases in small desert oases could not support large numbers of men and animals. Instead, they relied on speed, mobility, surprise, and their knowledge of desert routes, with their wells and patches of vegetation at distant intervals, for their effectiveness. Alexander's own cavalry forces did not have sufficient

11. 1–29), and Chorienes (C. 8. 2. 19–33) somewhat earlier than Arrian. Arrian remains the basis for Alexander's chronology, but Curtius provides an invaluable supplement.

26. For the route see above, p. 89.

27. See above, p. 33. When C. 7. 10. 15 and Pliny *NH* 6. 47 specifically state that Alexander was in Margiana and founded Alexandria Margiana, just as Alexander personally founded all his Alexandrias, I fail to see how it is possible to maintain that Alexander was never in Margiana and did not found the city of Alexandria Margiana, as does Schachermeyr, op. cit., 349, n. 416.

28. C. 7. 10. 15. Str. 11. 11. 5 is of no help in identifying the river.

29. Tarn, *Alexander*, Vol. 2, 8, n. 1; 310, n. 4; Tarn, *Bactria and India*, 113. A. 4. 6. 6.

numbers for his strategy to be effective, and he recruited powerful units of Sogdian, Bactrian, and Dahaean cavalry, which remained with the army throughout the rest of the expedition.[30] The Macedonians also required a communications network of fast messengers to relay word of a nomad attack to the regional cavalry commanders.

Hence, Spitamenes attacked a Bactrian outpost in western Bactria with some Massagetaean allies, killing its garrison, and advanced to Bactra. Here they were counterattacked by the garrison and later pursued by Craterus' force, which was operating in the vicinity.[31] Later, Spitamenes and his force crossed the Oxus and made a foray near the Bokhara Oasis. They were repulsed, however, by the nearby troops of Coenus and Amyntas who destroyed many of the invaders, and when the Massagetaeans learned that Alexander himself was approaching from the Kashka Darya, they slew Spitamenes.[32] He had been one of Alexander's most formidable opponents, not only because of his successful hit-and-run tactics but because he was able to maintain the loyalty of much of the Bactrian and Sogdian population against the Macedonian invader.

For the winter of 328–327, the army was divided between Bactra, Maracanda, and the region around Nautaca.[33] In the beginning of spring, the king advanced east from Nautaca to capture the Sogdian Rock, perhaps near Derbent,[34] and the mountain fortress of Chorienes near the Wakhsh River in Pareitacene, a wild, inaccessible mountainous region.[35] Winters here are severe, and all year long snow lies on the mountains, many of which approach 20,000 feet. It is not surprising, therefore, that the army suffered from spring

30. A. 4. 17. 3. These large units are still operating with the Macedonians in India (A. 5. 12. 2), although their strengths are never recorded.

31. A. 4. 16. 6; A. 4. 17. 1–2.

32. A. 4. 17. 4–7; C. 8. 2. 16.

33. C. 8. 2. 13; A. 4. 17. 3; A. 4. 18. 2.

34. The location suggested by von Schwarz, op. cit., 75, does not seem to me to resemble the description of the rock in A. 4. 18. 4–19. 4; C. 7. 11. 1–29, although it may have been near Derbent.

35. Von Schwarz, op. cit., 83, identified the second rock with Puli-Sangin on the Wakhsh. It was located near Hissar by J. G. Droysen, *Histoire de l'Hellénisme*, Vol. 1, trans. by A. Bouché-Leclercq (Paris, 1883) 477. The French edition of 1883–84 represents Droysen's final revision. For the nature of the country: Olufsen, op. cit., 8; W. Rickmer Rickmers, "The Fan Mountains in the Duab of Turkestan," *Geo. Journ.* 30 (1907) 357–371, 488f. The Wakhsh River, the largest tributary of the Amu, still retains the ancient name of the Oxus.

storms. Hephaistion had been ordered to Bactra to collect supplies for the army,[36] perhaps for its return across the Hindu Kush. Since the army recrossed the mountains in late spring[37] and harvests do not occur in the mountain valleys until July or August, the army could not forage for its grain supplies along the route—hence Hephaistion's order. After crossing the Hindu Kush by the Salang Pass, which took 10 days, Alexander arrived at the city of Alexandria, which he had founded before crossing the mountains in 329.[38]

Alexander now proceeded east down the Kabul (Cophen) River where he received the submission of several Indian tribes on the west side of the Indus and also the surrender of Taxiles, whose capital was some 25 miles east of the river.[39] In India, Alexander encountered some of the most formidable difficulties of his expedition, but the provisioning of his army was not among them. Fierce, independent tribesmen, rampaging elephants, excessive heat and rainfall, and his troop's mutiny at the Beas presented severe and ultimately insurmountable obstacles. Yet, because of the fertility and extent of the cultivable land in the Swat Valley, the Peshwar and Rawalpindi plains, and the submontane strip between the Jhelum and Beas Rivers, as well as the numerous large, navigable rivers, no supply difficulties were encountered in India.[40] The geographical problems concerning Alexander's route in India have been admirably treated by others, and no purpose would be served

36. C. 8. 2. 13.

37. Arrian 4. 18. 4 and 4. 22. 3 takes great pains to tell the reader that the operations against these fortresses occurred from early spring (e.g., late March or early April) to late spring (e.g., in June). It snows in this region all the time in spring, even as late as July (see geographical sources in n. 35), and because the army suffered in a snowstorm (A. 4. 21. 10) does not mean that these operations occurred in winter, as in Tarn, *Alexander*, Vol. 1, 72, n. 1.

38. Harvests: Thesiger, op. cit., 312–319. The Macedonians took a different and shorter route across the Hindu Kush than they had taken in 329 (Str. 15. 1. 26). Since the Shibar Pass is longer than the Khawak, this means that Alexander crossed by the Salang or Kaoshan, and, in all probability, the former, see above Chapter 4, n. 102.

39. A. 4. 22. 6.

40. O. H. Spate and A. T. A. Learmonth, *India and Pakistan* (London, 1967) 520–538. Despite a population of 25,000,000, the two provinces of Punjab and Sind today produce a surplus of 22,000 tons of rice and 80,000 tons of wheat, Government of Pakistan, *Pakistan* (Karachi, 1953) 225. The region was fertile and productive in antiquity: Str. 15. 1. 26; 15. 1. 28; 15. 1. 29; D. 89. 6. For Alexander's route: Str. 15. 1. 26; 15. 1. 32.

by repeating their conclusions here.[41] A brief outline will be sufficient.

In general, the climate and geography of the Indus watershed are similar to Mesopotamia's. Along the northern submontane region there is abundant rainfall in the winter and in the summer monsoon season so that dry farming can be conducted. Further south, however, below Peshwar, Lahore, and the Siwalik Hills, rainfall diminishes, and one enters the Great Thar Desert. Agriculture and human settlement in the southern region occurs only in the Indus Valley and its tributaries where irrigation is possible. Desert flanks the east side of the valley below the Salt Range and sterile mountain ranges to the west.[42]

After dismissing the Indian envoys who met him on the Kabul River, Alexander divided his army into two units. Hephaistion and Perdiccas were to proceed directly down the Kabul River through the territory of Peucelaotis to the Indus and subdue or receive the submission of the tribes along the way.[43] At the Indus they were to construct a bridge for the army to cross. Alexander himself took the rest of the army along the Kabul River to the Kunar (Choaspes), and crossing the Nawa Pass, he subdued the Aspasians, Assacenians, and Guraeans who had not submitted.[44] We have already noted that the king would never commit his entire force for a march through a region that had not surrendered to him in advance.[45] After capturing the mountain citadel of Aornos and receiving the surrender of Peucelaotis, the Macedonians advanced to the Indus. Because of the short distances between the navigable Indus, Jhelum (Hydaspes), Chenab (Acesines), Ravi (Hydraotes), and Beas (Hyphasis) rivers and the fertility and extent of the cultivated land,

41. The basis for the reconstruction of Alexander's operations in Punjab, like the basis for almost all meaningful archaeological research in India, Pakistan, and Southern Iran, was made by Sir Aurel Stein. His *On Alexander's Track to the Indus* (London, 1929) is still the fundamental work. His journey from Taxila to the battlefield of the Jhelum is given in his *Archaeological Reconnaissances in North Western India and South Eastern Iran* (London, 1937). See also Olaf Caroe, *The Pathans, 550 B.C.–1957 A.D.* (New York, 1958). The Macedonians' operation against the Mallians is analyzed in an excellent article by Muhammad Rafique Mughal, "Excavations at Tulamba, West Pakistan," *Pakistan Archaeology* 4 (1967) 18–21, which supersedes all previous discussions, based as it is on the most recent geographical and archaeological research.

42. Spate, op. cit., 498–616.   43. A. 4. 22. 7.
44. A. 4. 30. 9; A. 4. 23. 1.   45. See above, p. 72.

supplies were now brought to the army from subdued territory through which they had already marched. Supplies were collected by Craterus and Coenus[46] and brought by boat to where the army was about to ford a river. The provisions would then be used for the next advance into hostile territory beyond the river and the process repeated. Because of the limitations of overland transport in antiquity, this method of provisioning could only be used where the army was close to a seaport or navigable river.[47]

At the Beas the troops, wearied of constant marching through the hot, rainy Indian monsoon weather and fearful of the reports concerning Indian forces and elephants beyond the river, refused to march further. The Indo-Gangetic divide through which the army would have marched, had they gone on, was similar to the land through which they had already come: fertile, extensively cultivated, with abundant rainfall, and thickly settled.[48] In addition, there were many large, navigable rivers; the Sutlej, some 63 miles from the Beas, the Ghaggar, 40 miles further, the Sarasvati, another 25 miles, the Jumna, 30 miles, and the upper Ganges, about 50 miles from the Jumna. No logistic difficulties would have been encountered in the region ahead, had the army chosen to march further.

Alexander was now confronted with the decision of how to return to the center of his empire with his vast host, by this time approaching 120,000 combatants.[49] Doubtless many factors contributed to his decision to sail down the Jhelum and Chenab to the Indus and hence to the ocean,[50] but two in particular may be noted here. One of his considerations was certainly the ease of supplying his huge army by the navigable rivers, since the Macedonian flotilla of 2,000 vessels included a great number of transports and grain ships.[51] A second factor would have been the establishment of a defensible eastern boundary for his empire, if only temporarily until he could return. As we have noted, deserts, when remote from river or sea transport facilities, present the most formidable ob-

---

46. A. 5. 21. 1; A. 5. 21. 4.
47. For the limitations of land transport in antiquity, see Chapter 1.
48. Spate, op. cit., 534; B. B. Lal, *Ancient India* 10-11 (1954-55) 5-151.
49. See table 6.
50. E.g., Ernst Badian, "Alexander the Great and the Loneliness of Power," in Ernst Badian, *Studies in Greek and Roman History* (Oxford, 1964) 192-205.
51. A. 6. 2. 4; Arr. *Ind.* 19. 7.

stacles for the movement of an army.[52] By turning south and proceeding down the Indus Valley, the empire's eastern border would have marched with the Great Thar Desert, the most effective barrier for any army approaching from the east.

Retreating from the Beas, the Macedonians returned to the Jhelum and sailed down to the Chenab, through the Mallians' territory and hence down the Indus to the sea.[53] Since no logistic problems were encountered by the army in the Indus Valley, no time will be spent on their journey there.

Alexander's most formidable opponent was the Gedrosian Desert, which came closer to destroying him and his army than any enemy he ever encountered. It is important in analyzing this enigmatic campaign to distinguish Alexander's *plans* to cross the desert from the sequence of events that actually occurred. The problem with historical accounts of this campaign is that they simply record the events without attempting to understand their cause. However, a simple, coherent hypothesis can be formulated, based on the general principles used throughout this study, that offers an explanation for the astonishing sequence of events about to occur. Alexander did not uncharacteristically blunder his way into the desert without sufficient preparations and then muddle through; every last detail of the expedition was planned in advance. It was through the forces of nature, and not through a lack of knowledge concerning the difficulties of the march, that the expedition ended so catastrophically.

A thorough understanding of the Gedrosian campaign is important in evaluating Alexander's achievement as a general. The primary motivations for undertaking the campaign were probably twofold. First, Alexander wished to secure the southern boundary of his empire with the Indian Ocean, and, ironically, by having the army march along the Makran coast, its provisioning problems would be reduced by using sea transport. Yet, another reason for the expedition was probably Alexander's interest in the sea trade

---

52. See above, p. 21.

53. The recent study by Mughal, op. cit., 19–21, makes it clear that the city of Multan was nowhere near the Macedonian operations against the Mallians, as Alexander Cunningham, *The Ancient Geography of India* (London, 1871) 208–210 thought. Cunningham's book, like von Schwarz's, is out of date.

route with India. Like the Harappan seaports along the Makran and Persian Gulf connecting India and Mesopotamia a millennium earlier, Alexander planned to establish colonies along this coast and the offshore islands.[54] Rhambacia may be regarded as the first of these foundations, and the king believed that the coast could become as rich as Phoenicia. Communications with his Indian possessions would also be easier by sea than by the long, arduous land route.[55]

Preparations for the expedition had begun near Sindimana (perhaps to be identified with Sehwan), where the army was divided. Craterus took the battalions of Attalus, Meleager, and Antigenes, some archers, those Companions and Macedonians past service, and the 200 elephants (each required 500 pounds of grain and 60 gallons of water per day) to Zarangaea via Arachosia, while the king himself took the rest of the army down the Indus to the sea.[56] Thus, Alexander seems to have had not more than 87,000 infantry, 18,000 cavalry, and perhaps 52,000 noncombatants when he began the expedition into Gedrosia.[57] At Pattala (Bahmanabad), a fleet consisting of the largest and most seaworthy ships in the flotilla was fitted out for the sea voyage along the Makran coast.[58] Among the ships undertaking the sea voyage were 34 triremes, some 80 triconters, and approximately 400 merchant vessels of average size.[59] The average complement of a trireme was 200, including rowers and

54. A. 7. 19. 5.
55. Nearchus (Str. 15. 1. 5; A. 6. 24. 2; Arr. *Ind.* 20. 1) attributed nonrational motivations for Alexander's expedition into the Gedrosia: *pothos* and an emulation of Cyrus and Semiramis who also allegedly made the journey. This, however, is not correct (see p. 112), and it appears that it is no longer possible to accept the veracity of Nearchus' account of this expedition (see below, n. 83, and p. 141f.).
56. A. 6. 17. 3.
57. We estimate that Alexander had approximately 102,000 infantry and 18,000 cavalry before dividing his army at Sindimana (see table 6), and this means that the army he took into Gedrosia will have been this number minus the three phalanx battalions, some archers, and the retirees. Each phalanx battalion contained approximately 1,500 men (Marsden, op. cit., 65), and there seems to have been no more than 500 or so archers in all (Marsden, 66). There were about 10,000 retirees for whom Craterus was responsible (A. 7. 12. 1–3). For the approximate number of followers, see above, p. 13.
58. For the identification of Pattala: Herbert Wilhelmy, "Indusdelta und Rann of Kutch," *Erdkunde* 22 (1968) 183–184. The older spelling of Bahmanabad is Brahmanabad. Fleet: C. 9. 10. 3.
59. Triremes: Arr. *Ind.* 18. 3–10; triconters: A. 6. 2. 4; Arr. *Ind.* 31. 4; merchant vessels: see n. 63.

marines,[60] and thus the triremes will have had a crew of 6,800 altogether. The triconters will have had a crew of about 33 to 34 men apiece, and the cargo vessels needed no more than seven to eight sailors to work the sails and steer.[61] Troops were also carried on the ships, although there is no indication of how many.[62] One can see that there were at least 12,500 men in the fleet excluding the troops aboard the vessels, and an estimate of 7,000 to 8,000 for these will not be unreasonable, although their exact number is unimportant for our analysis.

At Pattala, Alexander collected four months' provisions for his army,[63] which would weigh in the vicinity of 52,600 tons. It was apparently the land army's responsibility to provide water for the expedition in certain sections of the route by digging wells on the coast. The rest of the army's water would be supplied from the Hab, Windar, Porali, Hingol, Maniji, Basol, Shadi Khor, and Dasht rivers which flow into the Makran coast. All these intermittent rivers would be full during the July monsoons, which is why Alexander planned to leave Pattala in mid-July, when the monsoons begin.[64] Hence, little water would need to be carried by the army. Since it was impossible to carry 52,600 tons of supplies overland for more than nine days because the pack animals and personnel would have consumed all the supplies they could carry by this time,[65] almost all the provisions were stowed aboard the fleet. For this was to be a combined land and naval operation with the army providing the fleet with water[66] and the fleet supplying the land army with grain, as we saw along the Thracian, Palestinian, and Egyptian coasts. It should be remembered that although the

60. John S. Morrison and R. T. Williams, *Greek Oared Ships* (London, 1968) 254; Hdt. 7. 184. 1–2.

61. On the size of ship's crews, see Lionel Casson, *Ships and Seamanship in the Ancient World* (Princeton, 1971) 314–321.

62. A. 6. 21. 3; Arr. *Ind.* 19. 7. Green, 558, n. 23 estimates 18,000 in the fleet.

63. A. 6. 20. 5. 152,000 personnel × 3 lb. grain × c. 120 da. = 27,360 tons. 18,000 cavalry horses × 20 lb. (both grain and fodder would be needed in this desert) × c. 120 da. = 21,600 tons; 3,040 baggage animals × 20 lb. × c. 120 da. = 3,648 tons. 27,360 + 21,600 + 3,648 = 52,608 tons. The average merchant ship could carry 140 tons, so 400 would be needed.

64. Rodman E. Snead, *Physical Geography Reconnaissance: Las Bela Coastal Plain, West Pakistan,* Louisiana State University Coastal Studies Series, no. 13 (Baton Rouge, 1966) 11–22; Str. 15. 2. 3.

65. See above, Chapter 1, n. 30.

66. A. 6. 24. 3.

fleet sailed through as desolate a stretch of ocean as the desert the Macedonian army marched through, its provisions never ran out—even though it was laid up for some three months before sailing in hostile territory from which it would be difficult if not impossible to procure supplies, and although the voyage itself took about 75 days.[67]

Once the supplies were marshaled and stowed aboard the fleet, it was ordered to sail alongside the army which would be marching along the coast.[68] The coastal route Alexander planned to follow was probably the caravan route taken by Sir Aurel Stein from Karachi to Ormara and followed by the Indo-European telegraph line.[69]

Remembering Alexander's logistic planning, we can now reconstruct this fateful expedition. In the beginning of his march, Alexander probably took nine days' supplies from Pattala and supplemented this from the territory of the Arabitae, who dwelt along the coastal plain to the Hab River, 187 miles from Pattala. Near the Hab, a detachment was ordered to dig wells along the coast for the fleet. After crossing the river, Alexander divided his army into three units to devastate the territory of the Oreitans, who had not surrendered to him.[70] The fleet had been delayed—temporarily, Alexander thought—because of the adverse winds, but supplies had been adequate for the army so far. Next, the Macedonians advanced to Rhambacia (Bela),[71] which Alexander wished to colonize because of its impressive position in the center of the most fertile and extensive cultivable land in the region.

Meanwhile, the Oreitans, having collected their forces, took a position blocking the Kumbh Pass, which formed the boundary

67. Str. 15. 2. 5. See Appendix 3 for the chronology of the campaign. This reconstruction is accepted by Green, 430f.

68. A. 6. 24. 3; Str. 15. 2. 4.

69. Rodman E. Snead, *Physical Geography Reconnaissance: West Pakistan Coastal Zone*, University of New Mexico Publications in Geography, 1 (Albuquerque, 1969) 4–5. Sir Aurel Stein, "On Alexander's Route into Gedrosia: An Archaeological Tour in Las Bela," *Geo. Journ.* 102 (1943) 193–227. Stein's is the most intelligent article ever written on Alexander's Gedrosian campaign; it is by a professional geographer who knew the Makran, from personal experience, like the back of his hand. If the telegraph line crossed Ras Malan, so could Alexander with the help of his road builders (A. 1. 26. 1) and perhaps with an assist from the fleet.

70. D. 104. 5–6; A. 6. 21. 3–5; C. 9. 10. 7.

71. For the correct identification of this site, see below Appendix 4, n. 81.

of the Oreitan and Gedrosian territories, leading from the Porali Valley to the Jhau tract.[72] When Alexander approached, however, they fled; but later their chiefs surrendered and were given terms. Alexander, becoming concerned about the fleet, wished to march along the shore, *but the fleet never came.* For, as it turned out, the very southwest monsoon that provided the army with water prevented the sailing of the fleet until October.[73] The southwest monsoon had just begun about the time Alexander began his march in mid-July,[74] and neither he nor Nearchus knew that the adverse winds would last until late October.

This was one of the greatest crises of his life; all Alexander's elaborate preparations were shattered, and he knew that whatever decision he made would cost the lives of three-quarters of his forces. It is a tribute to his spirit of determination that Alexander kept his head and escaped the desert with so much of his army. What were his options at this critical moment? There were three. First, he could remain where he was and wait for the fleet to arrive. However, it was not possible for his entire army to remain stationary in an area that had been devastated, and that, in any case, had only sufficient agricultural resources to support a few scattered towns.[75] Alexander had no idea what had happened to the fleet; it might have been destroyed by the hostile Indians at Pattala, in which case it would never come. It was just as well he did not wait, for it was now early August, and the fleet did not sail until late October.[76] Second, he could have marched back to Pattala. But it was 290 miles from Bela to Bahmanabad over territory that had been thoroughly devastated by the army.[77] Few, if any, supplies would remain in territory that was mainly desert and that had suffered the passage of an army containing 87,000 infantry, 18,000 cavalry, and as many as 52,000 followers. A march of 150 miles through the fearsome Kolwa depression was sufficient to cause the destruction of three-quarters of the entire land army: a 290-mile march to Pattala would

72. A. 6. 22. 1; Stein, "Las Bela," 217.
73. Str. 15. 2. 5; A. 6. 21. 3. See Appendix 3.
74. Jen-Hu Chang, "The Indian Summer Monsoon," *Geo. Rev.* 57 (1967) 394.
75. See above, p. 61.
76. See Appendix 3 for the chronology. The king had probably learned by this time, whether through communications with the fleet or through local sources of information, that the adverse winds would continue until October.
77. C. 9. 10. 7; D. 104. 4–5; cf. above, pp. 37–38.

have been fatal to the entire force. As Curtius put it, "they could neither remain where they were nor advance without danger of death; if they remained, famine, if they went on, a deadlier enemy, pestilence, afflicted them."[78] Given the circumstances, Alexander pursued the third and most feasible course: he left a detachment of the army behind in the Porali Valley and took the main army eastward to Pura through those inhabited regions of Gedrosia where supplies were most plentiful.[79]

After leaving Leonnatus in the Oreitans' territory with a small force, the king sent Thoas to reconnoiter the coast and report on conditions there.[80] He returned and told the king that the coast was desert, inhabited by only a few fishermen in huts made of fish bones (the same dwellings one saw here until recently). Learning this, Alexander took the army inland through the Kumbh Pass, which separated the Oreitans from the Gedrosians, and into the Jhau tract, where there is some cultivable land supporting a modest population: the "certain place where provisions were plentiful."[81] Up till now, supplies may have been barely adequate to support the army, but in the 150-mile distance from Jhau to Turbat, past the Nundara River, Awaran, and down the Kolwa depression, they would not find adequate supplies of grain, water, or fodder. This combined with the heat, burning sand, and improper diet caused the massive destruction of human life recorded by all our sources. After losing the track in an ocean of drifting sand, the army at last reached the vicinity of Turbat, the "halting place from where the sea is nearest,"[82] and the most extensively cultivated and populous region of the Makran. Here the remnants of the army amassed supplies of grain, dates, and sheep for the journey to Pasni. From this point on the coast, Alexander marched along the shore to the vicinity of Gwatar, a distance of some 136 miles which the army covered in seven days,[83] an indication of the speed of their forced march.

78. C. 9. 10. 13. The pestilence is the disorders caused by unwholesome and un-prepared food which took a heavy toll of life when combined with the other difficulties of the march.
79. For the rationale of Alexander's route through the Gedrosia, see Appendix 4.
80. A. 6. 23. 2.
81. A. 6. 23. 4.
82. A. 6. 23. 4.
83. A. 6. 26. 5. There are still two unanswered questions about this campaign. First, why was not the seasonal nature of the monsoons, which wrecked Alexander's planned synchronized coordination between the fleet and the army, known to

From this point, their supply problems would be minimal, if not completely eliminated.

It is a tribute to Alexander's leadership and organizational skill that one-quarter of his land army and his entire fleet did escape the

Nearchus or Alexander? It is possible that Nearchus knew the monsoons would delay his voyage but wished to kill Alexander by letting him starve in the desert. It is improbable, however, that Nearchus had collected more detailed intelligence concerning the climate than Alexander himself (see above, Chapter 2, n. 97). Also, the cooperation between the fleet and the army was not one-sided: it was apparently the army's responsibility to provide wells and anchorages for the fleet, a function they could not (and did not, as it turned out) fulfill if they had perished in the desert. It would be of no value to Nearchus to have the Macedonian army perish while he himself would have to sail along 500 miles of hostile coast alone. Also, it was possible that Alexander and a remnant of his army would escape the desert—which is what happened. If the king had the slightest suspicion that Nearchus had withheld intelligence from him concerning the monsoons, he would have no hesitation in inflicting a terrible penalty when the fleet returned. In fact, however, Nearchus was given the daughter of Barsine for a wife, which would make him the son-in-law of Alexander's mistress (A. 7. 4. 6), was decorated for his voyage (A. 7. 5. 6), and was later given a command in the fleet for Alexander's projected Arabian expedition (A. 7. 25. 4). The answer seems to be that Alexander did not receive adequate intelligence from the hostile Indians at Pattala. His guides for the expedition escaped, and new ones could not be found (C. 9. 9. 1). He could not find a pilot to sail down the Indus from the city, since all the Indians had fled at his approach (A. 6. 18. 4). Later, the fleet was damaged by an incoming tide, yet none of the Indians had bothered to tell Alexander of his error in anchoring in a tidal inlet. After the land army had left, the Indians began behaving like free men and tried to drive the fleet out of the harbor (Str. 15. 2. 5). Hence, neither Alexander nor Nearchus could be blamed for their ignorance of the monsoons, phenomena utterly unlike any meteorological event in the Mediterranean.

The second question that arises is why, if the expedition was to be a coordinated operation with the fleet supplying the army with grain, was not this fact noted by our sources, who, on the other hand, provide copious information on the land army's responsibility to supply the fleet with water? Indeed, we are treated to the astonishing spectacle of the land army, literally starving to death, providing magazines of provisions for the fleet (A. 6. 23. 4–5). Arrian's sources for this campaign were Nearchus and Ptolemy. Ptolemy, as we have noted (see above, Chapter 2, n. 137), is almost completely uninterested in logistic problems, and it would be remarkable if he made the Gedrosian campaign an exception. Nearchus was admiral of the fleet (Arr. *Ind.* 18. 4) and would have no interest in recounting his failure in provisioning Alexander's army. It appears that all was not well between Nearchus and Alexander when they were reunited in Carmania. Although Nearchus has told the tale (Arr. *Ind.* 36. 4), Alexander does not seem to have been pleased with his performance and threatened to remove him as admiral of the fleet. Indeed, Nearchus' account of Alexander's motive for the expedition, his planned coordination of the fleet and the army, and his own role in the operation, has been systematically and deliberately distorted (see also below, p. 141). Nearchus' reliability and veracity have already been dealt a mortal blow on other grounds by Ernst Badian, "Nearchus the Cretan," *Yale Class. Stud.* 24 (1975) 147–170.

desert despite hostile nature which destroyed his planning by holding up the fleet for three months. In a real sense, he had won a victory over the desert, not through planning and preparation as he had hoped, but through leadership, endurance, and a determination to get his men through. He was not motivated by *pothos*, or irrational impulsiveness, to cross the Gedrosia, but by a rational calculation of the best method to return his army safely to Mesopotamia. His planning did not succeed because of a gap in advance intelligence about the nature of the monsoon winds; it was not because of a defect of his personality.

From a logistic standpoint, after the tour de force of the Gedrosia, the rest of the campaign is an anticlimax. Yet, there still remain logistic and geographical problems to discuss. The first is the route from Gwatar to Pura, the district of the Gedrosian capital that the army reached after a 60-day march from the Kumbh Pass.[84] The easiest route and the one best supplied with provisions passes up the Chil River to the oasis of Qasrkand, from there to Champ, and hence to Bampur.[85]

After resting the force some time at Pura, Alexander marched to the Carmanian capital (Tepe Yahya?),[86] probably following the route past Kahnu. Here Alexander may have had his unhoped-for meeting with Nearchus, who had anchored his fleet at Old Hormuz. Well might the king rejoice at Nearchus' return, for he may have had half of the remaining army aboard his fleet.[87] From here, Alexander advanced to Pasargadae, taking with him some light infantry, the Companions, and part of the archers.[88] One of the reasons he took so few was probably the difficulty and barrenness of the

84. A. 6. 24. 1; P. 66. 3. Stein, "Las Bela," 222–223. The capital city of Pura (in the Bampur River Basin) has not been located, but the region is dotted with unexcavated sites.

85. Stein, "Las Bela," 222.

86. The Carmanian capital, where Nearchus may have been reunited with Alexander, is perhaps located at Tepe Yahya, *Iran* 7 (1969) 185. However, the site of the meeting may have been a coastal town (D. 106. 4) and Nearchus, once again, may have distorted the evidence to embroider his account of his dramatic meeting with Alexander by having the site inland, Badian, "Nearchus," 160f.

87. If Plutarch (66. 2; cf. A. 6. 25. 3) is correct, and there is no evidence that he is not, Alexander lost three-quarters of the land army in the desert. Hence, he may have had only 20,000 foot soldiers and 5,000 cavalry remaining with him at Carmania. We estimated that there were about 20,000 with the fleet (pp. 155–156).

88. A. 6. 29. 1.

terrain between Sirjan and Niriz to Pasargadae and Persepolis, the only feasible route.[89] Nearchus was ordered to continue his voyage from Harmozia to the mouth of the Tigris, while Hephaistion, with the baggage train, elephants, and the rest of the army, was ordered to march along the seacoast from Carmania to Persis since, according to Nearchus, the shore was "sunny and well supplied with necessities."[90] This is indeed an astonishing statement. The coast here, as Nearchus himself well knew,[91] was "sandy and sterile," and in fact the Iranian shore of the Persian Gulf is as much a desert as the Gedrosia, if not worse.[92] Thus, if the shore was "well supplied with necessities," it was only because they had been supplied by Nearchus and the fleet.

89. Harrison, op. cit., 120.

90. A. 6. 28. 7.

91. Arr. *Ind.* 40. 2; 37–38. It would not be possible for the coast between Bandar Abbas and Bushire to have been provisioned overland, since the sources of supply in Sitacene and Carmania are too distant. Any pack animal traveling in such terrain would need grain, fodder, and water, and would quickly devour the supplies it carried by the fourth day (see above, p. 21). This is why it was impossible for the army to have been supplied overland while marching through the desert, as related by D. 105. 7, and C. 9. 10. 17–18. For the probable interpretation of these passages, see Ernst Badian, "The Eunuch Bagoas," *CQ* 52 (1958) 147–150. Nearchus' description of the coast here certainly does not leave one with the impression that it was "well supplied with all necessities."

92. "Persis," *Encyclopaedia Britannica* 17 (1943) 611; Harrison, op. cit., 122; Naval Intelligence Division, *Persia*, 121–135; Schachermeyr, op. cit., pl. 24b.

6.
Conclusion

The major problem in attempting to understand the logistic system of the Macedonian army is not only the almost complete lack of interest by our sources in its functioning but also the fact that Alexander so capably directed its operation that logistics scarcely seems to have affected any of his strategic decisions. Yet, a deeper analysis shows this latter view to be false. Supply was indeed the basis of Alexander's strategy; and when the climate, human and physical geography, available methods of transport, and the agricultural calendar of a given region are known, one can often determine what Alexander's next move will be.

The Macedonians' logistic organization, developed by Philip, was fundamentally different from that of contemporary Greek and Persian armies. In Greek armies, the number of followers often approached the number of combatants; and rations, arms, and armor were carried by servants or baggage animals. Philip trained his soldiers to carry their full panoply as well as provisions, and he forbade carts and women to accompany the army. Much equipment was carried by a limited number of servants rather than by carts or pack animals. The consequence of Philip's reforms, which were continued as far as possible by Alexander, was a dramatic reduction in the size of the baggage train, and this had a momentous effect. It made the Macedonian army the fastest, lightest, and most mobile force in existence, capable of making lightning strikes "before anyone had time to fear the event." Alexander's astonishing speed, which so terrified his opponents, was due in no small part to Philip's reforms. Because many supplies were carried by the troops and a restricted number of servants, the Macedonian army would need far fewer pack animals than would other contemporary forces, which would reduce the problems of acquiring sufficient animals and feeding them among populations engaged in subsistence agriculture. In short, the logistic organization of Alexander's army was brilliantly adapted for campaigning in Asia, where the acquisition of pack animals and provisions would often be difficult in barren terrain and where speed and mobility were important tactical advantages.[1]

The two most significant obstacles to the supplying of the army were the limited capabilities of overland transportation and the subsistence level of most agricultural production in antiquity (which in turn was caused in large part by a lack of efficient transport). Because of the limitations of transport, the army could not remain self-sufficient for long distances when remote from navigable rivers or seaports. Hence, arrangements for the army's supply were made in advance with local officials, who regularly surrendered to Alexander before he entered their territory. In regions where local geographical conditions made the acquisition of supplies particularly difficult, Alexander would often take hostages or establish garrisons to insure their efficient collection.[2] When he entered the Iranian heartland, however, few surrendered to him in advance, and the army's provisioning problems were intensified. Alexander would never commit his entire army for a campaign into a region that had not surrendered to him in advance. Instead, he would first obtain intelligence concerning the routes, climate, and resources of the country and then strike out with a small, light force, while the main army remained behind at a base well supplied with provisions. Alternatively, he would divide the army into smaller units so that their diminished requirements could be more easily provided during their advance through the countryside. Supplies at such times would not be provided by markets, gifts, or requisitions, as before, but by pillaging towns and villages or foraging. Advance intelligence was always an essential factor in Alexander's successful operations.[3]

1. See discussion in Chapter 1.
2. See above Chapter 2, n. 79.   3 See above Chapter 2, n. 97.

Because of the subsistence level of most agricultural production in antiquity, most populations scarcely had enough food to feed themselves in the months before harvest. For this reason, the army would delay at its winter base until the harvest of winter wheat and barley were completed before undertaking its march.[4] The subsistence level of agriculture and the limitations of overland transportation made it impossible for the army to remain stationary for long periods when remote from sea or river transport. The radius from which supplies could be effectively carried overland to the army was only 60 to 80 miles, and the army's huge consumption rates would have quickly exhausted all the agricultural surplus within this limit. For these reasons, the Macedonians always wintered in regions that were populous and intensively cultivated, with easy access to a nagivable river or ocean port.[5] Where these conditions could not be fulfilled, the army would be divided into smaller units for the winter. Even locations where the army halted only for a few weeks would invariably be equipped with river- or sea-transport facilities. Because all agricultural production occurred within a limited radius of human settlement, the army always marched through populous regions wherever possible and not through uninhabited, open countryside.[6]

Alexander better understood the capabilities and limitations of his logistic system than perhaps any other commander, before or since. In this respect, he was aided by capable lieutenants, to whom the actual tasks of supply were delegated. Among these were certainly Parmenio and perhaps Craterus, Coenus, and Erigyius.[7] Their achievement becomes more impressive when one remembers the barren terrain through which the army often marched, the limitations of overland transport, and the low level of agricultural production they had to reckon with.

The terrain of the Persian Empire was in a real sense the Persian king's most formidable weapon. Its extensive deserts, salt wastelands, barren, impenetrable mountain ranges, rivers of salt water, severe climatic extremes, and the often vast distances between cultivated inhabited regions were immense obstacles to any invading army. Indeed, these factors were largely responsible for the failures of Crassus, Antony, and Julian. Yet Alexander was able to over-

4. See above p. 27, p. 61.
5. See above Chapter 3, n. 40.

6. See above p. 31.
7. See above Chapter 2, notes 53 and 54.

come these obstacles where other armies had failed because of his superior abilities in gathering intelligence, planning, preparation, and organization. In Cilicia, the king was even able to use logistics as a weapon against his opponent, forcing Darius to fight in unfavorable terrain.

The details of the Macedonians' logistic system given by Arrian, Curtius, Diodorus, Plutarch, and Strabo form a coherent and consistent pattern from which a meaningful hypothetical model can be reconstructed. They are also accurate and consistent when compared with other sources such as Polyaenus and Frontinus and with the known achievements of Alexander's expedition. Their descriptions of the types of pack animals used, the use of servants, the transporting of equipment, and of the troops carrying their own arms, armor, and rations (details unimportant in themselves) coincide in all our sources and form a firm basis for the reconstruction of Alexander's logistic organization.

The method used in this study has been to correlate the simple relationships of time, distance, consumption rates, and transport capabilities with Alexander's strategy, tactics, and the timing and direction of his marches. Perhaps this simple method could be of some value for the understanding of other ancient campaigns or any other problem concerning time, distance, and transportation.

It is hoped that this study has led to a greater appreciation of the very real difficulties Alexander had to face in directing the provisioning of his army. Even a daily march from one camp to the next required prodigious planning, preparation, and efficient logistic organization. The importance of geographical factors in Alexander's strategic decisions has also been stressed since "The locality is the surviving portion of the reality of an event that has long ago passed by . . . it often restores to clearness the picture which history has preserved in half-effaced outlines."[8] If this study contributes to a greater understanding of this complex man and his achievement, it has fulfilled its purpose.

8. Sir Aurel Stein, *Geo. Journ.* 80 (1932) 31.

Appendix 1
Rations

PERSONNEL

In order to sustain life, an individual must obtain sufficient protein and calories from the food he consumes. Sources in the U.S. Army Quartermaster Corps have informed me that the caloric content of an army ration needed to sustain a soldier in combat conditions is 3,600 per day.[1] A similar caloric requirement, 3,402 per day, is needed by a 120-pound individual engaged in carrying a moderate load for 8 hours in addition to other normal activities (other active work, 1 hr.; walking, 1 hr.; sedentary activities, 6 hr.; sleeping, 8 hr.).[2] Of course, individuals leading sedentary lives need fewer calories. The life of the Macedonian soldier was far from sedentary, however, and 3,600 calories per day is a realistic estimate for his needs. It should be remembered that the average daily caloric intake for a male in the United States during the last century was 6,000 to 6,500; for an adult female, 4,000 to 4,500. In addition to calories, at least 70 grams of protein per day are needed if one is to avoid the effects of malnutrition and starvation. The major staple of Alexander's troops would always have been grain products since wheat, barley, and millet were the most readily available forms of food to be found throughout their campaigns and the easiest to carry; once dried, they could be stored indefinitely, even in hot weather, unlike meat, fish, vegetables, or fruit.

When milled, 2.2 lb. (1 kg.) of wheat will weigh 2 lb. (900 g.) and contain 3,150 calories and 90 g. of protein.[3] The protein and caloric

1. U.S. Army Reserve Officers Training Corps Quartermaster, University of Texas, pers. comm. 1972.
2. Clark and Haswell, 11–13.
3. Clark and Haswell, 58; Philip L. Altman and Dorothy S. Dittmer, *Metabolism* (Bethesda, 1968) 26; Errett C. Albritton, *Standard Values in Nutrition and Metabolism* (Philadelphia, 1954) 115; Benjamin T. Burton, *The Heinz Handbook of Nutrition* (New York, 1965) 430.

content of both milled and unmilled grain is identical per unit of weight. But too often it is assumed, even by those who should know better, that this is the amount of absorbable calories and protein actually digested by the individual.[4] Few people eat raw grain or even flour, however, most consuming grains in the form of bread, biscuits, or porridge. The Macedonians' grain ration was consumed in the form of bread[5] and perhaps biscuits and porridge, as in the Roman army.[6] Many calories are lost in the production of bread so that 2.2 lb. of bread contains only 2,500 calories and 100 g. of protein.[7] In addition, because of the high cellulose content of grain, only 90 percent of the calories and 80 percent of the protein can be digested.[8] Hence, after the original kilogram of wheat is milled, baked, and digested, it only contains 2,025 usable calories and 80 g. of protein, so that 3.5 lb. of bread, manufactured from 3.9 lb. of grain, would have to be consumed to obtain 3,600 digestible calories. Three pounds of bread, the ration used in this study, contains 3,085 calories. Biscuits made from wheat contain about the same amount of protein and calories. In the process of cooking porridge, however, the caloric content of grain is sharply reduced to only 450 calories per kilogram.[9] Millet and barley have slightly more calories and slightly less protein per pound than wheat.[10] The soldier's basic grain ration would be supplemented where possible with meat, fish, vegetables, wine, fruit, olive products, and cheeses. Beef and cheese contain more calories and protein than an equivalent weight of bread, and the other products contain less. Olive oil also contains more calories than the other foods but no protein. However, meat would only be rarely obtainable by the Macedonians because few individuals engaged in subsistence agriculture can afford to possess many cattle or even goats or sheep for food consumption,[11] and both meat and cheese are difficult to preserve in hot climates. It is unlikely that flocks of sheep or cattle accompanied the army, and

4. Clark and Haswell, 58. One of the few errors in an otherwise excellent book.
5. D. 41. 7; C. 4. 2. 14.
6. Front. *Strat.* 4. 1. 6; cf. Xen. *Cyrop.* 6. 2. 31.
7. Burton, op. cit., 432.
8. Altman and Dittmer, op. cit., 291–292.
9. Ibid., 32.
10. Burton, op. cit., 430; Altman and Dittmer, op. cit., 26; Albritton, op. cit., 112.
11. Clark and Haswell, 24, 59–68, 212.

none are ever mentioned.[12] For the convenience of calculation we will estimate that the average food ration of Alexander's army (which was composed largely of adult males—the troops and their attendants—at all times) weighed 3 lb.

Grain rations in antiquity ranged from 1 *choinix* (1.92 pt. or 1.5 lb.) per day for Xerxes' troops to 4½ *choinices* per day for the Spartans.[13] Since the former is inadequate to support human life, it must have been supplemented. The ration of a U.S. soldier during the Civil War also weighed 3 lb.[14]

The water ration used in this study, 2 qt. per day, is taken from Maurice (p. 223). Since all water rations we use were taken from English sources, the British Imperial liquid measures will be retained for the convenience of calculation (1 imperial gallon = 1.20 U.S. gallons). These rations could be reduced for short periods depending on the climate and terrain through which the army marched. In a desert, while the food ration could be reduced for a short period, it would not be possible to reduce the water ration below 2 qt. per day. Sources in the U. S. Army Quartermaster Corps have informed me that water rations can be reduced in a desert only by troops who have conditioned themselves to go without water for extended periods of time. The normal water ration for troops in a desert is 10 litres per day (about 9 qt.).[15] Under actual desert marching conditions, a daily water ration of 2 imperial qt. has been shown to be inadequate even for individuals conditioned for desert journeys.[16] It is unlikely that the Macedonians received special training for desert warfare, and their ration could not be reduced below 2 qt. per day. This is especially true when one re-

12. Since all animals are inefficient converters of vegetable protein and calories, they need far larger quantities of protein and calories from grain and fodder in feeding them than one could obtain from eating their meat. Since, like horses, cattle and sheep will only eat during the day, large quantities of food must be carried for them (cf. Hallock, op. cit., 1780–1787). Hence, their presence would slow the army down and restrict its mobility.

13. Hdt. 7. 187. 1; Jardé, op. cit., 129; Thuc. 4. 16. 1.

14. Hard wheat flour, 18 oz.; fresh beef, 20 oz.; dry beans, 2.4 oz.; coffee, 1.6 oz.; salt, .64 oz.; vinegar, .32 gill; pepper, .04 oz., U. S. Army R.O.T.C. Quartermaster, University of Texas.

15. Ibid.

16. G. A. Hoskins, *Visit to the Great Oasis of the Libyan Desert* (London, 1837) 53–54.

members that they had to march for eight hours per day under a desert sun in extremely low humidity, subsisting on a diet of grain products, wearing their arms and armor, carrying other equipment, personal possessions, and provisions. Even in nondesert areas where the climate is hot—a description of virtually the entire march route —a reduction of water rations would be a severe hardship on the troops and animals.

The food ration we have allowed for the personnel—3 lb. per day, consisting largely of grain products—is inadequate to supply sufficient calories to the troops, and to reduce it still further would invite the effects of starvation and malnutrition if the reduction extended for long periods. It is injurious to the health and morale of troops to overwork them by making them carry heavy burdens and feeding them inadequate rations. If the reductions are extended for longer than a few days, undesirable effects will result: a lack of drive and initiative, avoidance of physical and mental effort, and excessive rest.[17] This is not the way to keep an army in fighting trim.

ANIMALS

In addition to horses for the cavalry, mules, horses, and camels were used as transport animals by the expedition. One should always remember in discussing food and water requirements for animals on a military campaign that "the conditions of service are totally different to, and much harder than, the normal work of the animal. The loads are, generally speaking, heavy, the marches long and often hurried, the opportunities for rest and grazing limited and the general wear and tear increased."[18] Under these circumstances, the animals require more water and more frequent watering than at any other time.

On a military campaign, a horse doing moderate work will need from 20–24 lb. of provisions or a daily ration of 24–32 lb. for hard work. Half this ration should be grain and the other half fodder.[19] Military practice has shown that the cavalry and transport horses

17. Clark and Haswell, 21.
18. Army Veterinary Dept., 289.
19. Ibid., 122; Isaac Phillips Roberts, *The Horse* (New York, 1905) 360–381; W. H. Jordan, *The Feeding of Animals* (London, 1905) 371–377; Altman and Dittmer, op. cit., 101; "Horse," *Encyclopaedia Britannica* 11 (1943) 757; Albritton, op. cit., 65.

will require from 5 to 15 gal. of water per day, depending on the temperature; the average quantity is 8 gal. per day.[20] Hot weather and hard work will almost double ordinary water requirements. Mules require about the same rations as a horse.[21] We will estimate that the average cavalry horse on Alexander's expedition consumed 10 lb. of grain, 10 lb. of forage, and 8 gal. of water per day: the ration of a medium size horse doing moderate work.

As Markham noted, the breeds and true sizes of ancient horses cannot be determined by references to works of ancient art, but only by careful measurements of their skeletal remains.[22] This is because in evaluating works of art, one must contend with the artist's traditions, his artistic style and conventions (such as isocephaly on the Parthenon frieze), his skill (or lack thereof), the limitations of his medium, and his knowledge of horses.[23]

Fortunately, the skeletal remains of large numbers of ancient horses have been excavated and studied, and they show that the size of the average horse has not changed from Alexander's day to our own. For example, Liepe's detailed catalog of the sizes of over a hundred fossil European horses from Neolithic times to the Middle Ages[24] records large, full-size horses, identical in size to the largest modern horses (massive draught horses excluded), as well as medium-size horses and small horses; just as one finds at present. One will note, for example, two horses from Roman Vindonissa of 160 and 167 cm. height at the withers (15½ and 16.1 hands respectively) that are as large as any modern Arabian, Thoroughbred, Standardbred, or Morgan. These two animals are not aberrations, for the table shows other large Roman and Iron Age horses as well.[25]

20. Army Veterinary Dept., 129.
21. Ibid., 272–273; Riley, op. cit., 43; Leonard, op. cit., 297.
22. S. D. Markham, *The Horse in Greek Art* (New York, 1969) 3.
23. An exception may be the famous Alexander Mosaic, since in this instance the artist, in accordance with the realistic conventions of Hellenistic art, has depicted all details with superb accuracy. He has depicted full-size, powerful cavalry chargers, fully as large as those of the early modern era.
24. Hans-Ulrich Liepe, *Die Pferde des Latène—Oppidums Manching*, Studien in vor-und frühgeschichtlichen Tierresten Bayerns, 4 (Munich, 1958) 17–19. Cf. M. Hilzheimer, "The Evolution of the Domestic Horse," *Antiquity* 9 (1935) 133–139.
25. At Roman Cambodunum, 161.5 cm.; at Linderbeek, 164 cm.; and at Iron Age La Tene, Engehabinsel, 164 cm. Cavalry horses in the nineteenth century averaged 14.3 hands for light cavalry and 15.3 hands for heavy cavalry, Maj. Gen. Sir F. Smith, *A Manual of Veterinary Hygiene* (New York, 1906) 761.

However, the Macedonians' use of various sizes and breeds of horses in the baggage train had no overall effect on their logistic system. Exhaustive tests, scientifically conducted under the auspices of the Army Veterinary Department of Great Britain, have shown that the weight a horse is capable of carrying or pulling is directly proportional to his body weight. The tests dynometrically measured the capabilities of 216 horses of different breeds and sizes, weighing from 840 lb. to 1,333.5 lb.[26] A horse's nutritional requirement of food is also directly proportional to his body weight.[27] Hence, if there were ponies in the Macedonian baggage train, say 75 percent of the weight of standard-size horses, they would only require 75 percent as much food, but they would also only be able to do 75 percent of the work of the larger horses. Therefore, the ratio between the animal's consumption rate and his carrying capabilities in pounds remains approximately the same (about 1 : 10), no matter what the size of the animal; and, of course, it is this ratio

26. Maj. Gen. Sir F. Smith, "The Relationship between the Weight of a Horse and its Weight-Carrying Power," *Journal of Comparative Pathology and Therapeutics* 11 (1898) 287–290; Maj. Gen. Sir F. Smith, "Maximum Muscular Effort of the Horse," *Journal of Physiology* 19 (1896) 224–226. One hundred thirty-six horses were measured for the weight they could carry and 80 for their draught capabilities. The ratio between the body weight and the weight capable of being carried under conditions of hard work averages about 5.757 : 1 or about 17% of the horse's body weight. The ratio between a horse's body weight and the weight capable of being pulled varies greatly depending upon the velocity he is required to achieve, the duration of time he is required to work, the condition and sizes of the axles and wheels of the vehicle he pulls, his harness, and road conditions. For example, a 10% grade is equivalent to increasing the load by 10%. Mud, sand, rocks, and other unfavorable conditions will also slow him down and reduce his work capabilities. At maximum effort, the best, most spirited horses are capable of pulling about 78% of their body weight for a few seconds on a smooth, level road. If the horse is to work eight hours per day, however, he can only pull a maximum of 8% of his body weight, or from 100 to 150 lb., depending on his size. If the horse is required to achieve a high speed, he can only pull 4% of his body weight, or about 40 lb. for a period of only 50 minutes. Note that a horse is capable of carrying more over long distances and slow speeds than he can pull and this was undoubtedly a significant reason for armies of preindustrial periods to prefer pack animals to wagons. Moreover, because of the inefficient throat and girth harness used in antiquity, a horse or mule may have been capable of pulling even less, Forbes, op. cit., 82–87. Naturally, horses are no longer used to carry military provisions, and this is why the relationships between his weight and carrying and draught capabilities have not received subsequent study, as far as I can determine.

27. Carl W. Gay, *Productive Horse Husbandry* (Philadelphia, 1916) 234; Roberts, op. cit., 364; Smith, *Veterinary Hygiene*, 116; or any standard handbook on the care and feeding of horses.

that determines how far the army can travel before the animals consume all the supplies they are capable of carrying.

Also, the use of smaller horses in the baggage train would not have significantly affected the army's gross consumption rates of food. This is because more small horses (or mules or camels) would be needed than standard-size horses to carry a given weight. For example, if an army detachment needed 3,000 lb. of supplies carried for one day, they would require 15 standard-size horses of 1,000 lb., capable of carrying 200 lb. apiece, or 20 ponies of 750 lb., capable of carrying 150 lb. apiece. Since the ratio between an animal's daily food requirements and carrying capabilities in pounds remains constant no matter what the size of the animal, both the 15 standard size horses and the 20 ponies would have consumed approximately the same amount of supplies per day; about 300 lb.

The requirements are higher for camels: 10 lb. of grain and 25 lb. of straw per day. If only 8 lb. of grain can be given, then 30 lb. of straw will be required; if only 6 lb. of grain, then 40–50 lb. of straw; if 4 lb. of grain, 50–60 lb. of straw; and if no grain can be given, 70 lb. of straw will be needed.[28] Concerning the watering of camels, "his powers or capabilities have been grossly exaggerated and the most culpable ignorance and negligence have been displayed."[29] Camels ought to be watered daily and will need 10 gal. although if the animal has gone three or four days without water, it may require 20 gal. at a time.[30] For the sake of convenience, we will estimate that the average pack animal's ration is that of a cavalry horse; but it must be remembered that because of the many camels with the expedition from Egypt onward, the hot climate of the march, and the heavy work required, this is a *minimum* ration and cannot be reduced without danger.

Unlike men, the physical condition of cavalry and transport animals cannot be restored by rest and proper diet after they have been worn out by several days of excessive work and inadequate rations; such treatment renders them unfit for further use.[31] This

---

28. Leonard, op. cit., 153–154; Army Veterinary Dept., 284–285.
29. Leonard, op. cit., 134.
30. Army Veterinary Dept., 285.
31. Ibid., 285, 302: "Whilst the animal is fit and in condition hardship and exertion can be borne without injury, but once the troop horse is sick, injured or exhausted, he is only an encumbrance to a fighting unit and has to be left behind,

is why "the transport animals of an army shall be regarded as worth their weight in gold, no care or supervision can be too great or too strict."[32] This statement, written about transport animals in the early part of this century, is even more relevant to Alexander's army, for the subsistence level of most agricultural production[33] and the barrenness of much of the terrain in Iran, Afghanistan, and Turkmenistan made suitable animals relatively scarce.

---

his place being filled by a fresh animal. . . . It is on this account that so much stress is laid [by the book] . . . on feeding and work under all circumstances, and to the directing attention to the prevention of injuries rather than to the treatment of those that have occurred." Cf. Leonard, op. cit., 201f.; A. 3. 30. 6.

32. Army Veterinary Dept., 199.

33. Clark and Haswell, 24, 212. Certain favored regions such as lower Mesopotamia, the lower Helmand River Basin, and the Indus River Basin could support a greater number of animals.

Appendix 2
The Site of the Pinarus

One frequently overlooked factor in studies concerning the location of the Pinarus River, where the battle of Issus was fought, is the relationship between time and distance.

After Alexander learned that Darius had crossed his rear and was descending south from Issus, he turned north from Myriandrus and encamped along the Pillars of Jonah Pass.[34] Now, it is 7.75 miles from the Pillars to the Payas River and 16.25 miles from the pass to the Deli Chai.[35] The Macedonian army left camp at dawn and descended through the pass in column, and when the plain widened, they deployed into a line.[36] It is easy for those unfamiliar with the time problem of an army marching through a pass to believe that the army could have deployed from a column to a line and then have marched 16 miles, all in one day. However, as Col. Sir Charles Wilson and Commandant Bourgeois observed long ago, this is impossible.[37] An army marching through a pass is like water flowing through a funnel: just as the volume of water flowing through the funnel per unit of time depends upon the narrowest constriction of the funnel, so the numbers of troops marching through a pass per unit of time depends upon the narrowest constriction of the pass. The narrowest part of the Pillars of Jonah

34. A. 2. 8. 1–2. See William Ainsworth, "Notes on the Comparative Geography of the Cilician and Syrian Gates," *JRGS* 8 (1838) 186 for the correct spelling of the Pillars of Jonah.

35. Naval Staff, *Asia Minor*, Vol. 4, pt. 2, 317–319. This source has measured the distance scientifically on the actual ground. It should be remembered that the Pillars of Jonah Pass is almost a mile high, Roman Oberhummer and Heinrich Zimmerer, *Durch Syrien und Kleinasien* (Berlin, 1899) 104.

36. A. 2. 8. 2.

37. Col. Sir Charles Wilson, "The Identification of the Pinarus with the River Payas," *PRGS* 6 (1884) 540–541; Dieulafoy, op. cit., 41–76. The methodology was first developed by Bourgeois and Dieulafoy, and by me independently in 1973. It obviously needs restating.

could allow no more than four infantry or two cavalry horses to pass abreast,[38] and hence, it would have taken 7½ hours for 40,864 infantry and 6,280 cavalry[39] to cross just the narrowest part of the pass if they marched at 4 miles per hour—a furious rate of speed considering that the pass is nearly a mile high—even though Alexander ordered his men to march through the pass on the double.[40] This is because 40,864 troops in sections of 4 will form a line 21 miles long, and 6,280 cavalry 2 abreast will form a column 9 miles long.[41] Hence, if they marched at 4 miles per hour, the column would take 7½ hours to pass a single point. Since the cavalry followed the infantry through the pass,[42] the cavalry's rate of speed would be determined by the infantry's rate.[43] As with water in a funnel, the march rate for the entire army will depend on how many soldiers and cavalry horses can cross the narrowest part of the pass per hour. We have repeatedly noted throughout this study that it takes a great deal of time to move large numbers of men and animals through constricted spaces.[44] Now, if the army began marching at dawn,[45] about 7:00 A.M. (the time of sunrise on November 15 for this latitude),[46] the last soldier and cavalry horse will

38. Dieulafoy, op. cit., 62.

39. For the numbers see table 4. Cf. Polyb. 12. 19. 3 who lists 42,000 foot and 5,000 cavalry.

40. C. 3. 8. 23. The average march rate for infantry is 3 mph. and 2.5 mph. over rough terrain, see table 7.

41. Maurice, 229.

42. A. 2. 8. 3; Polyb. 12. 19. 5; cf. C. 4. 12. 3; C. 6. 4. 15.

43. Obviously, the cavalry could not march faster than the infantry they followed in the column or they would trample the infantry. If, on the other hand, the cavalry delayed its march for 15 minutes until the infantry crossed the pass, allowing a gap of one mile between the rear of the infantry column and the head of the cavalry column, and then tried to catch up by trotting up the mile-high pass at 6 mph., no time would be saved. Simple arithmetic will show that in 30 minutes, the cavalry traveling at 6 mph. will collide with the rear of the infantry column traveling at 4 mph. and the cavalry would then be forced to march at the same rate as the infantry. Hence, no time would be saved by this maneuver since the cavalry would end up in the same place at the same time as if they had been marching right behind the infantry column at 4 mph. all along. The same result would occur if the cavalry waited 30 minutes or an hour for the infantry to cross the pass before it began its march. The cavalry did not march alongside of the infantry or ahead of it but behind it, and they did not line up abreast of the infantry until shortly before the battle was joined, A. 2. 8. 2–2. 8. 9.

44. See above, Chapter 3, n. 56.

45. A. 2. 8. 2.

46. Dieulafoy, op. cit., 63.

have crossed the pass at 2:30 P.M. If the Macedonians were then to march 16 miles to the Deli Chai, even at 4 miles per hour, they would reach that river at 6:30 P.M., one and a half hours after sunset,[47] whereas they would have reached the Payas (Pinarus) at 4:30 P.M. Even excluding the march through the pass, 16 miles was a good distance for the army to march in one day (see table 7). Were they, then, one and a half hours after sunset to fight a pitched battle? Even if the army left camp at 6:00 A.M.—one hour before sunrise—they still would not reach the Deli Chai until 5:30 at the very earliest, one-half hour after sunset.

The topography of the Payas also supports its location for the battle. Both the Payas and Deli have steep banks,[48] as recorded by the sources for the Pinarus, but only near the Payas is the ground considerably broken up by deep torrent beds, which, as Callisthenes, Arrian, and Plutarch noted, made the ground unsuitable for the deployment of cavalry on the Persian left wing.[49] This description does not apply at all to the Deli plain, which is completely smooth.[50]

The width of the battlefield recorded by Callisthenes and preserved in Polybius' polemical attack against him, 14 *stadia* (2,832 yards), better fits the Payas, which is about 3,828 yards,[51] than the Deli, which is considerably wider. Callisthenes' figure seems to be corrupt, however, perhaps through a scribal error or through a distortion of Callisthenes' measurement by Polybius in his biased attack. It is clear that the coastline of eastern Cilicia has neither advanced nor receded since Alexander's day. This is proven by the existence of no fewer than seven sites on the eastern edge of the Gulf of Alexandretta that were occupied from Alexander's era.[52]

47. Sunset occurs at 5:05, Ibid.

48. A. Janke, *Auf Alexanders des Grossen Pfaden* (Berlin, 1904) 54; A. Janke, "Die Schlacht bei Issus," *Klio* 10 (1910) 173; Naval Staff, *Asia Minor*, Vol. 4, pt. 2, 21.

49. Polyb. 12. 20. 4; A. 2. 8. 10; P. 20. 3.

50. William Ainsworth, "The Identification of the Pinarus with the River Piyas," *PRGS* 6 (1884) 468–469. He has often hunted badger over the Deli Chai Plain for many miles without encountering a single obstacle.

51. About 3,500 meters. F. W. Walbank, *A Historical Commentary on Polybius*, Vol. 2 (Oxford, 1967) 364, notes: "Even when all allowance is made for possible errors in copying and the manuscript tradition, this criticism of Callisthenes shows P. at his worst. His points are almost all trivial or fallacious; and his mathematical calculations are marred by egregious errors of logical reasoning and gross carelessness."

52. Seton-Williams, op. cit., 147–167. The sites are: Kinet (Nicopolis, occupied pre-Hellenistic through Byzantine); Payas (occupied Hellenistic to early nineteenth

Now, if the coastline had receded since antiquity (for whatever reason) these ancient ports would now be wholly or partly under water, which we see is not the case. If the coastline had advanced since Alexander's era, these sites, to be where they now are, would have been originally constructed under water, which is impossible. Not all measurements of distances preserved in ancient authors are accurate,[53] and this is one of them.

I pass over the fact that Curtius[54] reported that when the Macedonians were crossing the Pillars of Jonah, the Persians were 30 *stadia* (3.4 miles) away; that is, the advance divisions of the Persian army had deployed in front of the Payas, as the sources state.[55]

One can conclude that the Pinarus was the Deli Chai only by having the battle of Issus fought in the dark and by ignoring the laws of physics and the topographical information provided by the sources. Serious students of Alexander will avoid making such hazardous conclusions.

---

cent. A.D.); Iskanderun (Alexandretta, Hellenistic to modern); Ada Tepe (Hellenistic to Roman) Çokmeydan (Hellenistic to Roman); Seyithidir Merkadi (Hellenistic to Byzantine); Arsuz (Rhossus, Hellenistic to Roman).

53. Cf., e.g., Str. 15. 2. 11; A. 3. 8. 7; D. 68. 4; Pliny *NH* 6. 62 on the distance from the Jhelum to the Beas.

54. C. 3. 8. 23; cf. D. 33. 1.

55. A. 2. 8. 5; C. 3. 8. 28.

Appendix 3
Approximate Chronology of the Gedrosian Campaign

Mid-July:	Alexander leaves Pattala (Bahmanabad).
Late August:	Alexander reaches the border of the Oreitans and Gedrosians at the Kumbh Pass, 300 miles from Pattala.
Late October:	Nearchus begins his voyage, and Alexander arrives in Pura and rests the army.
Mid-December:	Alexander arrives at the Carmanian capital (Tepe Yahya?).
Mid-January:	Nearchus, having anchored at Harmozia after a trip of 75 days, is reunited with Alexander about 5 days later at the Carmanian Capital.

Alexander arrived in Pattala sometime in July of 325, around the heliacal rising of Sirius,[56] and probably left by mid-July. It was essential for Alexander to leave in July during the monsoon storms, for if he left much later, the ephemeral, intermittent streams, lakes, and wells of southern Baluchistan would all be dry.[57] Strabo is certainly correct in having Alexander march in summer to catch the rains.[58]

It took 60 days for Alexander to march from the border of the Oreitans' country at the Kumbh Pass to the capital of Gedrosia at Pura.[59] The location of Pura in the Bampur Basin is still unknown,

---

56. Str. 15. 1. 17.
57. Snead, *Las Bela*, 11–22, 58, 65; Stein, "Las Bela," 194, 214.
58. Str. 15. 2. 3.
59. A. 6. 24. 1; Str. 15. 2. 7. Strabo says ἀπὸ Ὠρῶν and Arrian, ἐξ Ὠρων. Is this reckoned from the beginning of the Oreitans' territory at the Hab, the border between the Oreitans and the Gedrosians at the Kumbh Pass, or somewhere in be-

but the march accomplished in the 60 days would be between 630 to 787 miles, depending on where in the 157-mile-long basin the capital was located. Alexander reached Pura about the same time Nearchus began his voyage in late October.[60]

The best fixed date for the expedition is the beginning of Nearchus' voyage, around the cosmical setting of the Pleiades.[61] The date of their cosmical setting would be around the fourth week of October in 325 B.C., when allowance is made, as usual, for haze and dust obscuring the horizon. October is also the month when the southwest monsoons cease and the wind circulation becomes northerly.[62] Nearchus wrote[63] that he began his voyage on the twentieth of Boedromion, which would be either September or October. By my count, Nearchus' voyage lasted about 75 days from Pattala to Harmozia.

Pliny[64] wrote that it was seven (lunar) months (about six of our months) after Alexander left Pattala that he and Nearchus were reunited at the Carmanian Capital. Thus, if Nearchus left in late October, his voyage lasted two and a half months, and it was about five days after he anchored that he met Alexander;[65] this would mean that Alexander left Pattala by mid-July and that they were reunited in mid-January. It seems that the king's estimate of four months' supplies needed to sustain the army during the march[66] was about correct.

---

tween? I believe it is reckoned from the border with the Gedrosians since this would better reflect a 60-day march to the Bampur Basin, considering the immense difficulties of the march, especially the deep sand, the fact that the expedition was lost for a time, and that they had to cross at least one mountain pass.

60. Str. 15. 2. 5.

61. A. 6. 21. 2; Str. 15. 2. 5. Strabo wrote that the voyage began when the Pleiades rose ἐπιτολή in the west. But stars, of course, like all other astronomical bodies, do not rise in the west; and, obviously, Strabo, like Arrian, meant when the Pleiades set in the west. For the date of the setting in antiquity see D. R. Dicks, *Early Greek Astronomy to Aristotle* (Ithaca, 1970) 36. The date is only approximate. The time for the march between Pattala and the Kumbh Pass includes the operations against the Oreitans, the refoundation of Rhambacia, and Thoas' reconnaissance.

62. Jen-Hu Chang, "The Indian Summer Monsoon," *Geo. Rev.* 57 (1967) 394; J. W. M'Crindle, *The Invasion of India by Alexander the Great* (London, 1896) 167. The monsoons begin here about July 15.

63. Arr. *Ind.* 21. 1.

64. *NH* 6. 100.

65. Arr. *Ind.* 33. 7, for the five-day journey from the anchorage.

66. A. 6. 20. 5.

Appendix 4
Alexander's Route
in the Gedrosian Desert

It is ironic that for the Gedrosian Desert, the most desolate and remote region traversed by the Macedonian army, we possess more detailed archaeological and geographical evidence for Alexander's route than for almost any other location. Thanks to the accounts of the march given by Arrian and Strabo as well as the archaeological and paleogeographical research undertaken in the last 40 years, Alexander's essential route can be accurately restored.

The Makran region has received exhaustive and diligent archaeological research, since, among other reasons, it was on one of the major trade routes between Mesopotamia and the Indus civilization. The surveys and excavations are concerned with all periods of the region's history. The first modern works were undertaken by Sir Aurel Stein.[67] As for so much of Iran, Afghanistan, and Pakistan, the research of this extraordinarily talented man forms the foundation for all subsequent studies of the Makran. More recently, Stein's pioneering work has been augmented by further survey work and excavations carried out under the capable direction of Fairservis, Dales, Raikes, and Field.[68] Supplementing the archaeological research, Snead has ably studied the region's

---

67. Sir Aurel Stein, *An Archaeological Tour in Gedrosia*, Mem. Arch. Surv. India, Vol. 43 (1931); "On Alexander's Route into Gedrosia: An Archaeological Tour in Las Bela," *GJ* 102 (1943) 193–227.

68. The research of Raikes and Fairservis is conveniently tabulated in Walter A. Fairservis, *The Roots of Ancient India* (New York, 1971) 406–408; Robert L. Raikes, "The End of Ancient Cities of the Indus Civilization in Sind and Baluchistan," *American Anthropologist* 65 (1963) 655–659; George F. Dales, Jr., "A Search for Ancient Sea Routes," *Expedition* 4 (1962) 2–11; Henry Field, *An Anthropological Reconnaissance in West Pakistan, 1955*, Papers of the Peabody Museum of Archaeology and Ethnology, 52 (1959); George F. Dales, "Harappan Outposts on the Makran Coast," *Antiquity* 36 (1962) 86–96.

geography[69] and shows conclusively that the configuration of the Makran coastline has changed considerably since Alexander's day, especially in Las Bela.

Today, there are two basic theories of Alexander's route, one proposed by Stein[70] and the other by Hermann Strasburger.[71] Strasburger wrote his first essay without having consulted Stein's works, both of which represent the most thorough geographical and archaeological studies on the Makran ever to appear. After reading Stein's studies, Strasburger wrote a second article which discussed the differences between his views and those of Stein.[72] Strasburger's route was based on the journeys of Miles and Goldsmid,[73] made over a hundred years ago when the geography of the Makran was still largely unknown. More recently, Hamilton[74] published a brief article in support of Strasburger's study. Hamilton is unaware of the recent research undertaken by Fairservis, Dales, Raikes, Field, and, most importantly, by Snead, although it was all published before his article appeared. There is no doubt whatsoever that Stein's route is the correct one.

The beginning of both routes is the same; both Stein and Strasburger follow Alexander to Lake Siranda and the Porali Valley of Las Bela (see map, p. 174). From here their routes diverge. Strasburger, first following Goldsmid, proceeds along the coast past Kandewari, up the Hingol River and Maniji stream, to avoid the

69. Rodman Snead, "Recent Morphological Changes Along the Coast of West Pakistan," *AAAG* 55 (1965) 648; *Physical Geography Reconnaissance: West Pakistan Coastal Zone*, University of New Mexico Publications in Geography, No. 1 (Albuquerque, 1969); *Physical Geography Reconnaissance: Las Bela Coastal Plain, West Pakistan* (Baton Rouge, 1966).

70. Stein, "Las Bela."

71. Herman Strasburger, "Alexanders Zug durch die Gedrosische Wüste," *Hermes* 80 (1952) 456–493. While I disagree with his route, which occupies only a short section of his article, the essay contains much of value. Another theory was advanced by T. Holdich, *The Gates of India* (London, 1910) 144–168, which was thoroughly demolished by Stein, "Las Bela," 204–208. Holdich's route passed along the Parkini River, and even M'Crindle, op. cit., 357, saw that this route bore no resemblance at all to the route described by the sources of Alexander's march, which was lacking water and passed through wide expanses of sand dunes.

72. "Zur Route Alexanders durch Gedrosien," *Hermes* 82 (1954) 251–254.

73. Capt. S. B. Miles, "Journey from Gwadur to Karachi," *JRGS* 44 (1874) 163–182; Maj. F. J. Goldsmid, "Diary of Proceedings of the Mission into Mekran for Political and Survey Purposes from the 12th to the 19th December, 1861," *JRGS* 33 (1863) 181–213.

74. J. R. Hamilton, "Alexander Among the Oreitae," *Historia* 21 (1972), 603–608.

obstacle of Ras Malan, and along the coast to Ormara. Although Strasburger believes that Alexander's main objective was to remain as close to the shore as possible so that the land army—marching through the desert—could supply provisions for the fleet, he next has Alexander following Miles' route, turning inland from Ormara up the Basol River to the Kech River and hence along the river to Turbat and south to Pasni. Stein follows Alexander to the Kumbh Pass into the Jhau tract, past the Nundara River into the Kolwa depression to Turbat, and hence down the Shadi River to Pasni.

Hamilton, supporting Strasburger's route, rejects Stein's observation that Alexander proceeded north from Lake Siranda to the vicinity of Bela because "it seems quite arbitrary to assume that he continued in a northerly direction rather than that he turned west." [75] Hamilton would look for Rhambacia, which Alexander refounded as an Alexandria, "between the Siranda Lake and Kandewari, north of the Miani Hor," [76] since the town was near the sea.

However, intensive geological investigation has shown that the shore line of Las Bela has advanced from between 20 to 30 miles in the last 2,000 to 5,000 years. [77] This is because the southwest monsoon and the prevailing westerly currents have deposited an enormous quantity of sand along the coast. In addition, the Porali River carries down a large volume of silt, and the land itself has been uplifted 200 feet or more since the recent past. [78] All these factors have contributed to the building up of the shoreline, which has occurred at a prodigious rate. For these reasons, the shoreline of the Porali Valley in Alexander's day was probably near Liari, some nine miles north of the present Miani Khor. [79]

Diligent archaeological research has shown, not surprisingly, that because of the rapid advance of the coastline, the southernmost archaeological site in the Porali Valley is Kaiara Kot—a medieval site a good 16 miles inland. [80] Thus, since the route Hamilton

75. Hamilton, op. cit., 607.

76. Ibid., 608.

77. Snead, "Morphological Changes," 648; *Las Bela,* 37, 65, 79, 83. As recently as 1890 the north shore of the Miani Lagoon was four miles north of its present location in some places.

78. Snead, *Las Bela,* 41.

79. Ibid. The Porali no longer reaches the sea because of a dam.

80. Stein, "Las Bela," 200; Fairservis, op. cit., 407.

would have Alexander follow after leaving the vicinity of Siranda Lake was under the Indian Ocean at the time, there is nothing at all "arbitrary" about Alexander marching north instead of west. In fact, it was the only possible decision he could have made. Since the area was under water in Alexander's day and exhaustive archaeological surveys have shown that the southern-most site is located at Kaiara Kot, Rhambacia cannot be on the north shore of the Miani Khor lagoon. Instead, as Stein observed long ago, the site of Rhambacia is located at Bela or its immediate vicinity.[81]

Hamilton next denies Stein's identification of the Kumbh Pass as the pass Alexander reached between the borders of the Oreitan and the Gedrosian territories.[82] The location of the Gedrosians' country is known from the study of the archaeology and human geography of Baluchistan.[83] They lived, in fact, in the Jhau tract and the Kolwa depression, and the pass the Oreitans blocked to prevent Alexander's approach had to be the pass between the Jhau tract and Las Bela—the Kumbh Pass.[84] The pass is not to be looked for near the coast, for this was the territory of the Ichthyophagoi;[85] the Gedrosians dwelt inland and north of the Fish-eaters.

There is abundant evidence from archaeology, human geography, and the literary sources on the route Alexander followed from the Porali Valley to Pasni. The route followed by Miles and Goldsmid bears no resemblance whatsoever to the descriptions of Alexander's route in the sources. First, when Alexander realized that the fleet would not be able to provision his army, he was faced with the decision of how best to supply his large force. Along the Macedonians' route, quantities of grain, dates, and sheep were

81. Stein, "Las Bela," 215; Fairservis, op. cit., 185.

82. Hamilton, op. cit., 607. See Stein's perceptive reconstruction for the correct location of this pass, "Las Bela," 216f.

83. Fairservis, op. cit., 406f.; Stein, *Gedrosia*; Stein, "Las Bela," 210. The Macedonians traversed the *Gedrosian* Desert. The Gedrosians did not dwell along or near the coast, the Ichthyophagoi dwelt here. The Gedrosians dwelt inland and north of the Fish-eaters, Arr. *Ind.* 26. 1–2; 32. 1.

84. Stein, "Las Bela," 216–217.

85. Arr. *Ind.* 26. 1–2; 32. 1. Hamilton, op. cit., 607, notes that Alexander's expedition saw mangroves (which only grow near the sea), and this invalidates Stein's route, which is away from the coast. However, the passage (A. 6. 22. 6) occurs *before* the expedition advanced into the desert (A. 6. 23. 1), and hence the trees were obviously seen in the Porali Valley. In any event, the expedition would have ample opportunity to observe mangroves along their 7-day coastal journey from Pasni to Gwatar (A. 6. 26. 5; Snead, *West Pakistan*, 7, 22, 34).

consumed.[86] As we have noted,[87] all agricultural production in antiquity occurred within a short radius of human settlements. Thorough archaeological surveys have shown that the human settlement of Baluchistan in Alexander's era, as today, occurred in the Jhau tract, the Kolwa depression, and the Kech River valley. Hence, in the Porali Valley—the Oreitans' territory—the king first sent Thoas to reconnoiter the coast, and he reported back that the shore was entirely desert.[88] Naturally, Alexander did not then take the coastal route but instead led his army inland[89] through the above-mentioned regions where provisions were most plentiful, although far from adequate to maintain the army. The army did not march in the Fish-eaters' country along or near the coast. Here, the only thing they could have eaten was fish, which is the one thing our sources do *not* record the army as having eaten.[90]

The idea that the army had to keep close to the shore to supply the fleet with provisions[91] is utterly false. The land army was literally starving to death in the desert and was in no condition to supply anything to anyone.[92] In fact, throughout the entire coastline of the Ichthophagai, there was not a single anchorage, well, or magazine of provisions set up by the land army for the fleet. Once Alexander understood that the fleet would be unable to provision his army because of the adverse winds, there was no reason for him to maintain close contact with the sea. All references to Alexander's need to keep close to the shore to provision the fleet are based on the account of Nearchus,[93] who by this method attempted to obscure his own responsibilities in supplying the land army. Arrian takes great pains to inform the reader that Alexander did not march along the coast of the Ichthyophagoi (which Goldsmid's route follows for some 100 miles from Kandewari to

86. A. 6. 23. 4 twice; A. 6. 23. 6.
87. See above, p. 31f.
88. A. 6. 23. 2.
89. A. 6. 26. 4; Str. 15. 2. 6.
90. Arr. *Ind.* 29. 9–16 for the diet of the Fish-eaters.
91. A. 6. 24. 3; Str. 15. 2. 4. from Nearchus. Strabo (15. 2. 4) wrote that Alexander kept no more than 500 *stadia* (57 miles) from the coast, "so that he could supply necessities to the fleet along the coast." This is absurd; it never in fact occurred, and the passage, based on Nearchus, is of no value. In any event, Stein's route is almost entirely within 57 miles of the coast. Also, the Macedonians could have no idea how far from the sea they were when they were lost and the sea was not even visible, Str. 15. 2. 6; A. 6. 26. 4.
92. A. 6. 23. 1; A. 6. 23. 4; A. 6. 24. 4; A. 6. 25. 1; Str. 15. 2. 5; Str. 15. 2. 6; C. 9. 10. 11–15; D. 105. 6; P. 66. 3.
93. A. 6. 24. 3.

Ormara) but in the Gedrosians' country, inland and north of the Fish-eaters.[94]

Another severe difficulty encountered by the troops was the lack of water along their route, which was fatal to a great many.[95] Now, if they followed Strasburger's suggested route up the Basol and Kech rivers, the only thing the army would be able to procure was water. There is no permanent settlement, ancient or modern, along the narrow, rocky gorges of the Basol River, and hence no grain or dates would be procurable here. Deep sand dunes were also a major obstacle, and their endless extent caused the guides to lose their way.[96] Now, there is no sand in the narrow, rocky gorges of the Basol and Kech rivers, but there are extensive areas of sand dunes in the Kolwa.[97] Arrian[98] wrote that the army's march deliberately followed even ground on account of the wagons, whereas Goldsmid himself wrote, "It is quite certain that this zigzag route (from the Hariani Gorge to Ormara) would be wholly impractical for troops."[99] Strasburger[100] wrote that Goldsmid's route would have just enough provisions to "allure" Alexander, whereas Thoas reported that the coast here was entirely desert[101] and Goldsmid noted that supplies here were barely adequate for a dozen men,[102] let alone for an army of 150,000 personnel and 18,000 cavalry horses. Along the inland march, Alexander first reached an area where grain was plentiful.[103] This describes the Jhau tract, where the cultivable land supported a modest population, and certainly not the coast from Kandewari to Ormara, the most desolate region of the Makran,[104] where the army would be lucky to find a few fish.

Strasburger[105] wrote that Goldsmid and Miles followed their routes with Alexander's march in mind. Miles does not mention

94. Arr. *Ind.* 26. 1-2; 32. 1.
95. A. 6. 24. 4; A. 6. 24. 5; A. 6. 24. 6; A. 6. 26. 2; Str. 15. 2. 6.
96. A. 6. 24. 4; A. 6. 25. 2; A. 6. 26. 4; Str. 15. 2. 6.
97. Stein, *Gedrosia*, 52-144.
98. A. 6. 25. 3.
99. Goldsmid, op. cit., 193.
100. Strasburger, "Zur Route Alexanders," 253.
101. A. 6. 23. 2.
102. Goldsmid, op. cit., 193-202.
103. A. 6. 23. 4.
104. Goldsmid, op. cit., 194; Snead, *West Pakistan*, 23-26.
105. "Zur Route Alexanders," 252.

any army, ancient or modern, throughout his account. Goldsmid[106] wrote that the route he took was impossible for an army and would be *fatal* in a heavy rain (we remember that Alexander made his march during the rainy season).[107] Neither officer mentions Alexander.

The routes of Goldsmid and Miles do not resemble the route followed by Alexander as described by our sources. Their routes were supplied with abundant water, little or no cultivable land, and no sand dunes. The Macedonian route traversed sand dunes, contained little water, but provided quantities of dates, grain, and sheep (hence cultivable land) and no fish. Had they marched along or near the coast, fish is all they could have eaten. It is only the route so ably reconstructed by Stein, based on the general principles of an army's requirements and the ancient human geography of Baluchistan, that corresponds to our literary evidence. Only by following Stein's route could the Macedonians hope to collect a fraction of the thousands of tons of provisions they needed and escape the desert. As Goldsmid himself wrote, the route he followed would be suicide for an army, to the last man and pack animal.

106. Goldsmid, op. cit., 193.
107. Str. 15. 2. 3.

Appendix 5
Statistical Tables

Table 1

The Army's Grain Requirement for One Day

	Numbers	Ration	Weight (lb.)
Personnel	65,000	3 lb.	195,000
Cavalry horses	6,100	10 lb.	61,000
Baggage animals	1,300	10 lb. (average)	13,000
Animals carrying provisions	1,121	10 lb. (average)	11,210

Note: Of course, it is impossible to determine whether each person and animal received his precise ration at any given time throughout the campaigns. Hence, these figures and others like them in subsequent pages are meant to indicate only the order of magnitude of the army's gross consumption. They are based on the nutritional requirements of men and animals discussed in Appendix 1. Furthermore, the army's gross requirements are not as important as the ratio between the army's carrying capability and its consumption rate of food and water.

Table 2

The Army's Grain and Forage Requirement for One Day

	Numbers	Ration	Weight (lb.)
Personnel	65,000	3 lb.	195,000
Cavalry horses	6,100	10 lb. grain 10 lb. forage	122,000
Baggage animals	1,300	10 lb. grain (average) 10 lb. forage (average)	26,000
Animals carrying provisions	1,492	10 lb. grain (average) 10 lb. forage (average)	29,840

Table 3

The Army's Grain, Forage, and Water Requirement for One Day

	Numbers	Ration	Weight (lb.)
Personnel	65,000	3 lb. grain ½ gal. (5 lbs.) water	195,000 325,000
Cavalry horses	6,100	20 lb. grain and forage 8 gal. (80 lb.) water	122,000 488,000
Baggage animals	1,300	20 lb. grain and forage (average) 8 gal. (80 lb.) water (average)	26,000 104,000
Animals carrying provisions	8,400	20 lb. grain and forage (average) 8 gal. (80 lb.) water (average)	168,000 672,000

Table 4

Approximate Troop Numbers in Alexander's Army: Hellespont to Gaugamela

Location	Reinforcements inf.	cav.	Losses inf.	cav.	Garrisons inf.	cav.	Reference
Hellespont advance expedition	10,000	1,000					D. 16. 91. 2; Green, 156
Expeditionary force	32,000	5,100					D. 17. 17. 3–5; J. 11. 6. 12
Granicus			9	120			A. 1. 17. 8
Sardis	300				all Argives		A. 1. 19. 6
Miletus			56		3000		A. 1. 20. 10– 1. 22. 7; A. 1. 23. 6
Halicarnassos						200	
Sagalassos			21				A. 1. 28. 8
Celaenae					1,500		A. 1. 29. 3

Gordion	3,150	500					A. 1. 29. 4
Near Issus	Agrianians				garrisons		C. 3. 9. 10; C. 3. 7. 7
Soli					garrisons		C. 3. 7. 2
Issus			1,000	200			P. Oxy. 1798
Sidon	4,000						C. 4. 3. 11; A. 2. 20. 5
Tyre	Greek reinforcements with Cleander and 3,000		400				C. 4. 3. 11; C. 4. 5. 18; A. 2. 24. 4
Egypt	400	500			4,000		A. 3. 5. 1; C. 4. 8. 4
Total:	52,850	7,100	1,486	320	8,500	200	
Sub Total: (Reinforcements minus losses and garrisons)	42,864	6,580					

Note: See note on tables 4 to 6, p. 151.

Table 5

Approximate Troop Numbers in Alexander's Army: Gaugamela to India

Location	Reinforcements inf.	cav.	Losses inf.	cav.	Garrisons inf.	cav.	Reference
Gaugamela	42,864	6,580	500				D. 17. 61. 3
Babylon					1,000		C. 5. 1. 43
Babylonia	13,500	2,100			2,000		D. 17. 69. 1; C. 5. 1. 43
Susa	cavalry and foot under Amyntas				4,000		A. 3. 16. 10; C. 5. 2. 16
Persepolis					3,000		C. 5. 6. 11
Media	5,000	1,000	some Thessalian cavalry and 11,200	600			C. 5. 7. 12; A. 3. 19. 5; C. 7. 3. 4; cf. A. 3. 19. 8
Hyrcania	1,500	mounted javelin men					C. 6. 5. 10; D. 17. 76. 2; A. 3. 23. 9; A. 3. 24. 1
Artacoana	5,600	930		40			C. 6. 6. 35; A. 3. 25. 2–5
Arachosia	11,200 and Arachosian and Parapanisadae cavalry	600			4,000	600	C. 7. 3. 4; A. 5. 11. 3; C. 7. 3. 5

							References
Oxus	900 oldest Macedonians and Thessalian volunteers						A. 3. 29. 5; C. 7. 5. 27
Maracanda			1,200	820			A. 4. 3. 7–4. 6. 2; cf. C. 7. 7.39
Jaxartes			100	60			C. 7. 9. 16
Bactra	19,400	2,600	100	67			C. 7. 10. 11–12; cf. A. 4. 7. 2; A. 4. 16. 7
Rock of Ariamazes			32				C. 7. 11. 19
Bactra				300			C. 8. 1. 3–5
Xenippa			80				C. 8. 2. 17; cf. A. 4. 17. 6
Gazaca			20				C. 8. 4. 13
Sogdia		Sogdian, Bactrian, Scythian, Dahaean cavalry			10,000	3,500	A. 4. 22. 3; A. 5. 12. 2
Total:	99,064	13,810	14,032	1,887	24,000	4,100	
Sub Total: (Reinforcements minus losses and garrisons)	61,032	7,823					

Note: See note on tables 4 to 6, p. 151.

Table 6

Approximate Troop Numbers in Alexander's Army: India

Location	Reinforcements		Losses		Garrisons		Reference
	inf.	cav.	inf.	cav.	inf.	cav.	
Massaga	61,032	7,823	25				A. 4. 27. 4
Peucelaotis					Macedonian garrison		A. 4. 28. 6
Aornos	Indians				guard		D. 17. 86. 3; A. 4. 30.4
Indus		1,000					A. 5. 2. 2; A. 5. 3. 6
Taxila	5,000				garrison		A. 5. 8. 5; A. 5. 8. 3
Jhelum			700	280			D. 17. 89. 3
Sangala			100				A. 5. 24. 5
Hydaspes	30,000 Asian 7,000 Greek	5,000					D. 17. 95. 4; C. 9. 3. 21; cf. C. 8. 5. 1
Mallians		2,500	25				C. 9. 7. 14; A. 6. 7. 4
Oxydracae		500					A. 6. 14. 3
Acesines					Thracian garrison		A. 6. 15. 2
Musicanus' city					garrison		A. 6. 15. 7
Musicanus' country					garrison		A. 6. 17. 1
Sudracae		1,330					C. 9. 8. 1
Pattala					garrison		A. 6. 20. 5
Total:	103,032	18,153	850	280			
Sub Total: (Reinforcements minus losses and garrisons)	102,182	17,873					

Note: See note on tables 4 to 6, p. 151.

NOTES ON TABLES 4 TO 6

It is not the purpose of this study to argue the numbers of combatants or followers in Alexander's army. It has been repeatedly stressed that the precise numbers in the army is not a major factor in calculating the capabilities and limitations of the Macedonians' logistic system. The most significant factor is the important ratio between the carrying capability of the system and its consumption rate. This relationship remains constant no matter how many personnel and animals are in the army (see above Chapter 1). Nevertheless, the figures in tables 4 to 6 are provided to give an idea of the order of magnitude of the army's requirements of food and water throughout the expedition. No claim is made for precision. The method used here is to list all numerical references to troops killed, established in garrisons, or enrolled in the army as reinforcements as given in our ancient sources. If the reader disagrees with these figures, he may substitute his own, whatever they may be based upon.

It has long been recognized that D. 17. 3–5 provides the most accurate troop total for Alexander's army at the Hellespont (P. A. Brunt, "Alexander's Macedonian Cavalry," *JHS* 83 [1963] 32–34; Green, 156; Marsden, op. cit., 24 f.), and it is in close agreement with the figures provided by Arrian. We also accept the arguments of Brunt that the advanced expedition operating in Anatolia under the command of Parmenio (D. 16. 91. 2) numbered approximately 10,000 infantry and 1,000 cavalry. Of course, Diodorus' and Arrian's figures were recorded before the army crossed the Hellespont (D. 17. 4; A. 1. 11. 3). We use, then, D. 17. 3–5 plus the troops in the advance expedition as our initial figure. The figures listed as reinforcements on the top of tables 5 and 6 were taken from the subtotals on tables 4 and 5 respectively.

The highest figures available from the sources have been used for the numbers of troops killed in battles. It is clear from the Athenian loss rate of 192 men at the battle of Marathon (Hdt. 6. 117—the figure would have been well known to all Athenians, cf. Thuc. 4. 101. 2; 5. 11. 2; 5. 47. 3), out of a total force of about 10,000 that the numbers killed on the winning side of a major battle need not be large. The Macedonians were, after all, victors. The ratio between killed and wounded seems to vary with the severity of the battles fought. Curtius (3. 11. 27) listed 4,500 wounded and 452 killed at the battle of Issus, which indicates the severity of that struggle, when Darius' experienced Greek mercenaries, seeing the phalanx charge broken by the steep banks of the Pinarus, inflicted heavy casualties on the Macedonians (A. 2. 10. 5–7; C. 3. 11. 5–6). When the fighting is not hotly contested, the ratio between killed and wounded can be about 1 : 5 (C. 8. 2. 18) or 1 : 6 (C. 7. 9. 16). When fighting is severe, the ratio is as high as 1 : 12 (A. 5. 24. 5). The highest casualty figure ever recorded for Alexander's campaigns is 1,200 infantry and 820 cavalry killed in the massacre of Andromachus' force near the Bokhara Oasis in Sogdia (A. 4. 3. 7–4. 6. 2; cf. C. 7. 7. 39).

Alexander left numerous garrisons behind in conquered lands. Yet many of these garrisons were temporary (e.g., the Allied Cavalry in Syria: A. 2. 13. 7; A. 3. 11. 10; at Celaenae: C. 4. 1. 35; and the garrisons established near Ora and Orabatis in India until these towns could be taken: A. 4. 27. 7; A. 4. 28. 5), and the troops were returned to the main army when their functions had been fulfilled. In addition, Alexander sometimes used local troops, not enrolled in his own army, for garrisons (A. 5. 24. 8). When the sources do not list the cavalry-infantry composition of the garrisons, all the troops will be listed as infantry for the sake of convenience. One must not assume, then, that all garrisons are necessarily composed of units from the Macedonian army, or that they were all permanent. We have included all garrisons established in Bactrian and Sogdian towns (e.g., C. 7. 10. 10; C. 7. 6. 10; A. 3. 29. 1) in the 10,000 infantry and 3,500 cavalry Alexander left behind in Sogdia and Bactria (A. 4. 22. 3).

Coenus (A. 5. 27. 6), in his speech to the king urging him to turn back from the Beas, noted that a great many troops were lost through illness, and no doubt this was true. Unfortunately, there are no references in the sources concerning the numbers lost through disease.

However, the Macedonian army often received massive reinforcements of native troops, but their numbers are unrecorded. The first of these reinforcements recorded are the mounted javelin men, whom Alexander recruited in Media or Hyrcania (A. 3. 24. 1). In Bactria and Sogdia, large, powerful cavalry units of Bactrians, Sogdians, Scythians, and Dahaeans were enrolled, and they play an important part in the battle with Porus (A. 4. 17. 3; A. 5. 12. 2). Forces from Arachosia, the Parapanisadae, and India were also enrolled (A. 5. 11. 3; D. 86. 3), but their numbers were never recorded. There is no possibility of estimating how many troops were lost in garrisons or through illness or were enrolled as reinforcements when their figures are not recorded by our sources. Hence, these tables can only give approximate figures.

There are only two passages from our ancient evidence which seem difficult to reconcile at first sight: C. 9. 3. 21 and D. 95. 4, for the reinforcements at the Hydaspes (which both mistakenly call the Acesines). However, there does not seem to be any real confusion. Diodorus recorded reinforcements of somewhat less than 6,000 cavalry, allied, and mercenary troops, and 30,000 infantry. The 30,000 infantry are those 30,000 Asian troops ordered by Alexander before he entered India (C. 8. 5. 1) in late spring of 327, who, naturally, did not arrive instantaneously (since it would have taken a considerable time to walk the distance) but at the Hydaspes in 326. The less than 6,000 cavalry of Diodorus are the 5,000 cavalry commanded by Memnon of Thrace recorded by Curtius, and the allied and mercenary troops are 7,000 foot soldiers from Harpalus recorded by Curtius. Curtius, having already mentioned the king's order for the 30,000 Asian infantry, does not record their number again when they arrived.

There are three, and perhaps four, external, independent checks on the accuracy and consistency of the figures in the tables, from reliable sources. The first is Polyb. 12. 19. 3, who recorded 42,000 infantry and 5,000 cavalry, a total of 47,000 men, at the battle of Issus in November of 333. Our table lists 40,864 foot and 6,280 cavalry, a total of 47,126, as the strength of the Macedonian army before that battle, or a difference of 0.3% from Polybius' total figure. The next check occurs for the battle of Gaugamela in late September or early October of 331, where Arrian (3. 12. 5) lists about (*amphi*) 40,000 infantry and 7,000 cavalry, or a total of about 47,000. Our table lists 42,864 infantry and 6,580 cavalry, or a total of 49,444, a total difference of 5%. Marsden (op. cit., 27f.), who has made the most thorough study on the numbers of troops at the battle, believes that the number of Macedonian infantry before that battle numbered about 43,000. Both Arrian (*Ind.* 19. 5) and Curtius (8. 5. 4) record the greatest number of troops in the Macedonian army in India as 120,000. Our Table 6 lists a total of 120,055 troops or a difference of .04%. In addition, the approximate numbers of troops, followers, and cavalry can be estimated at the time of the army's crossing of the Hindu Kush in late spring of 329 (see above, p. 95). As we have noted throughout this study, there is a real, measurable relationship between time, distance, and numbers. This relationship supports a total of about 100,000 troops and followers, and 12,000 cavalry horses, which is close to our estimate of 96,000 troops and followers and 10,000 cavalry. Our estimate did not include the numbers of pack animals. The rather close correspondence between these external checks and the figures in our tables leads us to believe that the error contained within them is not large.

Table 7

Alexander's March Rates

Location	Rate	Units	Reference
Pelinna—Border of Boeotia	18.9 mpd. (?)	whole army	A. 1. 7. 5
Onchestus—Thebes	10.5 mpd.	whole army	A. 1. 7. 7
Therma(?)—Sestos	16.2 mpd.	whole army	A. 1. 11. 5
Arisbe—Percote	7 mpd.	whole army	A. 1. 12. 6
Percote—Praktios River	c. 11 mpd.	whole army	A. 1. 12. 6
Sardis—Ephesus	15 mpd.	whole army	A. 1. 17. 10
Gaza—Pelusium	19.5 mpd.	whole army	A. 3. 1. 1
Paraetonium— Ammon Oracle	22.5 mpd.	small, light force	D. 49. 3–5
Assyria	c. 46 mpd.	cavalry only	A. 3. 15. 5
Babylon—Susa	12.3 mpd.	whole army	A. 3. 16. 7
Ecbatana—Rhagae	22 mpd. (?)	Companions' cavalry, mounted scouts, mercenary horse, part of phalanx, archers and Agrianians	A. 3. 20. 2
Rhagae—Airankief	34 mpd.	same as above	A. 3. 20. 2
Comisene	45 miles in c. 12 hours	500 mounted infantry	A. 3. 21. 9
Comisene	c. 33.3 mpd.	same as from Ecbatana—Rhagae	A. 3. 20. 2– 3. 21. 9
Parthia	34.4 mpd.	Companions' cavalry, mounted javelin men, archers, 2 phalanx brigades	A. 3. 25. 6
Sogdiana (Oxus to Nautaka?)	c. 37.5– 42.5 mpd.	3 regiments Companions' cavalry, mounted javelin men, 1 phalanx brigade, regiment of bodyguard, Agrianians, ½ archers	A. 3. 29. 7

Table 7 (Continued)

Location	Rate	Units	Reference
Sogdiana (Alexandria Eschate to Maracanda?)	43?–57.5 mpd.	½ Companions' cavalry, archers, Agrianians, lightest of phalanx	A. 4. 6. 4
Mallians' Territory	c. 30.6 mpd.	bodyguard, archers, Agrianians, 1 brigade infantry Companions, mounted archers, ½ Companions' cavalry	A. 6. 6. 2
Oreitans' Territory to Pura	10.5–13 ? mpd.	whole army minus fleet and Craterus' force	Str. 15. 2. 7; A. 6. 24. 1

NOTE ON TABLE 7

A great deal of confusion exists concerning the march rates achieved by the Macedonian army. This confusion is not the result of any lack of cataloging evidence (e.g., Neumann, op. cit., Milnes, op. cit.), but rather of a failure to understand what the evidence means.

As anyone delayed in heavy vehicular traffic knows, large groups of individuals move much more slowly than smaller groups. Likewise, large armies are slower than small ones (Maurice, 212). The reason for this is the length of an army's column while on the march. If Alexander's army had, say, 65,000 personnel and 6,000 cavalry, and the terrain allowed the personnel to march 10 abreast and the cavalry 5 abreast, their column would extend for some 16.5 miles (Maurice, 229). This excludes any space needed for baggage animals and animals carrying provisions. This column length has two significant implications for the army's march rate.

First, when the soldiers at the head of the column were filing into camp at the end of a day's march, those at the rear would not reach camp for over 5 hours if they marched at the standard march speed for infantry, 2.5 to 3 mph. (Maurice, 229; Neumann, op. cit., 197–198; Milnes, op. cit., 256, 3 mph. over open terrain and 2.5 mph. over difficult terrain). Thus, the army's marching time would have to be reduced to allow the troops at the end of the column to reach camp before nightfall.

However, much more significant are the halts that an army must make during its daily marches. First, an army must make at least one day's halt in seven days while on the march (Maurice, 212; Army Veterinary Dept., 136f., Clark and Haswell, 204). This is because horses and other baggage animals cannot withstand the pressure of riders or packs on their backs for more than five to seven consecutive marching days. If they are not rested, they will develop bleeding sores or physical damage, and will be unable to carry anything until they are completely healed. Additionally, horses and other baggage animals have large fodder requirements (see Appendix 1) and since they ought to be fed only during the day (hard-working horses, like hard-working people, need all the sleep they can get at night, Smith, *Veterinary Hygiene*, 145–148), it is necessary to allow one day's grazing in five to seven days or they will become malnourished and exhausted, becoming a burden that the army will have to leave behind. It is certain that Alexander or any competent commander would never allow such conditions to exist.

In addition to these day-long halts, the army will make several short halts during the course of its daily march. The Army Veterinary Department (137) recommends that one halt for a few minutes be made after the first one or two miles to adjust harnesses and tighten girths; a short halt of five to ten minutes every hour; and at two- to three-hour intervals, a long halt to feed the horses and off-saddle.

Since the cavalry and baggage regularly followed the infantry (A. 2. 8. 3; Polyb. 12. 19. 5; C. 4. 12. 3; C. 6. 4. 15), these halts would not impede the progress of the entire army. But if it were necessary for the entire army to halt during the course of their daily march for their midday meal or for some other reason, the following situation would occur. If the army had 65,000 personnel marching 10 abreast and 6,000 cavalry traveling 5 abreast, each file would contain 6,500 individuals and 1,200 cavalry horses. Now, when the individuals started on the march once more after a halt, the entire file would not begin marching instantaneously; first the first man would begin, then the second man, and so on until the last individual in the file began to move. If it took only a second between the time one soldier started and the next man in line began to march, it would take over two hours before the rear of the line began to move. Hence, wherever possible, the army would try to march with as broad a front as possible to reduce the length of its column. This is also why it was essential for road builders to precede the army on its march (A. 1. 26. 1; cf. Josephus, *BJ* 3. 6. 115–126), for if the army were held up only for a minute by some obstacle, it would still take the whole force a considerable time to begin moving again. It also explains why placing obstacles in front of a column of marching soldiers to impede their progress is a common and effective procedure (Huston, op. cit., 53). Of course, the same problem was faced initially each day when the army filed out of camp in the morning.

It is for these reasons that the march rate of a large army is utterly incommensurable with that of a small force. Hence, when comparisons are made between the march rate of Alexander's entire army (e.g., from Mallus to Myriandrus) and 6,000 light infantry and cavalry in light marching order under Masséna (e.g., Fuller, op. cit., 156) with no mountain passes to cross (T. A. Dodge, *Napoleon* [Boston, 1904] 382f.) we will reject them immediately. We will also reject the notion that an army of 47,000 combatants marching with elephants can achieve a march rate of 40 mpd. for seven consecutive days (Diod. 18. 44–45). No elephant, living or dead, could possibly achieve a rate of 40 mpd., or even 10 mpd. (Leonard, op. cit., 281f.). Nor when we read that Alexander made his *stathmoi*, or encampments, at intervals of 70 miles to conserve supplies in the Gedrosian Desert (Str. 15. 2. 6) will we believe that Alexander made his daily marches 70 miles long. *Stathmoi* have nothing to do with a day's march in this context: Cyrus also made his *stathmoi* longer while marching through the desert (Xen. *Anab.* 1. 5. 7); he did not make the days longer. It undoubtedly took the Macedonians three days of continuous marching to reach a site at a 70-mile interval where sufficient water and supplies would be available for a camp. No army even approaching the size of Alexander's beleaguered force in the Gedrosia could achieve a march rate of 70 mpd. Nor is comparison valid between Alexander's entire force and other armies supplied by fleets (cf. Polyb. 3. 39. 6), or those using different harnessing techniques or modern methods of transport.

Small, light units of Alexander's army were capable of great speed, as much as 40 or even 50 mpd. The maximum recorded rate for the *entire* army, however, is 19.5 mpd. and it is doubtful whether this rate could ever be surpassed under any conditions. Notably, when the army achieved this rate in the Sinai, it was provisioned by the fleet, and hence its transport problems were reduced. The army's average rate of speed over long distances, which included day-long halts every five to seven days, was about 13 mpd. (Therma-Sestos, Babylon-Susa, Oreitans-Pura). This would be equivalent to a 15-mpd. daily rate with one day's halt in seven. The army's daily rate for short distances, when long halts need not have been made, was about 14 mpd. (cf. Marsden, op. cit., 20, who estimates the Macedonians could achieve 15 mpd. for four to five days at a stretch). Averages, of course, are always imperfect reflections of reality, since they do not include the numerous political, strategic, climatic, geographical, and logistic factors that influence the decision of how far the army would march on a given day. Nevertheless, when we suggest approximate times the army took to march specified distances, these will be based on a daily march rate of 15 mpd. with one day's halt in seven. In table 7, when the exact routes Alexander traveled are unknown, a question mark is placed after the figure in the "Rate" column.

Table 8

The Bematists' Measurements

City	Pliny 6. 61-62		Strabo 11. 8. 9		Actual Distance (English miles)
	milia passuum	English miles	Stadia	English miles	
N. Caspian Gates–Hecatompylos			1960	225	227 main road
S. Caspian Gates–Hecatompylos	133	122			125 main road
Hecatompylos–Alexandria Areion	575 (565)	529	4530	521	531 Silk Route
Alexandria Areion–Prophthasia	199	183	1600 (1500)	184	189 Herat–Juwain
Prophthasia–Arachoti Polis	565	520	4120	474	525 Juwain–Kelat-i-Ghilzai
Arachoti Polis–Hortospana	250 (165, 175, 227)	230	2000	230	231 main road Kelat-i-Ghilzai–Kabul
Hortospana–Alexandria ad Caucasus	50 (variants)	46			47 Kabul–Begram
Alexandria ad Caucasum–Peucolatis	237	218			211 Begram–Charsada
Peucolatis–Taxila	60	55			69 Charsada–Taxila
Taxila–Hydaspes (Jhelum)	120	110			105 Stein's route
Alexandria Areion–Bactra–Zariaspa (the route is not recorded to have been followed by Alexander himself)			3870	445	438 via Kala Nau, Bala Murghab, Maimana, and Andkhui

Note: See note on table 8, p. 158.

NOTE ON TABLE 8

This table lists the distances of the routes traveled by Alexander as measured by his bematists Diognetus and Baeton and preserved in Pliny *NH* 6. 61-62. Another similar set of measurements given by Strabo 11. 8. 9 following Eratosthenes is also included. One may add yet another bematists' measurement, that between Thapsacus (Carchemish) and the ford of the Tigris where Alexander crossed (Abu Wijam) via Carrhae, Resaina, and Thilapsum (see above, p. 68).

The Roman mile is based on a foot of 296 mm., 5,000 of which make a *mille passus* of 1,480.0 meters or 1618.5 yards (Hultsch, *Metrol. Script.* 88f.; Dar.-Sag. s.v. mensura). The length of the Greek *stadion*, whether the race course or the measurement, is 600 Greek feet. The length of the foot, however, varied from place to place, but in the stadium at Athens, the distance between the starting and finishing lines is 606' 10" based on a foot of 308.3 mm. (William Bell Dinsmoor, *The Architecture of Ancient Greece* [New York, 1973] 251). One Attic *stadion* is one-eighth of a Roman mile (Pliny *NH* 2. 85) or 606' 10". Eratosthenes, Strabo's source, regularly used Attic *stadia*.

All routes in the table are measured from the main roads between the two locations as can be found on any map of the regions. We have found the Bartholomew World Travel Series maps for the Middle East and the Indian Subcontinent of value, supplemented by the regional maps in the Naval Intelligence Division series. The distance between Alexandria ad Caucasus and Charsada is measured along the bank of the Kabul River as suggested by Caroe, op. cit., 49. The route between Taxila and the Jhelum where Alexander crossed is taken from Stein, *N. W. India*, 1-44, and supported by Str. 15. 1. 32. The distance between the Jhelum and Beas rivers is recorded as XXXIVCCCXC miles and is obviously corrupt. The actual distance is about 150 miles. Numbers in parentheses refer to variant readings in the manuscripts. I see no evidence for a short Macedonian stade.

We do not wish to imply that Prophthasia is Juwain or that Arachoti Polis is Kelat-i-Ghilzai (although this latter identification has been made). Kapisa, the modern Begram, was long ago correctly identified with Alexandria ad Caucasus and Hortospana, with Kabul (Fischer, op. cit., 159, 168). For Peucelaotis, see Sir Mortimer Wheeler, *Charsada: A Metropolis of the North West Frontier* (Oxford, 1962). For Taxila, see Sir John Marshall, *Taxila* (Cambridge, 1951). The independent, external evidence for Alexander's route from Herat to Begram is discussed in Chapter 4, and it supports, and is supported by, the bematists' measurements and the actual distance of the route.

The overall accuracy of the bematists' measures should be apparent. The minor discrepancies of distance (only 1.3% from Herat to Begram) can be adequately explained by slight changes in the tracks of roads during the last 2,300 years. The accuracy of the measurements implies that the bematists used a sophisticated mechanical device for measuring distances, undoubtedly an odometer such as described by Heron of Alexandria (A. Neuberger, *The Technical Arts and Sciences of the Ancients* [New York, 1930] 215).

Note on the Maps

Because of the limitations of our sources, all routes depicted on the maps are only approximate. All the maps are original and may not be reproduced without permission.

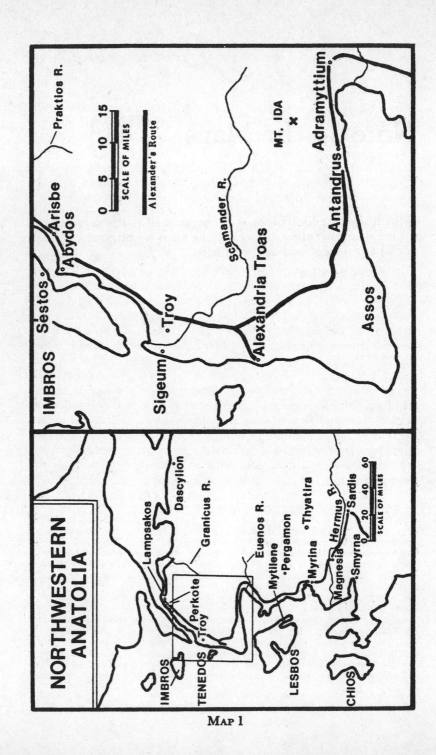

MAP 1

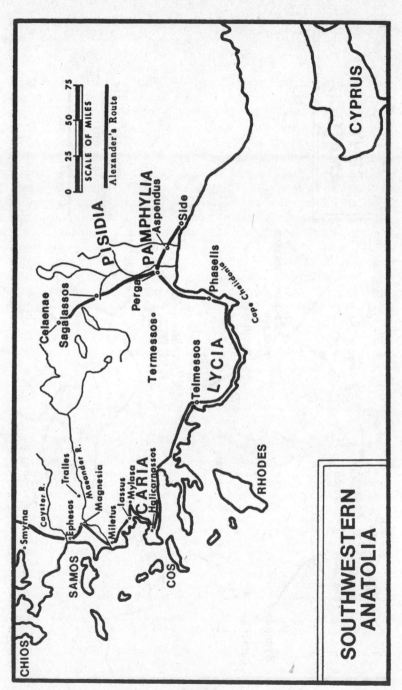

CHIOS

Smyrna

Cayster R.

Ephesos
Tralles
Magnesia
Maeander R.
Miletus
Iassus
Mylasa
CARIA
Halicarnassos

SAMOS

COS

RHODES

Telmessos
LYCIA

Termessos

Cape Chelidonia

Phaselis

Celaenae
Sagalassos

PISIDIA

Perga
PAMPHYLIA
Aspendus
Side

SCALE OF MILES
0 25 50 75
Alexander's Route

CYPRUS

SOUTHWESTERN
ANATOLIA

Map 2

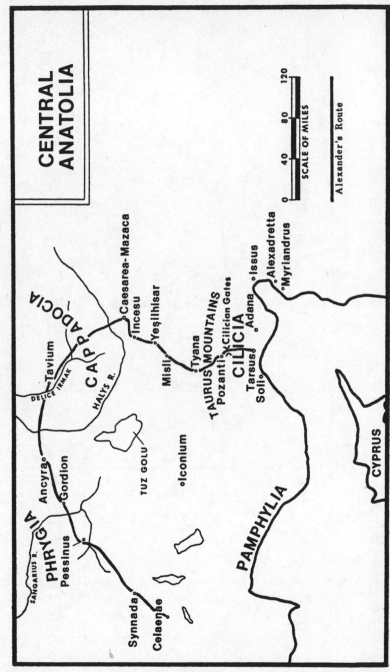

MAP 3

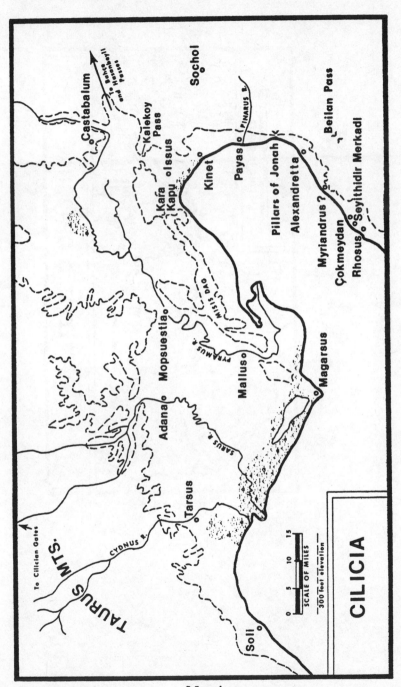

MAP 4

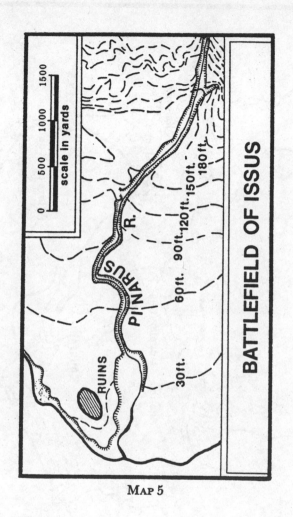

MAP 5

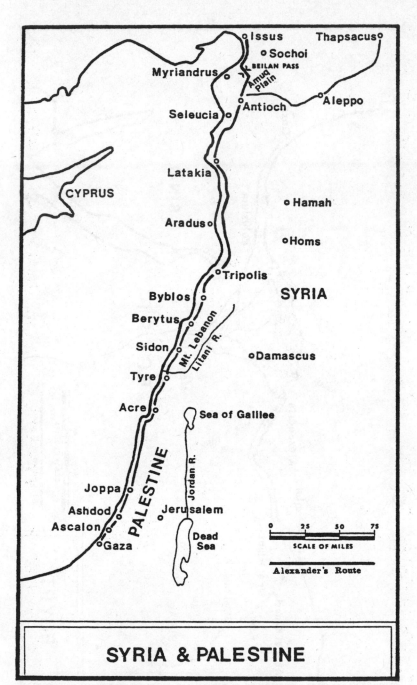

SYRIA & PALESTINE

MAP 6

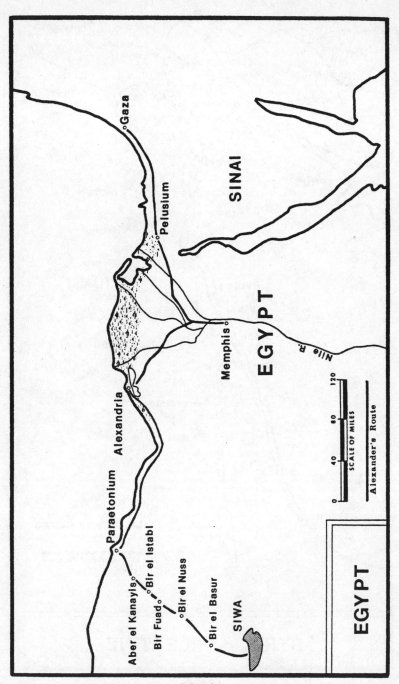

MAP 7

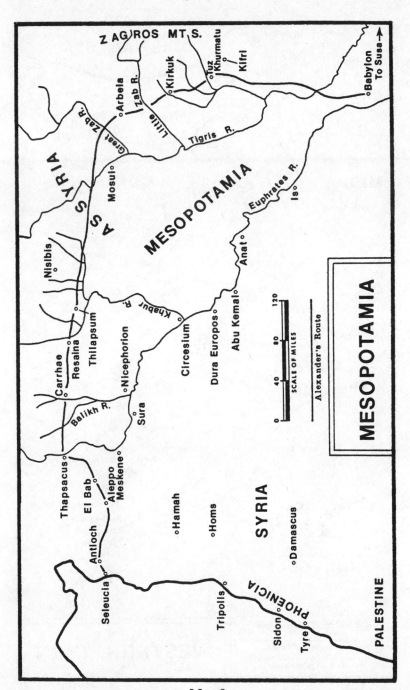

MAP 8

MAP 9

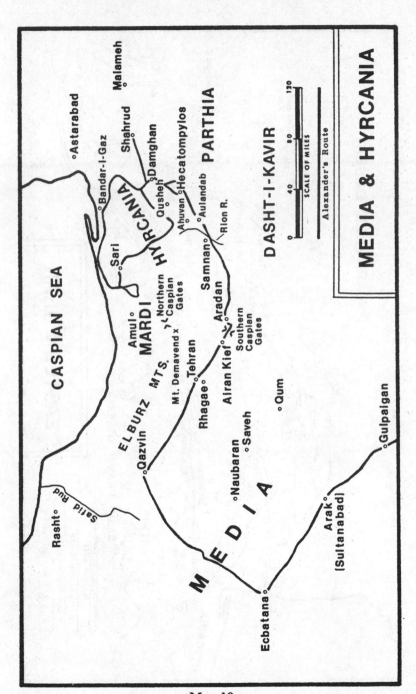

MEDIA & HYRCANIA

CASPIAN SEA

DASHT-I-KAVIR

PARTHIA

HYRCANIA

MARDI

MEDIA

ELBURZ MTS.

Malameh

Astarabad

Shahrud

Bandar-I-Gaz

Damghan

Qusheh

Hecatompylos

Ahuvan

Aulandab

Rion R.

Sari

Samnan

Amul

Northern
Caspian
Gates

Aradan

Mt. Demavend

Tehran

Southern
Caspian
Gates

Alran Kief

Rhagae

Qum

Naubaran

Saveh

Qazvin

Rasht

Safid Rud

Gulpaigan

Arak
[Sultanabad]

Ecbatana

SCALE OF MILES

Alexander's Route

40   80   120

MAP 10

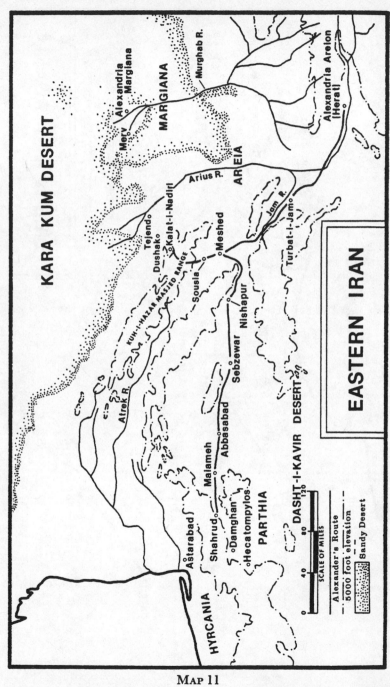

MAP 11

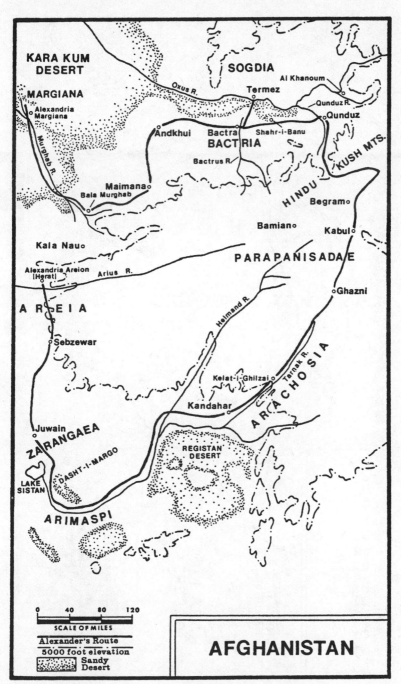

KARA KUM
DESERT

MARGIANA

Alexandria
Margiana

Murghab R.

Andkhui

Maimana
Bala Murghab

Kala Nau

Alexandria Areion
[Herat]

Arius R.

A R E I A

Sebzewar

Juwain

ZARANGAEA

DASHT-I-MARGO

LAKE
SISTAN

ARIMASPI

OXUS R.

SOGDIA

Al Khanoum

Termez

Qunduz R.

Qunduz

Bactra

BACTRIA

Shahr-i-Banu

Bactrus R.

HINDU

KUSH MTS.

Begram

Bamian

Kabul

PARAPANISADAE

Ghazni

Helmand R.

Kelat-i-Ghilzai

Tarnak R.

Kandahar

A R A C H O S I A

REGISTAN
DESERT

0   40   80   120

SCALE OF MILES

Alexander's Route

5000 foot elevation

Sandy
Desert

AFGHANISTAN

MAP 12

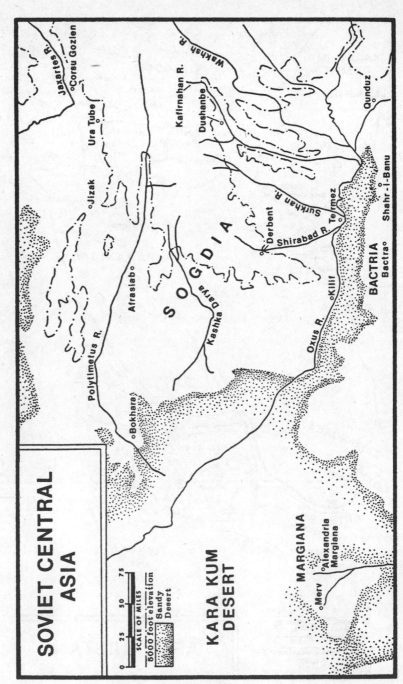

SOVIET CENTRAL ASIA

SCALE OF MILES

0   25   50   75

5600 foot elevation

Sandy
Desert

KARA KUM
DESERT

MARGIANA

Merv
Alexandria
Margiana

Corsu Gozlen

Jaxartes R.

Ura Tube

Jizak

Afrasiab

Polytimetus R.

Bokhara

Kashka Darya

SOGDIA

Kafirnahan R.

Dushanbe

Wakhsh R.

Qunduz

Derbent

Shirabad R.

Surkhan R.

Termez

Shahr-i-Banu

BACTRIA

Bactra

Kilif

Oxus R.

MAP 13

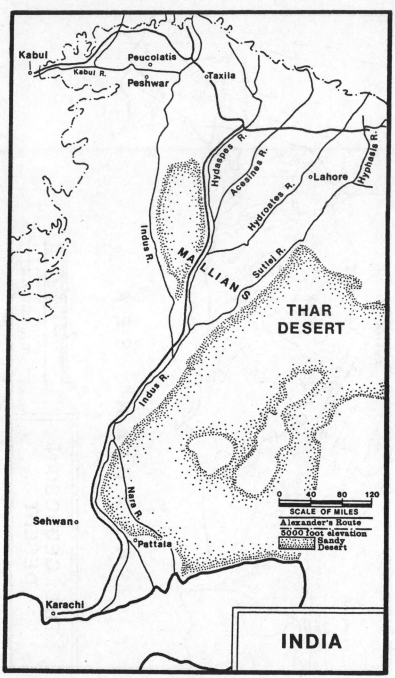

Kabul

Kabul R.

Peucolatis

Peshwar

Taxila

Hydaspes R.

Acesines R.

Lahore

Hydroates R.

Hyphasis R.

M A L L I A N S

Indus R.

Sutlej R.

THAR
DESERT

Indus R.

Nara R.

Sehwan

Pattala

0   40   80   120
SCALE OF MILES
Alexander's Route
5000 foot elevation
Sandy
Desert

Karachi

INDIA

MAP 14

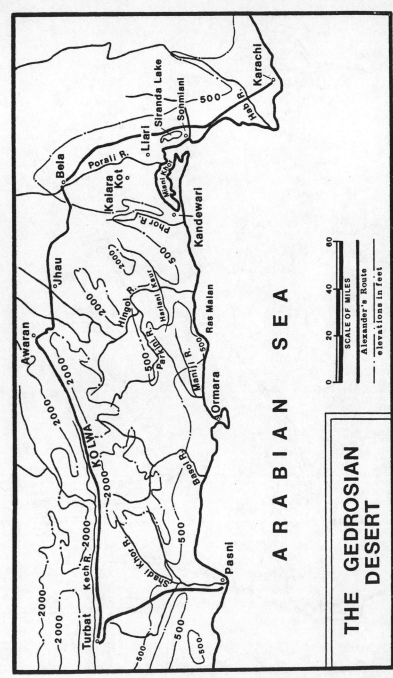

ARABIAN SEA

THE GEDROSIAN
DESERT

SCALE OF MILES

Alexander's Route
elevations in feet

MAP 15

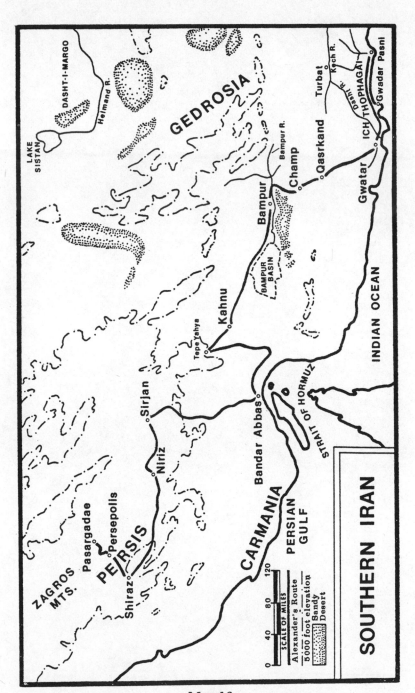

SOUTHERN IRAN

MAP 16

Bibliography

ANCIENT SOURCES

NOTE. Translations of ancient authors are based on the Loeb editions.

Arrian. *History of Alexander and Indica*, ed. and trans. E. Iliff Robson. 2 vols. Loeb Classical Library, London, 1929.

Curtius. *History of Alexander*, ed. and trans. J. C. Rolfe. 2 vols. Loeb Classical Library, Cambridge, Mass., 1946.

Diodorus Siculus, *Diodorus of Sicily*, Books 16. 66–95; 17, ed. and trans. C. Bradford Welles. Loeb Classical Library, London, 1963.

Frontinus. *The Stratagems and the Aqueducts of Rome*, ed. and trans. Charles E. Bennett. Loeb Classical Library, Cambridge, Mass., 1925.

Justin. *Epitome Historiarum Philippicarum Pompei Trogi*, ed. Otto Seel. Teubner Classical Texts, Stuttgart, 1935.

Pliny. *Natural History*, Books 3–7, ed. and trans. H. Rackham. Loeb Classical Library, Cambridge, Mass., 1942.

Plutarch. *Life of Alexander*, ed. and trans. B. Perrin. Loeb Classical Library, London, 1919.

Polyaenus. *Strategemata*, ed. Edward Woelfflin and John Melber. Teubner Classical Texts, Leipzig, 1970.

Strabo. *The Geography of Strabo*, ed. and trans. Horace Leonard Jones. 8 vols. Loeb Classical Library, London, 1917–1932.

Xenophon. *Anabasis*, ed. and trans. Carleton I. Brownson. 2 vols. Loeb Classical Library, Cambridge, Mass., 1922.

MODERN SOURCES

NOTE: This bibliography only includes sources cited in this work and is not exhaustive. Journal abbreviations follow those used in *L'Année Philologique* and the list of frequently abbreviated works on p. xiii.

Abel M. "Alexandre le Grand en Syrie et en Palestine." *Revue Biblique* 43 (1934) 528–545.

Ainsworth, William. "Notes on the Comparative Geography of the Cilician and Syrian Gates." *JRGS* 8 (1838) 185–195.

———. "The Identification of the Pinarus with the River Piyas." *PRGS* 6 (1884) 468–469.

Albaum, L. I., and Brentijes, B. *Wächter des Goldes: zur Geschichte und Kultur mittelasiatischer Völker vor dem Islam.* Berlin, 1972. 1972.

Albritton, Erret C. *Standard Values in Nutrition and Metabolism.* Philadelphia, 1954.

Altman, Philip L., and Dittmer, Dorothy S. *Metabolism.* Bethesda, Md., 1968.

Anderson, J. G. C. "The Road System of Eastern Asia Minor with the Evidence of Byzantine Campaigns." *JHS* 17 (1897) 22–44.

———. "Explorations in Asia Minor During 1898." *BSA* 4 (1897–98) 72–78.

Anderson, J. K. *Military Theory and Practice in the Age of Xenophon.* Berkeley, 1970.

Army Veterinary Department, Great Britain. *Animal Management.* London, 1908.

Atkinson, James. *Expedition into Afghanistan.* London, 1842.

Attagarryev, E., and Berdyev, O. "The Archaeological Exploration of Turkmenistan in the Years of Soviet Power." *EW* 20 (1970) 285–306.

Badian, Ernst. "Alexander the Great, 1948–67." *CW* 65 (1971) 37–56, 77–83.

———. "Alexander the Great and the Loneliness of Power," in Badian, Ernst, *Studies in Greek and Roman History.* Oxford, 1964, 192–205.

———. "The Eunuch Bagoas." *CQ* 8 (1958) 144–157.

———. "Nearchus the Cretan." *Yale Class. Stud.* 24 (1975) 147–170.

Barger, Evert. "Exploration of Ancient Sites in Northern Afghanistan." *Geo. Journ.* 93 (1939) 377–398.

Barthold, W. *Turkestan Down to the Mongol Invasion.* London, 1968.

Bauer, A. "Die Schlacht bei Issos." *Öst. Jh.* 2 (1899) 105–128.

Beek, Martin A. *Atlas of Mesopotamia.* London, 1962.

Belenitsky, Aleksander. *Central Asia.* Cleveland, 1968.

Belgrave, C. D. *Siwa: The Oasis of Jupiter Ammon.* London, 1923.

Bellew, Henry Walter. *From the Indus to the Tigris.* London, 1874.

Bellinger, A. R. *Essays on the Coinage of Alexander the Great.* Numismatic Studies, vol. 11. New York, 1963.

Beneviste, E. "La ville de Cyreschata." *Journal Asiatique* 234 (1943–45) 163–166.

Berve, H. *Das Alexanderreich auf prosopographischer Grundlage.* 2 vols. Munich, 1926.

Bevan, E. R. *The House of Seleucus.* 2 vols. London, 1902.

Bombaci, Alessio. "Ghazni." *EW* 8 (1957) 247–257.

Borza, Eugene N. "Alexander and the Return from Siwah." *Historia* 16 (1967) 369.

―――. "Cleitarchus and Diodorus' Account of Alexander." *Proc. Afr. Class. Assoc.* 2 (1968) 25–45.

―――. "Fire from Heaven: Alexander at Persepolis." *CPh* 67 (1972) 233–245.

―――. "Alexander's Communications." *Proceedings of the Second International Symposium on Ancient Macedonia.* Thessalonike, 1973.

Bossert, Helmut Th. *Journ. of the Turkish Hist. Soc.* 14 (1950) 661–666.

Braudel, Fernand. *The Mediterranean and the Mediterranean World in the Age of Philip II.* 2 vols. New York, 1972.

Brown, Truesdell S. *Onesicritus: A Study in Hellenistic Historiography.* Berkeley, 1949.

Brunt, P. A. "Alexander's Macedonian Cavalry." *JHS* 83 (1963) 27–46.

Burn, A. R. "Notes on Alexander's Campaigns, 332–330 B.C." *JHS* 72 (1952) 81–91.

Burton, Benjamin T. *The Heinz Handbook of Nutrition.* New York, 1965.

Butler, Howard Crosby. "Desert Syria: Land of a Lost Civilization." *Geo. Rev.* 9 (1920) 77–108.

Caroe, Olaf. *The Pathans: 550 B.C.–A.D. 1957.* New York, 1958.

Casson, Lionel. *Ships and Seamanship in the Ancient World.* Princeton, 1971.

Chang, Jen-Hu. "The Indian Summer Monsoon." *Geo. Rev.* 57 (1967) 373–396.

Chisholm, Michael. *Rural Settlement and Land Use: An Essay in Location.* London, 1968.

Clark, Colin, and Haswell, Margaret. *The Economics of Subsistence Agriculture.* London, 1970.

Conolly, Lt. Arthur. *Journey to the North of India Overland from England.* 2 vols. London, 1838.

Cook, G. A. *A Textbook of North Semitic Inscriptions.* New York, 1903.

Cordington, K. DeB. "A Geographical Introduction to the History of Central Asia." *Geo. Journ.* 104 (1944) 27–40, 73–91.

Cornwall, J. H. M. "A Journey in Anatolia." *Geo. Journ.* 64 (1924) 213–222.

Cunningham, Alexander. *The Ancient Geography of India.* London, 1871.

Curzon, Lord George N. *Persia and the Persian Question.* 2 vols. London, 1966.

Dales, George F., Jr. "A Search for Ancient Sea Routes." *Expedition* 4 (1962) 2–11.

———. "Harappan Outposts on the Makran Coast." *Antiquity* 36 (1962) 86–96.

De Planhol, Xavier. *De la plaine Pamphylienne aux lacs Pisidiens.* Paris, 1958.

Des Noettes, Lefebvre. *L'attelage: le cheval de selle à travers les âges.* Paris, 1931.

Dewdney, J. C. *Turkey: An Introductory Geography.* New York, 1971.

Dicks, D. R. *Early Greek Astronomy to Aristotle.* Ithaca, 1970.

Dieulafoy, Marcel. "La bataille d'Issus: analyse critique d'un travail manuscrit du Commandant Bourgeois." *Mem. Instit. Nat. France Acad. Inscr. et Belles-Lettres* 39 (1914) 41–76.

Dillemann, Louis. *Haute Mésopotamie orientale et pays adjacents.* Paris, 1962.

Dinsmoor, William B. *Archons of Athens.* Cambridge, 1931.

———. *The Architecture of Ancient Greece.* New York, 1973.

Directorate General of Antiquities, Iraq. *Map of Ancient Sites of Iraq.* Baghdad, 1954.

Dittberner, W. *Issos, ein Beitrag zur Geschichte Alexanders des Grossen.* Berlin, 1908.

Droysen, J. G. *Histoire de l'Hellénisme,* vol. 1. trans. A. Bouche-Leclercq. Paris, 1883.

Dupont-Sommer, A. "Une inscription araméenne inédite de Bahadirli (Cilicie)." *Jahrbuch fuer Kleinasiatische Forshung* 2 (1965) 200–209.

Dussaud, René. *Topographie historique de la Syrie antique et mediévale.* Paris, 1927.

Ehlers, E. "Klimageschichte und Siedlungsgang in vor— und frühgeschichtlicher Zeit in der Turkmensteppe Nordpersiens." *Arch. Mitt. Iran* 4 (1971) 7–21.

Elgood, P. G. *Egypt and the Army.* London, 1924.

Erinc, Sirri. "Climatic Types and the Variation of Moisture Regions in Turkey." *Geo. Rev.* 40 (1950) 224–235.

Evenari, Michael. *The Negev: The Challenge of a Desert.* Cambridge, 1971.

Fairservis, Walter A., Jr. "Archaeological Studies in the Seistan Basin of South Western Afghanistan and Eastern Iran." *Anthropological Papers of the American Museum of Natural History* 48.1 (1961).

———. *The Roots of Ancient India.* New York, 1971.

Farrell, W. J. "A Revised Itinerary of the Route Followed by Cyrus the Younger Through Syria." *JHS* 81 (1961) 153–155.

Field, Henry. *An Anthropological Reconnaissance in West Pakistan, 1955.* Papers of the Peabody Museum of Archaeology and Ethnology, vol. 52. 1959.

Finley, M. I. *The Ancient Economy.* Berkeley, 1973.

Fischer, Klaus. "Zur Lage von Kandahar an Landverbindungen zwischen Iran und Indien." *Bonner Jahrbucher* 167 (1967) 129–232.

———. "Preliminary Notes on Some Ancient Remains at Qunduz." *Afghanistan* 1 (1961) 12–13.

———. "Historical, Geographical, and Philological Studies in Seistan by Bosworth, Daffinà, and Gnoli in the Light of Recent Archaeological Field Surveys." *EW* 21 (1971) 45–51.

Fisher, W. B. *The Middle East: A Physical, Social, and Regional Geography.* London, 1961.

———, ed. *Cambridge History of Iran.* vol. 1. Cambridge, 1968.

Flottwell, V. "Aus dem Stromgebiet des Qyzyl-Yrmaq (Halys)." *Pett. Mitt. Ergänzungsheft* 24 (1894–95) 114.

Forbes, R. J. *Studies in Ancient Technology,* vol. 2. Leiden, 1965.

Foucher, A., and Bazin-Foucher, E. *La vieille route de l'Inde de Bactres à Taxila.* 2 vols. *MDAFA* 1 (1942).

———. "Notes sur l'itinéraire de Hiun-Tsang en Afghanistan." *Études asiatiques publiées à l'occasion du 25e anniversaire de l'Ecole française d'Extréme Orient,* vol. 1. Paris, 1925, 278–307.

Fox, Robin Lane. *Alexander the Great.* New York, 1974.

Fraser, P. M. *Ptolemaic Alexandria.* 3 vols. Oxford, 1972.

Freeman, Douglas Southall. *Lee's Lieutenants: A Study in Command.* 3 vols. New York, 1944.

French, D. H. "A Study of Roman Roads in Anatolia." *Anatolian Studies* 24 (1974) 143–149.

Frumkin, Grégoire. *Archaeology in Soviet Central Asia.* Leiden, 1970.

Fuller, J. F. C. *The Generalship of Alexander the Great.* London, 1958.

Galloway, J. P. N. "A Kurdish Village of North East Iraq." *Geo. Journ.* 124 (1958) 361–366.

Garstang, John. "Hittite Military Roads in Asia Minor." *AJA* 47 (1943) 35–62.

————, and Gurney, O. R. *The Geography of the Hittite Empire*. London, 1959.

Ghirshman, R. *Iran*. Baltimore, 1954.

Goetze, Albrecht. "An Old Babylonian Itinerary." *JCS* 7 (1953) 51–72.

Goldsmid, Maj. F. J. "Diary of Proceedings of the Mission into Mekran for Political and Survey Purposes from the 12th to 19th December, 1861." *JRGS* 33 (1863) 181–213.

Government of Pakistan. *Pakistan*. Karachi, 1953.

Grant, Col. J. A. "Route, March, with Camels, from Berber to Korosko in 1863." *PRGS* 6 (1884) 326–334.

Gray, John. *Archaeology and the Old Testament World*. New York, 1962.

Green, Peter. *Alexander of Macedon*. Harmondsworth, 1974.

Hallock, R. T. *Persepolis Fortification Tablets*. University of Chicago Oriental Institute Publications, vol. 92 Chicago, 1969.

Hamilton, J. R. "Alexander's Early Life." *GR* 12 (1965) 117–124.

————. *Plutarch Alexander: A Commentary*. Oxford, 1968.

————. "Alexander Among the Oreitae." *Historia* 21 (1972) 603–608.

Hamilton, William J. *Researches in Asia Minor, Pontus, and Armenia*. 2 vols. London, 1842.

Hammond, Norman. "An Archaeological Reconnaissance in the Helmand Valley, South Afghanistan." *EW* 20 (1970) 437–459.

Hancăr, Franz. *Das Pferd in prähistorischer und früher historischer Zeit*. Wiener Beiträge zur Kulturgeschichte und Linguistik, vol. 11. 1955.

Hansman, John. "The Problems of Qūmis." *JRAS* 100 (1968) 111–139.

————. "Elamites, Achaemenians, and Anshan." *Iran* 10 (1972) 101–125.

Harmand, J. *L'armée et le soldat à Rome*. Paris, 1967.

Harrison, J. V. "Some Routes in Southern Iran." *Geo. Journ.* 99 (1941) 113–130.

Herzfeld, E. "Sakastan." *Arch. Mitt. Iran* 4 (1932).

Hicks, E. L. "Recent Discoveries in Eastern Cilicia." *JHS* 11 (1890) 231–254.

Hilzheimer, M. "The Evolution of the Domestic Horse." *Antiquity* 9 (1935) 133–139.

Hlopina, L. I. "Southern Turkmenia in the Late Bronze Age." *EW* 22 (1972) 199–214.

Hogarth, D. G., and Wooley, C. L. *Carchemish*, vol. 1. London, 1914.

————. "The Geography of the War Theatre in the Near East." *Geo. Journ.* 45 (1915) 457–471.

Holdich, T. *The Gates of India*. London, 1910.

"Horse." *Encyclopaedia Britannica* 11 (1943).

Houtum-Schindler, Gen. A. "Notes on Some Antiquities Found in a Mound Near Damghan." *JRAS* 9 (1877) 425–427.

———. *Eastern Persian Irak.* London, 1896.

Howland, Felix. "Crossing the Hindu Kush." *Geo. Rev.* 30 (1940) 272–278.

Humulum, Johannes. *La géographie de l'Afghanistan.* Gyldendal, 1959.

Huston, James A. *The Sinews of War: Army Logistics 1775–1953.* Washington, 1966.

Imbrie, Maj. Robert Whitney. "Crossing Asia Minor: The Country of the New Turkish Republic." *National Geographic Magazine* 46 (1924) 445–472.

Jackson, A. V. Williams. *Persia, Past and Present.* New York, 1966.

———. *Constantinople to the Home of Omar Khyyam: Travels in Transcaucasia and Northern Persia for Historic and Literary Research.* New York, 1911.

Jacobsen, Thorkild, and Adams, Robert McC. "Salt and Silt in Ancient Mesopotamian Agriculture." *Science* 128 (1958) 1251–1258.

Janke, A. "Die Schlacht bei Issos." *Klio* 10 (1910) 137–177.

———. *Auf Alexanders des Grossen Pfaden.* Berlin, 1904.

Jardé, A. *Les céréales dans l'antiquité Grecque.* Paris, 1925.

Jarvis, Maj. C. S. *Yesterday and Today in Sinai.* Boston, 1932.

Jennings-Bramly, Wilfred. "A Journey to Siwah in September and October, 1896." *Geo. Journ.* 10 (1897) 597–608.

Joint Palestine Survey Commission. *Agricultural Colonization of Palestine.* Boston, 1928.

Jones, T. B. "Alexander and the Winter of 330–329 B.C." *CW* 28 (1935) 124–125.

Jordan, W. H. *The Feeding of Animals.* London, 1905.

Kinneir, John Macdonald. *Journey through Asia Minor, Armenia, and Kordistan.* London, 1818.

Kraus, W., ed. *Afghanistan.* Tuebingen, 1972.

Leaf, Walter. *Strabo on the Troad.* Cambridge, 1923.

Leonard, Maj. Arthur Glyn. *The Camel.* London, 1894.

Lessar, M. P. M. "M. P. M. Lessar's Journey from Askabad to Sarakhs." *PRGS* 4 (1882) 486–497.

———. "M P. M. Lessar's Second Journey in the Turkomen Country: Askabad to Ghurian near Herat." *PRGS* 5 (1883), 1–23.

Lewis, Robert A. "Early Irrigation in West Turkestan." *AAAG* 56 (1966) 467–491.

Lewy, Julius. "Studies in the Historic Geography of the Ancient Near East." *Orientalia* 21 (1952) 1–12, 265–292, 393–425.

Liepe, Hans-Ulrich. *Die Pferde des Latène-Oppidums Manching,* Studien an vor- und frühgeschichtlichen Tierresten Bayerns, vol. 4. Munich, 1958.

Litvinskij, B. A., and Tursunov, N. O. "The Leningrad Krater and the Louvre Sosibios Vase (Neo-Attic Art and Central Asia)." *EW* 24 (1974) 89–110.

Mallowan, M. E. L. "The Excavations at Tall Chagar Bazar and an Archaeological Survey of the Habur Region, 1934–35." *Iraq* 3 (1936) 1–59.

Markham, S. D. *The Horse in Greek Art.* New York, 1969.

Marquart, J. "Untersuchung zur Geschichte von Eran." *Philologus Suppl.* 10 (1907) 1–258.

Marsden, E. W. *The Campaign of Gaugamela.* Liverpool, 1964.

Marshall, Sir John. *Taxila.* 3 vols. Cambridge, 1951.

Marvin, Charles. *Colonel Grodelcoff's Ride from Samarcand to Herat through the Uzbek States of Afghan Turkestan.* London, 1880.

Maurice, F. "The Size of the Army of Xerxes in the Invasion of Greece, 480 B.C." *JHS* 50 (1930) 210–235.

McIntyre, James, and Richmond, I. A. "Tents of the Roman Army and Leather from Birdoswald." *Transactions of the Cumberland and Westmoreland Antiquarian and Archaeological Soc.* 34 (1934) 62–90.

M'Crindle, J. W. *The Invasion of India by Alexander the Great.* London, 1896.

Miles, Capt. S. B. "Journey from Gwadur to Karachi." *JRGS* 44 (1874) 163–182.

Milns, R. D. "Alexander's Pursuit of Darius through Iran." *Historia* 15 (1966) 256.

Miltner, Franz. "Alexanders Strategie bei Issos." *Oest. Jh.* 28 (1933) 69–78.

Morier, James. *A Journey through Persia, Armenia, and Asia Minor to Constantinople in the Years 1808 and 1809.* London, 1812.

————. *A Second Journey through Persia in the Years 1810 and 1816.* London, 1818.

Morrison, John S., and Williams, R. T. *Greek Oared Ships.* London, 1968.

Mounsey, A. H. *A Journey through the Caucasus and the Interior of Persia.* London, 1872.

Mouterde, R., and Poidebard, A. *Le limes de Chalcis.* Paris, 1945.

Mughal, Muhammad Rafique. "Excavations at Tulamba, West Pakistan." *Pakistan Archaeology* 4 (1967) 1–152.

Murison, C. L. "Darius III and the Battle of Issus." *Historia* 21 (1972) 399–423.

Murray, G. W. "The Land of Sinai." *Geo. Journ.* 119 (1953) 140–154.

Napier, Capt. G. "Extracts from a Diary of a Tour in Khorassan and Notes on the Eastern Alburz Tract." *JRGS* 46 (1876) 145–172.

Narain, A. K. *The Indo-Greeks.* Oxford, 1957.

Naval Intelligence Division, Great Britain. *Greece.* 3 vols. 1945.

———. *Turkey.* 2 vols. 1943.

———. *Syria.* 1943.

———. *Palestine and Trans-Jordan.* 1943.

———. *Persia.* 1945.

Naval Intelligence Division, Naval Staff, Great Britain. *A Handbook of Syria.* London, n.d.

Naval Staff, Intelligence Department, Great Britain. *A Handbook of Asia Minor.* 4 vols. London, 1919.

Neuberger, A. *The Technical Arts and Sciences of the Ancients.* New York, 1930.

Neumann, C. "A Note on Alexander's March Rates." *Historia* 20 (1971) 196–198.

Newton, C. T. *Discoveries at Halicarnassus, Cnidus, and Branchidae.* London, 1863.

Oakey, George. *Military Routes of Communication in Asia Minor.* M.A. Thesis, University of Pennsylvania, 1958.

Oates, David. *Studies in the Ancient History of Northern Iraq.* London, 1968.

Oberhummer, Roman, and Zimmerer, Heinrich. *Durch Syrien und Kleinasien.* Berlin, 1899.

O'Donovan, Edmond. "Merv and its Surroundings." *PRGS* 4 (1882) 345–358.

Olufsen, O. *The Emir of Bukhara and his Country.* Copenhagen, 1911.

Operations Research Office, U.S. Army. *Area Handbook, Iran.* Washington, 1963.

Oppenheim, A. Leo. *Mesopotamia: Portrait of a Dead Civilization.* Chicago, 1964.

Pearson, L. *The Lost Histories of Alexander the Great.* New York, 1960.

Pédech, P. "Deux campagnes d'Antiochus III chez Polybe." *REA* 60 (1958) 67–81.

"Persis." *Encyclopaedia Britannica* 17 (1943).

Poidebard, A. *La trace de Rome dans le désert de Syrie.* Paris, 1934.

Porter, Sir Robert Ker. *Travels in Georgia, Persia, Armenia, Ancient Babylonia.* 2 vols. London, 1822.

Pritchett, William Kendrick. *Ancient Greek Military Practices,* pt. 1, University of California Publications: Classical Studies, vol. 7. Berkeley, 1971.

Radet, G. "La dernière campagne d'Alexandre contre Darius." *Mélanges Gustave Glotz,* vol. 2. Paris, 1932.

Raikes, Robert L. "The End of Ancient Cities of the Indus Civilization in Sind and Baluchistan." *Amer. Anthropologist* 65 (1963) 655–659.

Ramsay, W. M. *Historical Geography of Asia Minor.* London, 1890.

———. "Cilicia, Tarsus, and the Great Tarsus Pass." *Geo. Journ.* 22 (1903) 357–413.

Richmond, I. A. "Trajan's Army on Trajan's Column." *BSR* 13 (1935) 1–40.

Rickmers, W. Rickmer. "The Fan Mountains in the Duab of Turkestan." *Geo. Journ.* 30 (1907) 357–371.

Riley, H. *The Mule.* New York, 1867.

Robert, L. "Contributions à la topographie des villes de l'Asie Mineure méridionale." *CRAI* (1951) 254–259.

Roberts, Isaac Philips. *The Horse.* New York, 1905.

Runciman, Steven. *A History of the Crusades.* vol 1. Cambridge, 1952.

Russell, Franklin. "The Road to Ur." *Horizon* 14 (1972) 90–103.

Scerrato, Umberto. "A Probable Achaemenid Zone in Persian Sistan." *EW* 13 (1962) 186–197.

———. "Excavations at Dahn-i Ghulaman (Seistan-Iran): First Preliminary Report (1962–63)." *EW* 16 (1966) 9–30.

Schachermeyr, Fritz. *Alexander der Grosse.* Vienna, 1972.

Schaefer, Ch. *Nouveaux Mélanges Orientaux.* Publications de l'Ecole des Langues Orientales Vivantes. Paris, 1886.

Schreider, Frank and Helen. "The World of Alexander," in National Geographic Society, *Greece and Rome, Builders of Our World.* Washington, 1968.

Seton-Williams, M. V. "Cilician Survey." *Anatolian Studies* 4 (1954) 121–174.

Smith, Maj. Gen. Sir. F. *A Manual of Veterinary Hygiene.* New York, 1906.

———. "Maximum Muscular Effort of the Horse." *Journal of Physiology* 19 (1896) 224–226.

———. "The Relationship between the Weight of a Horse and its

Weight-Carrying Power." *Journal of Comparative Pathology and Therapeutics* 11 (1898) 287–290.

Snead, Rodman. "Recent Morphological Changes Along the Coast of West Pakistan." *AAAG* 55 (1965) 648.

———. *Physical Geography Reconnaissance: Las Bela Coastal Plain, West Pakistan.* Baton Rouge, 1966.

———. *Physical Geography Reconnaissance: West Pakistan Coastal Zone.* University of New Mexico Publications in Geography, no. 1. Albuquerque, 1969.

Snodgrass, A. M. *The Arms and Armor of the Greeks.* Ithaca, 1967.

Spate, O. H., and Learmonth, A. T. A. *India and Pakistan.* London, 1967.

Spooner, Brian. "Arghiyān, the Area of Jārjam in Western Khurāssān." *Iran* 3 (1965) 97–107.

Stark, Freya. "Alexander's Minor Campaigns in Turkey." *Geo. Journ.* 122 (1956) 294–305.

———. "Alexander's March from Miletus to Phrygia." *JHS* 78 (1958) 102–120.

———. *Alexander's Path from Caria to Cilicia.* London, 1958.

Starr, Frederick S. "Mapping Ancient Roads in Anatolia." *Archaeology* 16 (1963) 162–169.

Staviskij, Boris J. "The Capitals of Ancient Bactria." *EW* 23 (1973) 265–277.

Stein, Sir Aurel. *An Archaeological Tour in Gedrosia,* Mem. Arch. Surv. India, vol. 43. 1931.

———. "On Alexander's Route into Gedrosia: An Archaeological Tour in Las Bela." *Geo. Journ.* 102 (1943) 193–227.

———. "Notes on Alexander's Crossing of the Tigris and the Battle of Arbela." *Geo. Journ.* 100 (1942) 155–164.

———. "An Archaeological Journey in Western Iran." *Geo. Journ.* 92 (1938) 313–342.

———. "An Archaeological Tour in the Ancient Persis." *Geo. Journ.* 86 (1935) 489–497.

———. *On Alexander's Track to the Indus.* London, 1929.

———. *Innermost Asia.* 2 vols. London, 1928.

———. *Archaeological Reconnaissances in North Western India and South Eastern Iran.* London, 1937.

Stewart, Lt. Col. C. E. "The Country of the Tekke Turkomans and the Tejand and Murghab Rivers." *PRGS* 3 (1881) 513–546.

Strasburger, Hermann. "Alexanders Zug durch die Gedrosische Wüste." *Hermes* 80 (1952) 456–493.

————. "Zur Route Alexanders durch Gedrosien." *Hermes* 82 (1954) 251–254.

Sumner, William M. *Cultural Development in the Kur River Basin, Iran: An Archaeological Analysis of Settlement Patterns.* Ph.D. Dissertation, University of Pennsylvania, 1972.

Sykes, C. "Some Notes on a Recent Journey in Afghanistan." *Geo. Journ.* 84 (1934) 327–336.

Sykes, P. M. "A Fifth Journey in Persia." *Geo. Journ.* 28 (1906) 560–592.

Tarn, William W. *Alexander the Great.* 2 vols. Cambridge, 1948.

————. *The Greeks in Bactria and India.* London, 1938.

————. "Two Notes on Seleucid History: Tarmita." *JHS* 60 (1940) 89–94.

Tegetmeir, W. B. *Horses, Asses, Mules, and Mule Breeding.* Washington, 1897.

Thesiger, Wilfred. "The Hazaras of Central Afghanistan." *Geo. Journ.* 121 (1955) 312–319.

Topographical Section, General Staff, Great Britain. *Sinai Peninsula Map,* 1: 250,000. n.d.

Torry, William. "Life in the Camel's Shadow." *Natural History* (May 1974) 59–68.

Toynbee, Arnold J. *Between Oxus and Jumna.* Oxford, 1961.

Treidler, Hans. "Paraetacene." *RE Suppl.* 10 (1965) 478–482.

Trousdale, William. "The Homeland of Rustam." *ILN* (December 1975) 91–93.

Tscherikower, V. "Die hellenistischen Städtgrundüngen von Alexander dem Grossen bis auf die Römerzeit." *Philologus Suppl.* 19.1 (1972) 1–216.

Von Hagen, Victor W. "The Horror of the Tomissa Crossing." *Geographical Magazine* 48 (1976) 278–281.

Von Schwarz, Franz. *Alexander des Grossen Feldzüg in Turkestan.* Munich, 1893.

Von Stahl, A. F. "Notes on the March of Alexander the Great from Ecbatana to Hyrcania." *Geo. Journ.* 64 (1924) 312–329.

Warner, Arthur George, and Warner, Edmond. *The Shahnama of Firdausi.* 3 vols. London, 1908.

Welles, C. B. "The Discovery of Sarapis and the Foundation of Alexandria." *Historia* 11 (1962) 271–298.

"Wheat." *Encyclopaedia Britannica* 23 (1943).

Wheeler, Sir Mortimer. *Charsada, a Metropolis of the North West Frontier.* Oxford, 1962.

White, Lynn. *Medieval Technology and Social Change.* Oxford, 1963.

Wilhelmy, Herbert. "Indusdelta und Rann of Kutch." *Erdkunde* 22 (1968) 179–191.

Willcocks, Sir William. "Mesopotamia: Past, Present, and Future." *Geo. Journ.* 35 (1910) 1–18.

Williams, John. *Two Essays on the Geography of Ancient Asia.* London, 1829.

Wilson, Sir Arnold T. *Persia.* London, 1932.

Wilson, Col. Sir Charles. "The Identification of the Pinarus with the River Payas." *PRGS* 6 (1884) 540–541.

Wilson, H. H. *Ariana Antiqua.* London, 1841.

Wright, W. *Catalogue of Syriac Manuscripts in the British Museum,* vol. 3. London, 1872.

Young, Rodney S. "Gordion of the Royal Road." *Proceedings Amer. Philosoph. Soc.* 107 (1963) 348–364.

———. "The South Wall of Balkh-Bactra." *AJA* 59 (1955) 267–276.

Index

Ai Khanoum: 97n.111
Alexandria Areion: 33n.36, 85, 85n.
69, 91n.89, 157
Alexandria, Egypt: 33n.36, 63n.54, 158
Alexandria Eschate (Corsu Gozien?):
99, 103, 103n.19, 154
Alexandria by Oxus. See Termez
Alexandria Margiana (Giaur Kala):
33n.36, 105n.27
Alexandria Troas: 33, 33n.36
Aleppo: 41n.79, 65, 65n.63
Alliance: logistic significance of, 9,
40–41, 56. See also Surrenders
Amanic Gates. See Bahçe Pass, Hasan-
beyli Pass
Ammon, oracle of Zeus. See Siwah
Arachosia, Arachosian: harvest date
in, 93; mentioned, 28n.14, 78n.36,
111, 148, 152
Areia: 2, 15, 23n.37, 78, 80, 85, 87, 90,
91, 91n.89, 93n.92
Artacoana: 47, 87, 89, 90, 91, 148

Babylon: 11, 11n.1, 33n.36, 42, 42n.
91, 43n.91, 61, 64n.61, 66, 67, 70, 71,
71n.1, 78n.33, 148, 153, 156
Bactra: 61n.41, 97n.111, 98, 98n.113,
99, 101, 101n.7, 104, 106, 107, 149,
157
Bactria, Bactrian: climate and terrain
of, 96–97; mentioned, 2, 6, 7, 13,
41n.79, 75, 79, 86, 86n.76, 87, 89,
90, 90n.86, 91, 93n.92, 95n.102, 96–
98, 106, 151, 152
Baggage animal. See Camel, Donkey,
Horse, Mule, Ox

Bahçe Pass: 49, 50, 51, 53n.137
Beilan Pass: 44, 44n.97, 50, 51n.131,
54
Bematists: 4, 33n.36, 68, 85, 85n.69,
157–158

Camel: carrying capability of, 14, 14n.
11; feeding of, 18, 129; mentioned,
3, 14n.10, 15, 15n.12, 23, 29, 35, 40,
54, 58n.25, 62, 63, 63n.52, 63n.53,
79, 126
Cappadocia: 6, 37, 41, 42
Caria: 11, 12n.5, 35, 43n.94
Carmania: 2, 116n.83, 117, 117n.86,
117n.87, 118, 118n.91, 135, 136
Cart: use of, 12, 14, 15–16, 17n.19, 22,
24, 24n.39, 24n.40, 119. See also
Wagon
Caspian Gates: southern, 47, 80–83
passim, 85, 157; northern, 83n.61,
157
Castabalum (Bodrum): 48, 49, 50, 53n.
137
Cilicia: 38, 39, 42–53, 71n.3, 122, 133
Coenus: 12n.2, 72, 72n.6, 82, 83, 87,
106, 109, 121, 152
Comisene: 71n.3, 72n.5, 153
Craterus: 36, 36n.54, 72, 72n.6, 87, 89,
90, 106, 109, 111, 111n.57, 121
Cyropolis: 103

Damascus: 15n.12, 54, 65, 65n.63
Dascylion: 30, 31, 32, 32n.34
Dasht-i-Kavir: 3, 36n.55, 60n.39, 82
Deli Chai: 131, 133, 133n.50
Dividing of army: logistic significance

of, 9, 36, 36n.55, 61, 72, 120, 121; mentioned, 104, 106, 113
Donkey: 14, 14n.10, 16n.15, 19, 23

Ecbatana (Hamadan): 35, 74–80 *passim*, 86n.76, 153
Egypt: harvest date in, 64; mentioned, 6, 11, 11n.1, 14, 15, 59, 60n.38, 61n. 40, 62, 64, 78n.33, 100, 112, 147
Elburz Mountains: 81n.52
Erigyius: 36, 36n.54, 121
Euphrates River: 5, 8, 8n.16, 24, 42, 43n.91, 64–69 *passim*

Fleet: Macedonian, 9, 11, 34, 35, 41n. 79, 46n.106, 58, 58n.26, 59, 60, 62, 64, 66, 111–118 *passim*, 141, 155, 156; Persian, 33, 34
Followers: numbers of, 11–14; mentioned, 3, 16n.18, 18, 23, 24, 40, 47
Foraging: 2, 30, 72, 72n.6, 103, 107, 120
Forced march: logistic significance of, 60n.39; examples of, 9, 39, 69, 69n. 80, 115

Garrisons: logistic significance of, 9, 41, 41n.79, 120; other examples of, 87, 103n.16, 105, 151, 152
Gaugamela: 3, 13, 17n.19, 35, 36n.53, 67, 70, 70n.80, 71n.3, 78n.33, 148, 152
Gaza: 28n.15, 40n.78, 41n.79, 57, 58, 59, 60, 64, 153
Gedrosia, Gedrosian: terrain and climate of, 112–118; location of, 140–142; mentioned, 1, 5, 10, 13n.8, 15n. 13, 41n.79, 59, 60n.39, 94n.98, 110–118, 135–143, 155
Gifts of provisions: 41, 41n.82, 72, 120
Gordion: 37, 42, 43n.91, 43n.94, 61, 61n.41, 147
Grain. *See* Wheat

Halicarnassos: 34, 34n.46, 35, 43n.94, 56, 146

Halys River: 37, 38, 39, 40n.78, 41, 41n.79
Hamah: 41n.79, 65, 65n.63, 66n.65
Harvest dates: significance of for tactical planning, 27–28, 37, 121; dates of in individual regions, see under the region
Harvests: 4, 9, 30, 32, 33, 45, 57, 59, 68, 68n.77, 78
Hasanbeyli Pass: 49, 50, 51, 53n.137
Hecatompylos: 47, 78, 80, 83, 85, 93n. 92, 157
Helmand River (Etymandrus): 8, 9n. 16, 32n.30, 92, 93, 130n.33
Hephaistion: 41n.79, 72, 72n.6, 107, 108, 118
Hindu Kush: 64n.56, 90, 93–97 *passim*, 102, 107, 107n.38, 152
Horse: carrying capability of, 14, 128–129; size of ancient, 14n.11, 127–129; feeding of, 18, 126–129; mentioned, 3, 14n.10, 15, 15n.15, 16, 16n.15, 17, 19, 21, 22n.35, 23, 26, 29, 37n.66, 45, 54, 60, 63, 63n.52, 65n. 61, 68, 81, 95, 96, 96n.106, 102, 102n. 13, 104n.23, 126–129, 145, 154, 155
Hostages: logistic significance of, 9, 41, 41n.79, 120; mentioned, 11
Hyrcania, Hyrcanian: 13, 13n.5, 79, 80, 83, 84, 85, 85n.67, 93n.92, 148, 152

Ichthyophagoi: location of, 140, 140n. 83, 141
Ilium: 31, 33
Indus River: 8, 9n.16, 32n.30, 38n.67, 107–111 *passim*, 130n.33, 137, 150
Intelligence, advance: 2, 2n.8, 4, 42n. 91, 43, 44n.97, 49, 51, 51n.128, 71, 72, 73, 83, 104, 116n.83, 117, 120, 122
Isfahan (Gabae): 41n.79, 75, 77n.28, 79
Issus (Kara Huyuk): battle of, 3, 15, 15n.12, 35, 36n.53, 43n.91, 43n.94, 47, 49, 50n.125, 52n.137, 54, 66n.65, 67, 80n.46, 134, 151, 152; town of, 44, 44n.96, 48–51 *passim*, 131, 147

Jaxartes River (Syr Darya): 99n.2, 103, 103n.18, 149
Jhelum River (Hydaspes): 3, 85, 107, 109, 110, 134n.53, 150, 157, 158

Kabul: 93, 93n.94, 94, 94n.98, 107, 108, 158
Kalat-i-Nadiri: 47, 60n.39, 87–91 *passim*
Kandahar: 93, 94, 94n.98
Kara Kapu Pass: 43, 49, 49n.120, 50, 50n.125, 52
Kara Kum Desert: 13, 41n.79, 86n.76
Kashka Darya (Ochus River?): 100, 102–106 *passim*
Khawak Pass: 94, 95n.102, 107n.38
Kolwa: 114, 115, 142
Kumbh Pass: 113, 115, 117, 135, 135n.59, 136n.61, 139, 140

Las Bela. *See* Oreitans
Litani River: 55, 58
Lycia: 35, 35n.53, 36, 36n.56, 57

Magarsus (Dort Direkli): 44, 46
Magazines of provisions: 9, 40, 41, 60, 76, 87, 116n.83, 141
Makran. *See* Gedrosia; Ichthophagai
Mallus (near Kiziltahta): 44n.97, 45, 46, 46n.105, 47, 48, 49, 50, 52
Marakanda (Afrasiab?): 47, 61n.41, 99, 103–106 *passim*, 149, 154
Margiana (Merv Oasis): 90, 104, 105, 105n.27
Market: 41, 72, 120
Media, Median: 71n.3, 74, 75, 77–80 *passim*, 148, 152
Memphis: 63, 63n.54
Mesopotamia, Mesopotamian: climate and terrain of, 66–68; harvest date in, 67; mentioned, 9n.16, 12, 32n.30, 37, 38n.67, 70n.90, 71n.3, 108, 111, 117, 130n.33, 137
Miletus: 34, 34n.46, 36n.55, 43n.94, 146
Mopsuestia (Misis): 49, 49n.120, 50, 52
Mule: carrying capability of, 14; feed-ing of, 18, 126–127; mentioned, 3, 14n.10, 15, 16, 16n.15, 19, 23, 24n.38, 26, 29, 35, 45, 63, 79, 129
Multan: 110n.53
Myriandrus (Ada Tepe?): 47, 47n.108, 48, 49, 51, 51n.131, 52, 131

Nautaka: 61n.41, 99, 102, 102n.12, 106, 153
Nearchus: 7, 8, 114, 116n.83, 117, 117n.86, 118, 118n.91, 136, 141, 141n.91
Nile River: 24, 32n.30, 38n.67, 41n.79, 61, 62, 64

Ochus River. *See* Kashka Darya
Oreitans: 72n.5, 113, 114, 115, 135, 135n.59, 136n.61, 140, 141, 154, 156
Ox, oxen: 12n.4, 14, 14n.10, 15, 15n.15, 16n.15, 23
Oxus River (Amu Darya): 61n.40, 64n.56, 99, 101–106 *passim*, 153

Pack saddle: weight of, 15n.11
Palestine, Palestinian: harvests in, 64; mentioned, 3, 5, 55–58, 64, 112
Pamphylia: 35, 36
Parapanisadae: harvest date in, 94, 107, 107n.38; mentioned, 85n.67, 93, 93n.94, 94, 94n.101, 148, 152
Parmenio: 12n.2, 30, 32n.34, 35, 35n.53, 36, 36n.56, 43, 44, 44n.97, 48, 49, 50, 52n.137, 54, 78n.36, 79, 80, 121, 151
Parthia, Parthian: 2, 71n.3, 75, 78, 79, 80, 84, 85, 91n.89, 153
Pattala (Bahmanabad): 111, 111n.58, 112, 113, 114, 116n.83, 135, 136, 136n.61, 150
Persepolis: 35, 41n.79, 73–79, 94n.98, 118, 148
Persis: harvest date in, 73, 77; climate and terrain of, 74–78; mentioned, 10, 35, 35n.53, 36n.55, 61, 61n.41, 70, 71–78, 118
Philotas: 13n.5, 15n.13, 72, 72n.6, 93n.92

Phoenicia, Phoenician: harvest date in, 56; mentioned, 11, 11n.1, 60n.38, 63n.54, 65, 66, 111
Phrygia, Phrygian: harvest date in, 37; mentioned, 35, 37, 38
Pillaging: 72, 72n.6, 77, 120
Pillars of Jonah Pass: 44n.97, 48, 50n. 125, 51, 52, 131, 131n.34, 131n.35, 134
Pinarus River (Payas): 51, 51n.132, 52, 131–134, 151
Pisidia: 36
Polytimetus River. *See* Zeravshan River
Ptolemy, son of Lagus: 6, 8, 52n.137, 72, 72n.6, 102, 116n.83
Pura: 115, 117, 117n.84, 135, 136, 154, 156
Pyramus River (Ceyhan or Jihan): 49, 49n.119, 50

Rations: men, 123–126; animals, 126–130; mentioned, 12n.4, 13, 18, 20n. 30, 21, 21n.32, 22n.35, 23, 40, 60, 83, 96, 119
Requisitions: 29, 30, 41, 41n.82, 56, 72, 120
Rhagae: 80–83 *passim*, 153
Rhambacia (Bela): 111, 113, 136n.61, 139, 140
River transport: 26, 27, 45, 61, 70, 109, 121

Saddle bags. *See* Pack Saddle
Salang Pass: 95n.102, 107, 107n.38
Sardis: 30, 30n.23, 31, 32, 33, 43n.94, 146, 153
Sea transport: 2, 3, 26, 27, 45, 46n.106, 55, 61, 65, 109, 110, 121. *See also* Fleet; Ship
Seistan: harvest date in, 93; mentioned, 8, 9n.16, 91, 92n.91, 93, 93n. 93, 94n.98. *See also* Zarangaea
Ship: 26, 26n.3, 28, 30, 31, 34, 46n.106, 58n.26, 66, 111, 112, 112n.63. *See also* Fleet; Sea transport

Sinai: climate and terrain of, 60; mentioned, 3, 5, 20, 41n.79, 59, 59n.33, 64, 156
Siwah (Oracle of Zeus Ammon): 61–63, 64n.54, 85n.67
Sochoi (Darab Sak): 42–46 *passim*, 51n.131, 53n.137
Sogdia, Sogdian, Sogdiana: operations in, 99–106; climate and terrain of, 100–102; mentioned, 2, 36n.55, 61, 71n.3, 72n.5, 86n.76, 149, 151, 152, 153, 154
Sousia (Tus): 13, 60n.39, 78, 78n.36, 80, 85–89 *passim*, 91
Surrenders: logistic significance of, 1, 9, 41, 41n.81, 120; other examples of, 55, 71, 72, 72n.6, 84n.63, 101, 114. *See also* Alliance
Susa: 35, 61n.40, 71–73 *passim*, 75n.22, 77, 78n.33, 79, 148, 153, 156
Syria, Syrian: harvest date in, 56; operations in, 54–55; mentioned, 41n. 79, 46n.106, 58, 65, 65n.61, 66, 66n. 65, 67n.74, 78n.33, 151

Tarsus: 37, 42, 44, 45n.102, 46, 46n. 105, 49n.119, 61, 99
Taxila: 85, 150, 157, 158
Termez (Alexandria by Oxus, Demetria): 33n.36, 101, 101n.7, 102n.13
Thapsacus (Carchemish): 64–69 *passim*, 158
Therma: 26, 27, 28, 29
Tigris River: 5, 8, 8n.16, 24, 33n.36, 65n.61, 65n.64, 66n.68, 68, 69, 70, 70n.86, 118, 158
Tyana: 39, 40, 40n.78, 41n.79
Tyre: 32n.30, 41n.79, 54, 56, 57, 59, 61n.40, 63, 64, 64n.60, 64n.61, 99, 147

Uxians: 23n.37, 72, 72n.5, 77

Wagon: use of, 12, 15–16, 128n.26; mentioned, 13, 14, 23, 46, 47, 51n.

131, 60, 86, 86n.76, 142. *See also*
Cart
Wheat: yield rates of, 38, 38n.67; nutritional value of, 123, 124; mentioned, 45, 81n.51, 93, 104, 107n.40,
121, 123, 125n.14
Winter: provisioning problems in,
27n.4, 61, 61n.40, 121; mentioned,
4, 10, 13, 35, 36, 37, 74, 75, 78, 91,
106, 108

Zadracarta (Sari): 84, 85, 93n.92
Zagros Mountains: climate and terrain
of in winter, 74–75, 78, 79; mentioned, 3, 67
Zarangaea: harvest date in, 93; mentioned, 2, 61n.40, 91, 92n.91, 111.
See also Seistan
Zeravshan River (Polytimetus): 100,
102n.12, 103n.17